Neither Root Nor Branch

The Disaster Manual for Depression

By
Mary Jane Grange, R.N.

About the Cover

Authors usually try to represent their entire book by the picture which they have chosen for their book cover. A picture is worth a thousand words. My picture on my book cover follows this tradition. Step parents, and even biological parents, have become like driftwood–neither root nor branch. Step parents are expected to accent their homes while confined to a corner of their property and then walled-off with stone walls. Step parents are expected to watch others bloom, but not bloom themselves. Our physical and spiritual hearts do not have the strength or capacity for this mistreatment. The Lord expects fruit on these branches. (John 15:5; Malachi 4:1-6; <u>Doctrine and Covenants</u> 2:1-3) Like Ephraim and Manasseh, parents and step parents must become branches that grow over the wall. (Genesis 49: 22-25)

Copyright Information

To My Posterity

and to the

Physician in Charge of Our Care

With Thanks and Deep Affection

Acknowledgments

To John Thomas Hinshaw, thank you for rescuing a frightened teenager by giving to me my first Book of Mormon. Thank you for walking several miles in a Wyoming snowstorm to buy that 65 cent Book of Mormon for me. Instead of giving me a beer, a pill, the "smooth talk" of males, or something worse, you gave me a "Pearl of Great Price." Because of this "Pearl of Great Price," we can both make it through the buffetings of Satan. You will always be affectionally known as Jack and will be remembered forever.

To my husband, Joseph E. Grange, thank you for your efforts in two marriages. Thank you for always giving your two wives your hands of mercy. If anyone knows you, your have large hands. We love you very much.

To Owen and Colleen Asplund and family, thank you for not leaving me neither root nor branch. You are a great example for the families of the world, and it was not that difficult either. Thank you for your encouragement in the writing of these books and the review of my manuscripts.

To Morris Kjar, thank you for teaching me how to study all of the Pearls of Great Price in my life and showing me how to recognize them. Thank you also for checking my manuscripts.

To Ron Collins, thank you for keeping my computers and printers going. To Glen Cameron, thank you for help in designing my book cover and also keeping my printers and computers going.

To Pres. Keith Yorgason, thank you for reviewing my manuscripts and giving me suggestions and encouragement.

All footnotes from individuals or companies are used with permission. The text of the four scriptures, The Holy Bible, The Book of Mormon, The Doctrine and Covenants, and The Pearl of Great Price are in public domain. I do not translate doctrine for The Church of Jesus Christ of Latter-day Saints. I do try to apply its teaching to my life.

Mary Jane Grange, R.N.

Table of Contents

Let Not Your Heart
Be Troubled:
Ye Believe In God,
Believe Also In Me.

–Jesus Christ
John 14:1, The Holy Bible

Prologue

I am a registered nurse who retired from Latter-Day Saints Hospital (LDS) in Salt Lake City, Utah, to marry a man with eight children. His first wife passed away with cancer. Like all families and step families, we had our challenges. During my nursing career, I noticed that addictions, depression, and suicide were increasing in families and step families over the years. I did not know why. When it was my turn to experience the challenges that these families and step families were experiencing, I decided quickly that I did not want to respond to our difficulties with these methods of escape. It took me a little while to get a handle on this experience. I pondered and prayed a lot about this matter.

When I felt depression coming on, I prayed to know what was happening to us. I, of course, prayed to discover how to fix our family. I began noticing others were having the same problems that we were having. The failures were as similar as a script. Only the names were changed. It appeared no one was concerned about the step families of the world. These kinds of casualties were expected. Step families are not viewed as fixable anymore by the families and step families of the world. Families and step families were told to tough it out and to get second and third jobs by counselors in order to tough it out. We may not realize it, but we are writing off a very large segment of our population.

Many people feel step families have no value anyway. Gouging family members, especially step family members, has become a way of life. Paychecks are created or extended by gouging others. It seems that we are now a country that is no longer a country who has a system of government of the people, by the people, for the people. We are a country who controls people with wounds of the people, by the people, for the people. If it is in our favor, the end justifies the means. We have systems in society which do this gouging very well, too. We blame many people for these wounds and our actions, especially our parents and step parents. The President of the United States is blamed for all of our failures. Being a scapegoat is not the role of the Father of our Country or the fathers and step fathers in our homes.

We take pill after pill for our wounds and our attention deficit disorders. Many of these medications are not legal. We go to every sports function and watch every movie that is released from Hollywood year after year. It does not matter how old you are. When you watch people play sports or act in movies and who have attention deficit disorders year after year, what do you get over the years? You guessed it. You get family members with the same kinds of attention deficit disorders and depression. The attention deficit disorders and depressions are worse in step families because step mothers are not allowed to care for their step family. Biological children no longer respond to their parents the way they used to do before their parents become step parents. Children and parents in step families never get to experience the family experience which the Creator of this world planned for all of us.

Before, my step family was created, I saw in the hospitals and doctors' offices the effects of the world that was so attractive. I became bored with the way that the world and Hollywood wanted me to respond to my problems so their problems could be fixed. Their ideas were not helping my family or me anyway. Like all parents in all nations, I wanted a different world for my family. I tried to take my family to a different world. They did not want that better world.

7

I decided to search some textbooks about the problems that I was experiencing in my life. These textbooks are interesting. There are many different teachers, but they teach the same theme. The theme of their teachings do not change year to year, even as the spokesperson changes. Even the spokespersons are gathered under one great Teacher. These spokespersons seek to gather us under this great Teacher. Their words are the textbooks that we now call the scriptures. The spokespersons are known as prophets.

I used The Holy Bible, The Book of Mormon, and The Doctrine and Covenants, and The Pearl of Great Price to fix my problems. Instead of reading the scriptures alone, I read them together. I noticed common threads which helped me in my step parenting process. I am hoping these scriptures will help you, too.

I am not teaching you false doctrine. You can look up these scriptures yourself. To save space, I did paraphrase. We will be learning concepts in scripture line up line, precept upon precept, here a little, and there a little as the prophet Isaiah advised. The scriptures will make more sense and will be easier to remember. This is what will help you. After all, you are getting wounds heaped on wounds with irrational reasoning on top of irrational reasoning many times in your life. Parents and step parents might as well know the mysteries of raising children and step children, living with a spouse, improving oneself, and enduring to the end all at the same time. This comes precept by precept so our inexperienced minds can absorb these concepts.

The topics which we will be discussing are intense. Depression, drug and alcohol addictions, and suicidal thoughts are intense. Go as fast or as slow as you want. There are questions for you to answer at the end of each chapter. I know you are busy and may not have the time to answer these questions with long essays. Writing does help relieve stress. These questions are your layers of stress. You will be able to think of more questions and become aware of more layers of stress. I recommend a private notebook to keep track of your answers.

These questions are not designed for you to beat up on yourselves. You have had enough of that. I know these questions will cause many tears in both men and women. It is okay to cry. You are not a failure because your children and step children hate you and are doing things to aggravate you. The only way that you can change your children and step children is to change and improve yourselves and your homes.

I have written two other books in this manner. One book is on step parenting, and the other book is on attention deficit disorders. Parents and step parents deal with many problems in second and third marriages. There are many pits created to destroy your step family. A step mother may have multiple biological children, multiple step children, and multiple spouses with attention deficit disorders. This is why she becomes overburdened and depressed. Step fathers are becoming more and more depressed. Roles are switching. Mother is working more and harder for the family than father. Both mother and father always want to make their families and step families better. Better cannot happen this way.

I am a member of The Church of Jesus Christ. I do not have the authority or stewardship to speak for the President or members of The Church of Jesus Christ. I understand this. I do feel impressed to try and assist the step parents of the world with the wisdom that I have learned in my step parenting and nursing experiences and experiences with the scriptures. I hope this helps you. You certainly will always have someone praying for you. I do not want my books to replace the scriptures. There are many more things in the scriptures than what I have been able to tell you. These things will help you   The Savior is a better teacher than I am. Pray for His assistance. Isaiah told us:

3 He is despised and rejected of men; a man of sorrows, and acquainted with grief:
and we hid as it were our faces from him; he was despised, and we esteemed him not.
4 ¶ Surely he hath borne our griefs, and carried our sorrows: yet we did esteem him
stricken, smitten of God, and afflicted.
5 But he was wounded for our transgressions, he was bruised for our iniquities:
the chastisement of our peace was upon him; and with his stripes we are healed.

Isaiah 53:3 - 5, The Holy Bible

Despised, rejected, sorrowful, acquainted with grief, no acknowledgment, smitten of God, and afflicted sounds like step parenting. This also sounds like depression. You may not realize it, but Christ is our spiritual step parent. Heavenly Father taught Christ how to be our spiritual step parent as well as the Savior of God's children. Heavenly Father taught Christ how to handle all of the burdens and sorrows of mankind at the same time. This is quite a task. Ask any mother of a large family. She can tell you how hard it is to bare the burdens of one family.

Christ bore all of our sorrows, yet we esteemed him not. Many of us consider His ways as failures. We forget His voluntary mission was to be crucified to save us all. This was accomplished. Christ and His ways are not failures. Christ and His ways can help us out of depression. We can carry our burdens with grace as He did. We do not have to place our burdens on others' shoulders.

Our Heavenly Father and His Son, Jesus Christ, have created a time for us to grow up in private. Only four generations approximately will know of our struggles. It is not helpful to us to carry on our personal struggles and family battles for an eternity. Personal failures and family battles keep us from the peaceable things of His Kingdom which we will be relying on for an eternity. I suspect our family and step family battles will remain in the telestial and terrestrial kingdoms. We will not be allowed to progress to the Celestial Kingdom without mercy, love, and forgiveness for each other.

61 If thou shalt ask, thou shalt receive revelation upon revelation, knowledge
upon knowledge, that thou mayest know the mysteries and peaceable things—
that which bringeth joy, that which bringeth life eternal.

Doctrine and Covenants 42:61

Christ managed anger, sorrow, depression, and grief with the same principles He teaches us in scripture. I encourage you to look up the words in these principles also in Webster's Dictionary. We speak in slang so much. We do not know what these words really mean anymore. Our experiences are too limited to completely rely on our knowledge.

*Walking Backward*s. One of the first tasks that we accomplish in life is learning how to walk with stability. The infant accomplishes this task by learning how to hold his head up without support, rolling over, sitting, standing, and then baby steps. Each action strengthens a specific group of muscles. All of these muscle groups are needed for walking. When babies first learn to crawl, they crawl backwards. Our bodies were created so we could walk forward. We may occasionally back up, but I suspect we walk forward over ninety-five percent of our time on Earth. Our eyes are placed in the front of our bodies. Our feet and toes are placed forward on our legs. Even our ears are placed in a manner that we can sense our balance while walking forward. Can you imagine how uncomfortable life would be to walk backwards all our life?

Our spirits want to walk forward, too. We must learn to walk forward spiritually, morally, psychologically, emotionally, financially, in service, sacrifice, persistence, in work, in faith, in love, in mercy, and in forgiveness as well as physically. These are our spiritual muscle groups which need strengthening. If you are depressed, you are walking backwards and need to give this up. Our spirits can walk backward so much that we become amoral and emotionally and financially drained all the time. We do not develop the spiritual muscle that is created by love, mercy, and forgiveness. We can find the same grace that the Savior had. We will give up some things so we can add other things to our lives which will give us experience and help us feel better. We are going to start with the story of the Creation. Notice the patterns.

Chapter One

The Creation of Ourselves

In my first two books, I talked about how to balance our lives. If we are going to balance anything, we must first create a space for something in our lives. Creating space for something or someone takes time and effort. The story of the creation applies to our life as well as the creation of the world. This story will tell us how to create space for some very important things and people in our life. Our bodies and minds were created in a similar manner. Likewise, families and step families are formed in the same manner.

Our texts will be Genesis in The Holy Bible and The Book of Moses and The Book of Abraham in The Pearl of Great Price. We are going to learn about the steps in creation. Genesis describes the creation. Moses and Abraham were prophets who were shown the world from the beginning to the end. Their books in The Pearl of Great Price talk about the organization of the world. There were purposes that God wanted to accomplish. Each plan had many steps to complete these purposes before God's day was done. Jehovah, the God of the Old Testament, called these steps, days and years. Jehovah is the Son of God or Jesus Christ. Jehovah had many steps within these first days. Remember. His time is not calculated the way we calculate time.

> *1 AND then the Lord said: Let us go down. And they went down at the beginning, and they, that is the Gods, organized and formed the heavens and the earth.*

> *Abraham 4:1, The Pearl of Great Price*

On the first day, when the Earth was without form and void, God created light. There has to be a balance between light and darkness. Germs and mold grow readily in dark, moist places. The Creator's efforts would have been destroyed by germs and mold. Man, woman, and animals would become sick. Food and water would spoil before the humans and animals of the Earth could harvest it, eat it, or drink it. With too much light, our skins would burn. There would be droughts in every place of the Earth. Food could not be established for us. Trees and plants which balance oxygen and carbon monoxide would wilt. The moisture of the Earth would evaporate. We need a proper balance of light and darkness for vision to take place.

Notice. Darkness was brought upon our Earth, and light was created before the sun, moon, and stars were placed upon the Earth. The Creator of this world, Jesus Christ, is the Light of this world. The Creator of this world allows darkness to come into our life if we do not follow Him. He allows light in our lives if we do follow Him. He simply has to withdraw from us because of our behavior to remove the light from us. His light is the truth we yearn for and which makes us free.

When we are without form and in a void, Light and Day are there for us. Voids in humans cause feelings of darkness, desolation, emptiness, and a feeling that time stands still in our deprivation and desolation. A vacant stare is a void. Things around us have no effect or are useless to us. Our passing or death creates a void in our family. Our Creator knew there would be many times that His children would feel desolate and experience a great sense of loss as the histories of our families, communities, and nations unfolded. In Genesis 1:4 - 5, God divided the light from the darkness. He called the light Day, and the darkness, he called Night.

Special days and nights are capitalized. They are known as proper nouns. They would remain capitalized in the same sentence or paragraph if the author was describing the same special event. It would be interesting if the word, Day, which is capitalized meant a person, particularly Jehovah or Jesus Christ, and the word Night, meant Satan. This would be similar to a verse found in the New Testament, John chapter 1, verse 1.

1 IN the beginning was the Word, and the Word was with God, and the Word was God.
2 The same was in the beginning with God.
3 All things were made by him; and without him was not any thing made that was made.
4 In him was life; and the life was the light of men.
5 And the light shineth in darkness; and the darkness comprehended it not.

John 1:1 - 5, The Holy Bible

God appointed the Creator of this world, Jesus Christ. The principles of Heaven which were with God, the Father, in the beginning were given to Jesus Christ. The authority for this world was turned over to Jesus Christ. In Him, life and light are found before anything else.

On the second day, God divided the waters from the waters. He first placed a firmament in the midst of the waters. Firmament is the heavens or atmosphere. Jehovah then divided the waters from the waters. He divided the waters below the ground from the waters above ground.

Most people think this is the time when creeks, streams, rivers, lakes, seas, and oceans were formed. Make your self a glass of ice water with ice cubes. Fill the glass only about half full. Look at it. The waters are separated or divided from the waters. If you had to describe this separation of waters from the waters in your glass, how would you describe it? The description is something that you first learned in science–solid, liquid, and gas. The ice cubes are the solids, the water is the liquid, and the seemingly emptied space above the water is the gas. Small atoms of hydrogen, nitrogen, and oxygen are going back and forth in solution.

With solids, liquids, and gases, the Creator of this world, Jesus Christ, could manage many things. He could manage temperature, humidity, evaporation, condensation, climate, quality of the soil, etc. Most of all, the Creator could provide a safe environment for all of the various microorganisms that would inhabit the Earth. There could be a balance between new life and old life. There was a manner to clean the living and decay the things which had died.

It is amazing to see that for the most part, the harmful gases are underground and the gases that we need to breathe are above ground. When man would breathe, he would inhale oxygen and nitrogen and exhale carbon dioxide. The combination of these gases do not ignite every time man would build a fire for warmth and cooking. However, when we breathe, the air we take in must have moisture and some warmth. Otherwise, our respiratory passage ways would become very dry and plugged with a very dry mucous plug.

6 ¶ And God said, Let there be a firmament in the midst of the waters, and let it divide the waters from the waters.
7 And God made the firmament, and divided the waters which were under the firmament from the waters which were above the firmament: and it was so.
8 And God called the firmament Heaven. And the evening and the morning were the second day.

Genesis 1:6 - 8, <u>The Holy Bible</u>

On the third day of creation, God gathered the waters. He also gathered moisture in the clouds. He gathered the water in streams, creeks, rivers, lakes, seas, and oceans. Where did the Creator of this world gather the ice? You guessed it–at the North and South Poles. He also gathered snow and ice in clouds. It is interesting to note, this gathering of moisture in rivers and clouds took place to collect moisture in one place and transport it to another place. There is a balance in watering and draining the land–just like in our bodies.

The gathering of the solids, liquids, and gases, or the waters help maintain a steady temperature on the land. Our bodies function at a temperature of 98.6 degrees. We have muscle and fat layers to maintain this temperature when the temperatures are higher and lower. If our muscle is not able to maintain this body temperature, the layer of fat on our bodies increases to insulate or maintain a temperature of 98.6 degrees Fahrenheit.

9 ¶ And God said, Let the waters under the heaven be gathered together unto one place, and let the dry land appear: and it was so.
10 And God called the dry land Earth; and the gathering together of the waters called he Seas: and God saw that it was good.
11 And God said, Let the earth bring forth grass, the herb yielding seed, and the fruit tree yielding fruit after his kind, whose seed is in itself, upon the earth: and it was so.
12 And the earth brought forth grass, and herb yielding seed after his kind, and the tree yielding fruit, whose seed was in itself, after his kind: and God saw that it was good.
13 And the evening and the morning were the third day.

Genesis 1: 9-13, <u>The Holy Bible</u>

On the fourth day, God created a power source for the earth that had risen among the gathered waters. The power sources are the sun and the moon. The sun has dominion over the day. The moon has dominion over the night. Stars were placed in the heavens. Light and dark were divided and gathered like the waters were divided and gathered.

In the dominions of the sun and moon, we have days, months, seasons, and years. We have light and heat during the day and night. The sun is far enough away so its heat cannot heat and inflame the harmful underground gases. There is moisture in the air so oxygen and nitrogen

13

will not be ignited or dry out our respiratory passages. Our bodies also receive certain vitamins from the sun. We are comforted by the heat and light of the day.

The Lord placed these lights in the Heavens, not just for time, or heat, or light, but for signs. Signs take the place of words or communicate thoughts and feelings. Signs give grounds for believing in the existence or presence of something else. Some important signs that we are aware of are rainbows, the Star of the Nativity, earthquakes, and the darkness that occurred at the Savior's death. There are signs for the Second Coming of Christ. Do you know them?

14 ¶ And God said, Let there be lights in the firmament of the heaven to
divide the day from the night; and let them be for signs, and for seasons,
and for days, and years:
15 And let them be for lights in the firmament of the heaven to give light
upon the earth: and it was so.
16 And God made two great lights; the greater light to rule the day,
and the lesser light to rule the night: he made the stars also.
17 And God set them in the firmament of the heaven to give light
upon the earth,
18 And to rule over the day and over the night, and to divide the light
from the darkness: and God saw that it was good.
19 And the evening and the morning were the fourth day.

Genesis 1:16 - 19, The Holy Bible

On the fifth day, the Earth was ready for life. Creatures in the water and of the sky were created and placed here first. Herbs and grasses were created for their homes and food. This could be to test the Earth to see if the Earth was ready to support both animal and plant life.

More than likely, the animals in the water were our first water-purifiers. Small microorganisms eat decaying material. Larger animals eat them to keep a balance. Birds had to have a way of being sustained until the insects were formed. Animals in the water and the fowls of the sky were given the commandment to be fruitful and multiply and fill the seas. Animals to this day recognize their Creator of this world in some way, usually by the way they turn in their nest. Animals face east.

20 And God said, Let the waters bring forth abundantly the moving creature
that hath life, and fowl that may fly above the earth in the open firmament of heaven.
21 And God created great whales, and every living creature that moveth, which
the waters brought forth abundantly, after their kind, and every winged fowl
after his kind: and God saw that it was good.
22 And God blessed them, saying, Be fruitful, and multiply, and fill the waters
in the seas, and let fowl multiply in the earth.
23 And the evening and the morning were the fifth day.

Genesis 1:20 - 23, The Holy Bible

On the sixth day, the Lord brought forth every living creature on the land. This included cattle, every creeping thing, the beasts of the Earth, and finally man and woman. Every living thing and their anatomy were created in a size that would not give them an overdose of the things they ate and breathed in. Organs had to be a certain size and shape to function. In addition, every living thing including insects were given a way to defend themselves, but man was given dominion over every living creature in the air, in the sea, and in the sky. Man was also given ways to defend himself. He was made in the image of God. God's ways of peace defend man.

24 ¶ And God said, Let the earth bring forth the living creature after his kind, cattle, and creeping thing, and beast of the earth after his kind: and it was so.
25 And God made the beast of the earth after his kind, and cattle after their kind, and every thing that creepeth upon the earth after his kind: and God saw that it was good.
26 ¶ And God said, Let us make man in our image, after our likeness: and let them have dominion over the fish of the sea, and over the fowl of the air, and over the cattle, and over all the earth, and over every creeping thing that creepeth upon the earth.
27 So God created man in his own image, in the image of God created he him; male and female created he them.
28 And God blessed them, and God said unto them, Be fruitful, and multiply, and replenish the earth, and subdue it: and have dominion over the fish of the sea, and over the fowl of the air, and over every living thing that moveth upon the earth.
29 ¶ And God said, Behold, I have given you every herb bearing seed, which is upon the face of all the earth, and every tree, in the which is the fruit of a tree yielding seed; to you it shall be for meat.
30 And to every beast of the earth, and to every fowl of the air, and to every thing that creepeth upon the earth, wherein there is life, I have given every green herb for meat: and it was so.
31 And God saw every thing that he had made, and, behold, it was very good. And the evening and the morning were the sixth day.

Genesis 1: 24 - 31, The Holy Bible

On the seventh day, God rested. When the host, or a very large number of people and animals were grouped together, God rested. However, God was not idle. God blessed and sanctified the day of rest. Mist watered the whole Earth at His command.

1 THUS the heavens and the earth were finished, and all the host of them.
2 And on the seventh day God ended his work which he had made; and he rested on the seventh day from all his work which he had made.
3 And God blessed the seventh day, and sanctified it: because that in it he had rested from all his work which God created and made.
4 ¶ These are the generations of the heavens and of the earth when they were created, in the day that the LORD God made the earth and the heavens,

5 And every plant of the field before it was in the earth, and every herb
of the field before it grew: for the LORD God had not caused it to rain
upon the earth, and there was not a man to till the ground.
6 But there went up a mist from the earth, and watered the whole face of the ground.
7 And the LORD God formed man of the dust of the ground, and breathed into
his nostrils the breath of life; and man became a living soul.

Genesis 2:1 - 7, <u>The Holy Bible</u>

By now, I imagine you are wondering why have I included the story of the creation in a disaster manual for depression. If we want to become a living, productive soul, we must follow the same steps the Creator of this world followed. *First,* when we are without form and void and darkness has over taken our life, we must create or produce light in the darkness that has overtaken our soul. No one is going to do this for us. No one can do this for us. The Lord placed us in families while we learn how to make room for light within ourselves. The light of the Savior's gospel is the best light.

Second, we must divide the waters from the waters above ground and below ground. We must learn how to deal with public and private matters appropriately. In order for our personalities to come forth, we must divide the solids, liquids, and gases in our life. Friendships will not take precedence over the family that you were born into or that was created by your marriage. There is a lot of hot air in the world. People can and want to inflame you to control you, especially if you have something good to offer your family and the world. There are always going to be people that want to separate us from the solids in our life.

Third, we gather the solids, liquids, and gases in our life. First, we must know how to recognize the solids, liquids, and gases in our life. This dividing and gathering of the waters from the waters will bring us more solids, liquids, and gases into our life. I gathered my solids in a family and then in my elementary, junior high, high school, and college educations. This time of education was followed by experience in a career in nursing and then marriage. I gathered myself spiritually in The Church of Jesus Christ and in some of the temples belonging to The Church of Jesus Christ. I now have firm ground to stand on.

Fourth, we must decide on a power source for our lives. A proper power source brings heat, light, comfort, seasons, days, and years, not just dominion over us. Your power source must give you a balance between watering and draining the solids, liquids, and gases in your life. If forms of darkness such as drugs, alcohol, and movies and television are your power sources, you are adding multiple sources of dominion and darkness.

In order to resupply someone else, we must have a fuel source which can resupply ourselves. This is why we follow the Savior. This is why repentance, forgiveness, and mercy work in easing depression.[1] The Savior is our endless fuel supply. The types of spiritual fuel that we have at our disposal depends on the commandments, ordinances, and covenants which we are willing to "store and use." If we depend on commandments of men, this fuel source will end with time. Instead of adding cupfuls of fuel from the Savior, we add talents and oil by drops.

---

[1]Mark 4: 26-27, <u>The Holy Bible</u>, p. 1247.

Fifth, we must create life in the waters and manage the creatures of the water and sky.
We do not have much contact with animals of the water and fowl of the sky, unless we work in one of the occupations that deals with this kind of wild life. There are many marine fishermen, hunters, biologists, ichthyologists, and forest service employees. We may only be fisherman and hunters at heart, but we have to understand that we have dominion over these animals. They and the sports around them are not to have dominion over us. We have to leave a certain amount of fish and microorganisms in the seas, fowl in the air, wildlife, trees, and plants of the various lands for animals and plants to replenish the Earth. For most parents and step parents, the creatures they will try to manage are their spouse and children who can be found on land, sea, or in the sky.

Sixth, we become fruitful, multiply, replenish, and subdue ourselves. We do this with steps 1 - 5 and step 7. However, we must learn how to be fruitful, to multiply, to replenish, and to subdue the Earth and the creeping things in our lives–even when our fruits do not want to be multiplied, replenished, and subdued.

If we are fruitful, we are productive. Like fruit trees, we bear fruit, not just flowers and leaves. If we are productive, the things we do are profitable for ourselves, families, step families, and others. Multiply means an increase. This can be in numbers, degrees, and efforts. Our children and step children should increase their efforts until they have families which increases their productivity. The word "replenish" means to resupply. We get further on a full tank of gas rather than a half-full or empty tank. Efforts and food resupply our empty tank spiritually.

Subdue is an interesting word which has many definitions. You will become acquainted with them in your life time–hopefully not all at once. Our Heavenly Father gave us agency to subdue ourselves so we could put ourselves under subject and not be compelled to be subjected. Our development and happiness depends on whom we subjected ourselves and who compels us.

There have been so many wars between countries and families before and after I was born. It appears to me that most countries, families, and step families believe that subdue only means to control others. If you are trying to be another source of dominion in another's life, this only brings depression. It will not bring the satisfaction in life that you are seeking. If I had to describe subdue myself, it would be with one word–tame. We cannot teach our children to be tame or gentle if we ourselves are not tame and gentle. Many families are trying to tame their children with Darkness with a capital D.

Seventh, we must rest on the seventh day or the Sabbath Day. The Lord rested after he gathered the hosts for the Earth. After we have gathered the many hosts in our life, we must rest, bless them, and sanctify them. A "mist" must come into our lives to give ourselves and the hosts that we have gathered the living water that is needed to be living souls. We cannot replenish and subdue without rest. We cannot drain the heartaches of life without rest on the Sabbath Day.

Pattern. There is a pattern for us to follow–be fruitful (produce), multiply (increase), replenish (restore), and then subdue (tame). This pattern occurs in plants, animals of the sky, sea, land, and in man and woman. The Savior followed this pattern also. This is the pattern we teach our children. Replenish always comes after fruitful and multiply. Subdue always comes after replenish. Fruitful means a time of great productivity. Subdue means to make less severe or soften. Fruit trees are pruned and their fruit is thinned, or they produce small, hard fruit. We also must be able to recognize when fruit in ourselves needs to be pruned for a good harvest.

17

Most people feel that being fruitful means having children, grandchildren, etc. We need to be productive before we can handle a family. Reproduction occurs in the multiply step. Our families will be growing. It is better for families if we learn how to make an increase in our life before we are responsible for a family that is continually changing.

In what areas of our life are we going to have a great productivity–enough to gather and divide? I believe these areas are the physical, emotional, social, intellectual, financial, moral, psychological, spiritual, and work, service, sacrifice, persistence, and obedience parts of our physical bodies and our personalities. We are to be fruitful or productive, then multiply, replenish, and subdue these areas. If we do not, we receive conflict and depression.

Since you have burdens to bear in this life, it is time for you to get acquainted with them, especially the burdens which cause depressions. Depressions are plural because there are many things which make you depressed. These depressions accumulate in layers very quickly. If you are depressed, I know that you are hurting and are crying a lot. It is okay to cry. Let's divide the waters from the waters, your tears. There are tears of happiness and tears from depression. Notice the pattern. This is your beginning pattern. This is the pattern to use when forming your family or step family.

Light and Darkness. *Do you prefer to learn from the Darkness in your life or the Light in your life? Are you willing to create Light in your life? How do you create life in your family? Are you trying to calm or gather children and step children with the Darkness of this world?*

Divide the waters. *What makes you cry? Divide your tears into the solids, liquids, and gases in your life? Where are you placing the ice of your life? Does the ice, hot, cold, or lukewarm gases have dominion over your joys in your life?*

Gathering yourself. *After dividing your waters from the waters, do you have enough good waters to gather yourself and family in from the cold of the world? Who does your family or step family gather under? Where are you going to find the living waters which the Savior told us about?*

Fuel Source. *What or who has become your fuel source? This determines how you are gathered as a family. Does your fuel source give you organization and solid ground to stand on in your life? Can your fuel source supply an unending amount of fresh, living water to you?*

Dominion. *What or who has taken dominion over you? Who do you rightfully have dominion over? Are you trying to establish dominion over others to control them?*

Management. *Are you trying to manage yourself and your family or step family on light and fresh water or the dark, polluted water, and harmful gases of life? Can you recognize the difference between public and private matters? Can you manage your family without rules?*

Subdue. *If depression has overtaken your life, how are you trying to subdue yourself, your spouse, and your fruits? Are you trying to subdue yourself without that period of productivity? Do you have something to multiply other than grief and anger? Are you trying to subdue yourself and others without being tame and gentle?*

Rest. *Are you willing to rest from the oppositions in your life to decrease your cares and sorrows and improve your health? Rest increases our facilities. We are not trying to be perfect. We are trying to become whole. If you are unable to follow the pattern of the Lord in the creation of all things, you will become depressed. Our depressions come because we have not learned our spiritual synonyms and antonyms.*

Chapter Two

Our Spiritual Synonyms and Antonyms, Part One

My teachers in elementary school in Sheridan, Wyoming, drilled my classes on synonyms and antonyms as much as they did multiplication tables. I feel that I am a better reader because of this instruction. At the time, I got bored with synonyms, words that have the same or similar meaning, and antonyms, words that have the opposite meaning. Of course, we were talking about cats and kittens or cats and dogs back then. I always wondered why my teachers wanted me to learn the difference between cats and dogs so much.

I help my grandchildren with their reading. I realized they were having difficulty understanding what they were reading. They did not understand the synonyms and antonyms in the material. Thus, the story was not interesting. It was a battle to get them to read. I realized this is why my elementary teachers and even some high school teachers taught me how to recognize synonyms and antonyms in the material I was reading. Understanding synonyms and antonyms helped me in other subjects such as mathematics, algebra, and history.

I wondered if it was that way in life. Synonyms and antonyms teach us how to discern between good and bad–just like opposition does. Individuals become depressed because they call synonyms, the antonyms of life, and the antonyms of this world, the synonyms of life.

Think back when you have been instructed on new or difficult things. Your teacher asked questions about the subject he was teaching you. He asked questions that could not be answered by "yes" or "no" answers. The teacher told stories pertaining to the subject that he was teaching in which his students could relate. This put his students at ease. The students *began thinking* on the same wavelength as the teacher. The teacher could find out what we knew about the subject and what we wanted or needed to learn. The teacher could broaden or increase our knowledge base about the subject. A good teacher always includes synonyms and antonyms to see how much the students are understanding. Synonyms and antonyms are the basics of comprehension.

The Greatest Teacher of all time, Jesus Christ, taught in the same manner. Christ taught His children by comparisons. The Savior showed us where and how to change through parables. He taught us about these changes, and He gave us the agency and time to change. Christ taught us about opposite things also. Opposition has to be identified for us so we can avoid opposition, not embrace opposition. There is a difference.

With synonyms and antonyms, Christ could instruct beginners, His disciples, in Christianity, as well as those who were experienced, His apostles, in the principles of Heaven. Christ also knew that He would be teaching more of His brothers and sisters by scripture. With synonyms, or parables, Christ untangled His own teachings that had been encumbered over time.

The synonyms and antonyms of life are called parables. Parables are short stories in which comparisons are used to illustrate a message with the story. The message is not always religious. Parents tell stories to their children all the time. They want their children to change and understand why there is a need for change. Parents and step parents are not skillful in parables because they do not give children agency and time to change. Parents also do not have the same expert consistency as the Savior. The story has to apply to different situations, but stay the same.

We have been taught that depression is an overwhelming sadness that incapacitates individuals. From the verse below, I wonder if depression is a synonym for temptation. Our sadness comes from guilt, being caught, desiring things that harms us, and the consequences we must bear. It would be interesting if there was a parable for every different type of depression, our temptations. With parables, we embrace the Kingdom of Christ instead of embracing opposition and depression. We find and choose the way God made for us to escape. (covenants)

13 There hath no temptation taken you but such as is common to man:
but God is faithful, who will not suffer you to be tempted above that
ye are able; but will with the temptation also make a way to escape,
that ye may be able to bear it.

1 Corinthians 10:13, The Holy Bible

The Savior began His comparisons or parables with the Parable of the Sower and the Seed. I will, too. Think of your gardens as you read this parable. Your successes and failures in your garden happened for a reason. Most likely, your failures began with the seed and where you planted the seed.

The Parable of the Sower. A sower or gardener went forth to sow or to plant seeds in the ground. Some seeds fell by the way side. The fowls came and devoured the seeds. Some seeds fell upon stony places. There was not much earth. These seeds sprang up quickly, but when the sun came up, they were scorched and withered away because they had no roots. Some seeds fell among thorns. The thorns choked the seeds. Some seeds fell on good ground. This ground was soft and had nutrients in the soil. These seeds brought forth much fruit, some a hundred fold, some sixty fold, and some thirty fold.[2]

At this point, the Apostles asked the Savior why He was teaching in parables. They did not understand why the Lord was teaching by comparison any better than children in a classroom. There has been much debate on why Jesus taught each generation of His younger brothers and sisters by parables. In my various Sunday School classes, I have been taught that Christ had to veil the meaning of His parables to protect Himself and those listening to Him in a politically dangerous environment. Veiling encumbers His teachings. Christ would not veil His teachings while stating that we did not understand things. Jesus Christ was given power over death. He decided when it was time for him to lay down His life and rest from the opposition in the world.

Jesus tells us in Matthew 13 why He taught us in parables.[3] First, we do not know the mysteries of Heaven. Second, we see not and hear not, so we do not understand. Third, our hearts our waxed gross. Fourth, our ears are dull of hearing. Our eyes have closed lest we

---

[2]Matthew 13:3-9, 18-23, The Holy Bible, p. 1209-1210.

[3]Matthew 13:11-17, The Holy Bible, p.1210.

20

should understand and be converted, and He should heal them. Fifth, what we have shall be taken away if we do not use it. Christ does not want that to happen. He wants us to be joint-heirs with Him. In short, we have our protective defenses up. The parables help us set aside those many defense mechanisms that we have accumulated. We discard the natural man in us and ease our anxieties with parables.

After explaining why He taught in parables, the Savior explained the Parable of the Sower. The Savior explained that the seed by the wayside, probably the hard paths in the garden, is like one who hears the word of the kingdom and does not understand the word. The wicked one comes and catches away that was sown in his heart. The Savior explained that the seed that falls into stony places is the same that hears the word with joy. However, there is not much ground for seed among the thorns. He may hear the word. The cares and riches and the deceitfulness of the world chokes the seed. The seed is unfruitful. When tribulation comes, they are easily offended or angered.

Families and step families resemble The Parable of the Sower. The seed of parents, step parents, children, and step children have fallen by the wayside, in stony places, and among the thorns. They have heard the word of God, but do not understand it. The word may fall on deaf ears. Naturally, Satan is not going to let the word, especially a testimony of Jesus Christ take root. Through anger and jealousy, family members devour the good seeds planted in their hearts and family by telling themselves these seeds are not relevant for the times, nor are they the truth.

Individuals who stonewall others are like the seeds in stony places. They did not partake of the teachings of the Son, Jesus Christ, which also involves obeying a parent and a step parent. Thus, these individuals do not have enough spiritual soil for the seeds given to them to make roots. These seeds in our children and step children grew quickly, but when the stresses of life, the heat of the day, come to them, and it will, they are scorched with anger. These plants had no roots for their fuel source to provide nutrients. They withered away.

Many of our children and step children have decided to live among the thorns of this world. The thorns of this world can provide for them what parents and step parents will not. It does not matter that the thorns of this world chokes and intimidates them. Our children and step children learn to choke and intimidate others.

Some seeds fell on good ground. These seeds brought forth much fruit, some a hundred fold, some sixty fold, and some thirty fold.[4] There are children and step children who manage to overcome the opposition in families, step families, and the world. They become successful. They allowed the good ground of family, church, school, and friends to nourish them. They also nourished others.

Many parents and step parents have sown good seeds in their children and step children only to have those seeds devoured in the power struggles and secret combinations of step families. Parents and step parents become isolated, manipulated, and stonewalled. Parents and step parents are not allowed to educate, comfort, and soothe their children and step children. Step children are not allowed to follow good advice of a step parent or be comforted by their step parent. All become neither root nor branch and wither with some form of depression and even suicidal thoughts.

---

[4]Matthew 13:8, The Holy Bible, p. 1209.

It is interesting to note that the harvest in good seed is some hundred fold, some sixty fold, some thirty fold. In other words, we will harvest more of some things than others. We do not need to harvest one hundred fold of zucchini, eggplant, or Brussel sprouts. We would need to harvest a hundred fold in fruit and wheat. We will not harvest as much peas, beans, beets, and potatoes as fruit, corn, and wheat. Is the harvest of your life in balance? Are you harvesting more bills, pop, candy, drugs, alcohol, sports, and recreation than fruits, vegetables, grains, education, work, and the gospel of Jesus Christ? Is this why you and your family struggle with depression and temptations?

We always have a harvest. Like the parable of the sower, the fruits of anger, jealousy, and depression are also some one hundred fold, some sixty fold, some thirty fold. We do reap what we sow. (Galatians 6:7, The Holy Bible; Doctrine and Covenants 6:33-34)

If you want to be a root and branch in the generations of your family and step family, you have to be willing to harvest the fruits of your seeds. This requires effort, work, sacrifice, and persistence. You must be able to recognize when it is the correct time to harvest.

The Wheat and the Tares. There is a comparison or parable about the sower and kinds of seeds planted. A man sowed good seed into good ground. While the householder slept, an enemy came and sowed tares into the wheat field. When the wheat began to sprout, the man realized there were tares in the field also. Tares are poisonous or noxious weeds. Tares can be anything that you do not want growing in a particular garden or field.

Servants asked the householder if he had planted good seed in his field. If so, where did the tares come from? The owner of the field replied, "An enemy hath done this." The servants asked if they should gather the tares, bundle them, and burn them. The householder told them to not gather the tares at this time. When the servants would pull the tares out, the wheat would be lost, too. The owner of the field lets the tares remain with the wheat. At the time of harvest, the servants will bundle the tares and burn them.[5]

Many parents and step parents have tares growing within their families. They have shed many a tear and offered many prayers in behalf of children and step children who would rather spread noxious, destructive weeds within their family and community. Families and step families have family members who would rather be calmed by noxious weeds than the gospel of Jesus Christ. The Savior knows that parents and step parents love their families and would be lost without all their family members.

If you are getting no where with your family, it is easy to become depressed. It is very depressing to realize you have tares in your family, especially if everyone blames you for the behavior and fruits of a tare. It is depressing to be called a tare when you are trying so hard to produce a crop of wheat in your family or step family.

The Savior knows that everyone has wheat and tares within themselves. The Savior loves the wheat in us more than He wants to punish the tares within us. The wheat, the good, and the tares, the bad, of every family will be gathered without religious instruction by society. When society separates the wheat from the tares, society has a tendency to call the wheat of your family, tares, and call the tares of your family, wheat. (Isaiah 5:20) This is why the Savior instructed the prophets to identify the wheat and warn us about the tares.

---

[5]Matthew 13:24-30, The Holy Bible, p. 1210.

The Savior has limits. At some point, no matter how difficult, you and your family members have to decide if you are going to be a wheat or a tare. No one can do this for you. The Savior does not allow parents or spouses to make this decision for their children and spouses. When individuals are given their final reward for their productivity, efforts, increases, and gentleness in this life, they will be gathered according to the parable of the Wheat and the Tares.[6]

The Sheep and the Goats. At the time of the Second coming, nations will be gathered before the Savior. I suspect that nations with be gathered according to the wheat and tares within them. Those having wheat, those who keep the commandments and His covenants, will be known as the sheep. Nations with tares, those who reject the commandments and are stubborn towards the covenants of God, will be known as goats. The sheep inherit the Kingdom which our Heavenly Father has prepared for us from the beginning. (Matthew 25:32 - 34) This is why all nations are entitled to hear the Gospel of Jesus Christ.

Mothers readily understand the wheat and tares. This is why Mother cannot stand anyone punishing her child, even the child's father. She has planted much wheat among her child's tares. No one is going to destroy her child's "wheat." Loving the "wheat" in your spouse more than hating their "tares" is what makes for a happy marriage. Hopefully, there is some wheat in your spouse or child to love, not just tares. There are limits for tares in a child even for mother.

It is our responsibility to discover and protect the "wheat" in ourselves and families and to discover the ways to eliminate the "tares" within ourselves. It is our responsibility to instruct our families, particularly children and step children and our grandchildren about the wheat and the tares they will experience in their life. They will have less tares if they plant a crop of wheat. Tares do not go away by ignoring them or re-labeling tares as wheat or agency or rights. Our depressions are not decreased or eliminated by adding more tares to our life. This increases burdens which increases our layers of depression. There is a way to eliminate tares.

Through parables, Christ teaches us that we can eliminate the tares in our life with repentance. When we or our children have fallen by the wayside, among the stony paths, and fall among the thorns of life, there is always repentance. Repentance is within our grasp, even when an enemy to God and family has sown tares within us. The parables are all about repentance– how we have been repenting and how we should repent.

Christ is under the same obligation to preach repentance to His brothers and sisters as we are. Christ does not remove our tares harshly by upbraiding us. The Savior eases us into repentance with His parables. Christ wants to ease burdens with repentance, not create burdens with repentance. Faith in ourselves and Him come this way. This brings many blessings into our lives and the lives of others.

The sun rises and sets in their children and step children for most parents and step parents. However, for many parents and step parents, their sunrises and sunsets are not so pretty. At sometime in our life, we and our children fall into all the synonyms and antonyms which Christ taught His brothers and sisters. There are parables for these situations. We will be discussing them in subsequent chapters. There are too many to put in one chapter.

In latter day scripture, the Savior told all of us, including parents and step parents, to: "reproving betimes with sharpness, when moved upon by the Holy Ghost; and then showing

---

[6]Doctrine and Covenants 101:65, p. 199.

forth afterwards an increase of love toward him whom thou hast reproved, lest he esteem thee to be his enemy." (<u>Doctrine and Covenants</u> 121 :43) Every parent and step parent wishes they could be this skillful in teaching their children this way, especially when they have a wayward child or wayward spouse. With every parable, we have an example of how to do this. Notice. We show an increase in love not rewards or a decrease in love. All adults and children have many layers of wax accumulating over his or her heart since birth. It takes a lot of patient chastening to get the many layers of wax and grossness to melt.

Without Christ's parables, the spiritual synonyms and antonyms of our lives, we are ever learning, but not able to come to the knowledge of the truth. Individuals cannot learn faith, love, respect, mercy, and forgiveness by limiting our comparisons to apples and oranges, dogs and cats, cookies and cakes, sports and recreation, or movies and television. What truth do we need to learn? Faith in Jesus Christ, repentance and forgiveness, love and charity, mercy and justice.

The Savior received much grief for teaching us about the principles and mysteries of Heaven–faith, repentance, charity, forgiveness, mercy, and justice. In our settings of life, there are many who do not want us thinking like the Savior did. They do not want us to teach or learn our spiritual synonyms and antonyms. If we begin thinking like the Savior did, we might act like the Savior did. If we act like the Savior does, we will have some of his grace and stature.

Stop here. It is now time to think about the seeds that each family member sows in their families and step families and communities, the ground they are growing in. As we do this, we will discover there are tares growing among your wheat. What kind of seeds have you and your children cast within themselves and with others? Are these seeds worthy to plant? Are parents and step parents the sowers of the family and step family, or are children and step children the gardeners? You know how children garden.

Has your seeds fallen by the wayside, in stony places, among the thorns, or on good ground? Are you able to create life in these types of ground? Who or what is devouring the good seeds which you and each family member plants? I suspect that we get experience in each of these types of ground.

How are you managing your seeds in the various kinds of soil? Can you and your family members tell the difference between these four types of soil? Are you willing to transplant a seedling to good ground? It takes work. The seedling could be yourself. Remember the pattern in the steps of the creation as you now try to create your family garden.

List the wheat and the tares that are growing in each family member. In spite of our best efforts, all of us have tares. We also have wheat. Do the tares outnumber the wheat in your family? Are you or anyone in your family becoming a stubborn goat who will eat anything or a sheep who knows and follows the shepherd? Who has sowed the tares among your family members? How can you help family members and yourself grow more wheat than tares? Are you aware that repentance, mercy, and forgiveness eliminates the tares in families and your self?

Are you willing to harvest your wheat, or do you leave it on the ground in the elements? Do you harvest your tares instead of your wheat because tares takes less effort and are more exciting? Are you trying to harvest a one hundred-fold crop, a sixty-fold crop, or a thirty fold crop of tares? Are you trying to harvest a one hundred-fold crop with a thirty-fold planting? Your crop failures will be frustrating and depressing if you do. Your ground will become so hard that even tares will not grow in them.

Chapter Three

Our Spiritual Synonyms and Antonyms, Part II

In the first chapter on synonyms and antonyms, we briefly discussed the seeds that are planted, the types of ground in which they are planted, and the wheat and the tares that grow in the ground. In part two, we will discuss our reactions to the harvests or lack of harvests in ourselves and others. Parents and step parents work hard at transplanting a seedling to good soil. Their seedlings prefer the wayside, stony places, or life among the thorns. Parents and step parents respond with feelings of shock, anger, betrayal, and grief. They bargain with a seedling to get the seedling to move to better ground. When this does not work, parents become more angry and depressed. The synonyms for anger, betrayal, grief, and depression are rents. A rent is a tear, hole, or gap in cloth or relationships. The most famous rent was in the curtain of the temple when the Savior died. The world suffers with the rent between the Savior and Satan.

Rents. In two of His parables, the Savior compares an unsightly patch and an ineffective, useless bottle. The Savior reminded us that we cannot patch old material with new material and have the item look good. The tear in the material will increase. Men cannot put new wine in old bottles. Bottles will break in the fermentation process. If bottles are not sealed or have tiny rents, air and bacteria enter and contaminate the juice. We, of course, are thinking patches and are wondering why the Savior is teaching about wine in a parable when fermented juice is against His Word of Wisdom.

> *16 No man putteth a piece of anew cloth unto an old garment, for that which is put in to fill it up taketh from the garment, and the rent is made worse.*
> *17 Neither do men put new wine into old bottles: else the bottles break, and the wine runneth out, and the bottles perish: but they put new wine into new bottles, and both are preserved.*
> Matthew 9:16 - 17, <u>The Holy Bible</u>

These parables are not talking about the same kind of rents. It would be interesting if the Savior was comparing tears in clothing from normal use and wear with the rents caused by family conflicts. Conflicts can be so bad that the step family splits in pieces. We used to call the rents in our families, generation gaps. The generation gap could be in chronological age or mental age. Now, we call them dysfunctional families.

Families become unattractive with generation gaps. The younger generation tries to put new material, alcohol, drugs, fornication, adultery, homosexuality, abortion, lack of education, etc., into old material, a family with parents and growing children, who are trying to mature and receive an education. Parents and step parents know the things which cause generation gaps or rents will effect young children deeply, as well as themselves and their wayward child. Parents and step parents become angry and feel betrayed. As they teach siblings, children, and step children about the harmful effects of this new material, the gaps or rents become larger in their families and step families. They become dysfunctional and ineffective families and step families.

Tailors and seamstress' do not patch old material with new material. The strength of the new material causes a larger tear. I have seen this occur in tents. The old material could not withstand the wind. The new material was strong enough to withstand the wind, but was sucked through the old material causing a larger tear.

When I learned to sew, I learned how to put material in other material to make a dress. There were steps to this process. Pieces of material in the form of a dress were cut out and sewed together at the shoulders. Necklines were completed before I sewed the side seams of the dress. Cuffs were sewn on before I sewed the sleeves together. Waistlines, necklines, collars, and cuffs required facings and interfacing. Even buttonholes had to be stabilized with thread and sometimes an interfacing between two layers of material. Some dresses required an entire inner lining. This is like making two dresses and putting one into the other. With all this work, I assure you that I did not use new material to line old material for the clothing I made.

As I learned the concept of putting material into other material, the necklines, collars, cuffs, pockets, waistbands, and buttonholes in the dresses formed and looked nicer. I quit trying to save money by cutting out patterns anyway I wanted and by omitting interfacing in waistbands, cuffs, and collars. As a result, my daughter's outfits did not tear as often. Her dresses which required an entire lining were not as limp after washing. I did learn to avoid the patterns that required an entire lining of the dress. The dresses that I did make for my daughter would have looked terrible if I had used new material for the lining and interfacing of her necklines, collars, sleeves, and cuffs. There would have been no shape, flexibility, or grace to the dress.

I imagine the Savior watched His mother and father sew. Mary probably had to patch her family's clothing several times. Men are tailors, too. The Savior's father, Joseph who was a carpenter, probably sewed things to carry his carpentry tools or to make shade in his shop or in the area he was working. Being married to a carpenter, I know all carpenters do this. Mary and Joseph may have sewed or repaired a tent for their family.

Mary also made dresses for her self and her daughters and cloaks and trousers for her sons and husband. She, too, placed rents or gaps in the material. These tears or rents were needed if the material was to be made into clothing for her family. However, if Mary wanted these gaps to remain a certain size, her gaps needed facing and interfacing, too. These gaps became necklines, holes for sleeves, waistlines, and buttonholes. She placed a facing made out of the same material so the neckline did not tear beyond the desired size. Mary washed her clothing in streams. The clothing would tear easy or fray when washing, especially in the gaps.

If a seamstress used new material to line old material to save the dress, the new material would be on the inside and the old material would be on the outside. The old material would fray as it rubbed against the new material. This would expose the underside of the new material.

A seamstress using silk material in a dress or shirt has to be careful. Silk is a beautiful, but delicate material. Silk dresses also need binding, facings, and interfacing. A needle placed through silk leaves a hole the size of the needle. The thread must stay there. There is no forgiveness with silk. Otherwise, the finished dress has a lot of little needle holes where adjustments were made. The dress would not be so attractive. Seamstresses using silk usually make an entire different dress out of other material before they make the dress out of silk. This is similar to our bodies in this life and what our bodies will be like after our resurrection. In this life, we learn the correct measurements of our dress, the bindings, the cuffs, the collars, the interfacing, the hems (limits). We decide what fabric to use in our dress and how we will line the collars, cuffs, necklines, and hems. We learn to repair the tears.

The concept of binding, lining, facing, and interfacing is not new nor is it limited to material and clothing. Shelves are more sturdy with a backing material on the back. This material may only be one fourth of an inch thick. Books have binding. Blankets loose their shape, become limp, and wear easy without bias tape. Fractured vertebrae in spinal column are fused with "new" material from a donor or the patient's hip. Unfortunately, the spine continues to fracture above and below the fusion. This is most likely due to the strength of the new material used to fuse the injured area in the spine.

With what have you lined, faced, and interfaced the natural rents and the unnatural rents in yourself and your family? Are you trying to patch your life back together with new material on old material? When there are conflicts in your self and your home, are you seeking things that will render you and your family ineffective? The fruits of your labors will not be lost if you line yourself and your family with the gospel of Jesus Christ. The gospel of Jesus Christ is the same, yesterday, today, and forever. This is where your hidden treasures lie, not by the wayside, in stony places, or among the thorns. Of course, if you have many rents in your family, you may feel the need to seek many treasures.

Christ has several parables about treasures. Christ explains the kingdom of heaven *is like* a treasure found in a field. When a man, possibly a farmer or shepherd, finds a treasure that was hidden, he rehides it. He is joyful and sells all that he has and buys the field. (Matthew 13: 44) A merchant man is looking for goodly pearls. When he finds that one pearl of great price, he also sells all that he has and buys the pearl of great price. (Matthew 13:45-46)

> *44 ¶ Again, the kingdom of heaven is like unto treasure hid in a field;*
> *the which when a man hath found, he hideth, and for joy thereof goeth*
> *and selleth all that he hath, and buyeth that field.*
> *45 ¶ Again, the kingdom of heaven is like unto a merchant man, seeking*
> *goodly pearls:*
> *46 Who, when he had found one pearl of great price, went and sold all*
> *that he had, and bought it.   Matthew 13:44 - 46, <u>The Holy Bible</u>*

Since we are talking about the kingdom of heaven, most of us are thinking this field is a field with good ground, and the treasure is the gospel of Jesus Christ. The man liked the treasure so much. He rejoiced at finding the treasure. He even re-buried the treasure and sold all that he had to buy this field. Some treasures in this life have been deliberately hid in the field so we will buy the field. We may buy the field over and over and never take possession. Some have had to sell all they had to partake of the gospel of Jesus Christ. However, the gospel of Jesus Christ is not to be hidden within us.

As I look around the environment that I live in and watch the environment which is portrayed to me in the newspaper, movies, and television, there are a lot of people who have many different treasures. These treasures are very important to them. They need them for comfort, satisfaction, status, or a distraction from their hurt and pain. Their treasures may have come from a field by the roadside or the wayside, a field of stones, a field of thorns, or good ground. They hoard these kinds of treasures to comfort themselves and take their mind off of their suffering. The treasure which they have buried is themselves.

Many have thrown valuable treasures away because they could not recognize a treasure when they had it in their grasp? Families and step families have buried family members, sometimes literally in a field. Do you recognize a treasure in your possession? What kind of field has it come from? Are you burying the treasures within yourself with depression? Have you cast away or buried the treasures of your family for a treasure from the wayside, stony places, and thorny places? Do your treasures need to be sorted and some cast away because they are not really treasures? It your treasure something you just want to hang onto because you might make something out of it someday.

Sorting. When people are angry and feel betrayed in the relationships of their family, they sort things out in their mind. They try to cast the bad away. Mankind has always had trouble sorting mankind. They hoard things, but will cast away anyone who upsets them immediately. People can hoard feelings for years. Some call this rumination. I call it grudges. In our grudges, we forget that we are casting away a parent, step parent, spouse, child, sibling, step sibling, or grandparent. Naturally, we expect that God will do the same.

> *47 ¶ Again, the kingdom of heaven is like unto a net, that was cast into the sea, and gathered of every kind:*
> *48 Which, when it was full, they drew to shore, and sat down, and gathered the good into vessels, but cast the bad away.*
> *Matthew 13:47 - 48, The Holy Bible*

In these parables, fishermen cast a net into the sea. They gather fish of every kind. When the boat is full of fish, they gathered the good fish into vessels and threw away the bad fish. The Savior explains this will happen also at the end of the world. The wicked will be sorted from the just. (Matthew 13:44 - 49) How did the fishermen decide what was a good fish and what was a bad fish? They were all living when they were caught in the net so they were not spoiled. I suspect it was what would sell on the market. Some fish may have been poisonous. The weight of a large amount of fish in a net damages the fish on the bottom.

Seek Understanding. When generation gaps cause large rents in families and step families, everyone desires understanding. Children and step children expect parents and step parents to conform to children's wishes. To children, this is understanding. If children do not receive the understanding they want, they expect mother and father, step mother or step father to sort and discard their own children or spouse. Children and step children often expect the neighborhood and the world to conform as they expected their parents and step parents to conform. Unnecessary and vengeful sorting stonewalls the neighborhood and the world.

Jesus asked if we understood all these things. I suspect that we do not. Our idea of a kingdom is a king or queen, a monarchy. Christ is not here nor did He die to change Himself. This life is for us to change. Christ taught us how to change through parables. The Kingdom of Heaven is us. This is how the Savior sees us. We are brothers and sisters who resemble: old and

28

new material, broken bottles, fish of every kind, and treasures. We are not yet perfected, but we have an older brother who thinks we all are a treasure. He is a Treasure that should be kept close to our hearts and minds and followed.

> *51 Jesus saith unto them, Have ye understood all these things?*
> *They say unto him, Yea, Lord.*
> *52 Then said he unto them, Therefore every scribe which is instructed*
> *unto the kingdom of heaven is like unto a man that is an householder,*
> *which bringeth forth out of his treasure things new and old.*

Matthew 13:51 - 52, The Holy Bible

Most all of us are scribes. We can read, write, and keep records in some manner. We keep track of our treasures. Grudges can become treasures. We have been instructed in the Kingdom of Heaven with Christ's parables. There are times and ways to sort treasures. We can trade some treasures for other treasures that we and our families can use and be benefitted by. Sorting creates space for more treasures. It does not help to hoard the bad and discard the good in our lives. The bad will overtake the good. It always does. Are you willing to sort the good treasures from the bad or ineffective treasures in your life? Are you willing to bring out the old and new things in your treasures that you have sorted? If not, you will be depressed. Naturally, we have to account for the treasures we did obtain or did not obtain or sort.

Accounting. Mankind expects mankind to make an accounting of their mistakes when they disagree or are angry with them. We tend to give our view of justice with a heavy hand of justice, instead of mercy. Compassion makes others think that we are weak and vulnerable.

The Kingdom of Heaven *is* like a certain king who wanted an accounting of his servants. A servant who owed the king ten thousand talents was brought to the king. The servant could not pay his debt to the king. His lord commanded that he, his wife, and children be sold and the payment made. The servant fell down, worshiped him, and said, "Lord, have patience with me, and I will pay thee all." The lord of that servant was moved with compassion and forgave the debt. The same servant found one of his fellow servants which owed him a hundred pence. He took *him* by the throat, and said: "Pay me that thou owest." His fellow servant fell down at his feet, and asked: "Have patience with me, and I will pay thee all." The first servant refused. He cast his fellow servant into prison till he should pay the debt. Other fellow servants saw what happened and told their lord what was done. His lord called him and said: "O thou wicked servant, I forgave thee all that debt, because thou desiredst me: Shouldest not thou also have had compassion on thy fellow servant, even as I had pity on thee?" His lord was angry and delivered him to the tormentors, till he could pay all the debt. Christ said that my Heavenly Father will do unto you, if ye do not forgive every one their trespasses. (Matthew 18:23 - 35)

One day, we are going to stand before our Lord. All of us owe Him a debt that we cannot repay. In spite of our ways and ideas, our Lord keeps trying to make things better for us. There are people on Earth to whom we owe debts. We cannot repay them. Some of these people are parents and step parents, not movie stars or football players. Are you willing to stand before the Lord with a long lists of debts which you could not forgive parents and step parents, siblings or

29

step siblings, or a spouse, but you could forgive your favorite movie star of many things? If so, you will be delivered to the tormentors. Its called depression. With depression, your only option in life is to try to balance hate for yourself and hate for others with hate.

How much mercy have you given to others? How much mercy do you give yourself? Do you expect more mercy for you than you give others? Do you give less mercy to yourself than what all God's children deserve? Would you like to have more mercy? Begin with the Ten Commandments. This brings you and your family much mercy. All commandments of Christ bring mercy to ourselves and others. Mercy is the benefit of this kind of service.

Pass By Others. About twelve years of age, children begin to pass by parents for peers. Parents can be hurt, sick, and need help. Children continue to pass by parents. A spouse can pass by their spouse for drugs, alcohol, adultery, homosexuality, and pornography. This kind of life is more exciting and urgent than a life with parents and spouse. After giving us The Parable of The Good Samaritan, children and step children and adults do not think the Lord will notice their behavior with each other.

The Story of The Good Samaritan. The story of the Good Samaritan begins with a lawyer. The Story of the Good Samaritan is Christ's final answer to the lawyer. It is a story about passing by others.

A lawyer, tempting Christ, asked Christ what he should do to receive eternal life. Christ told the lawyer to love thy God with all thy soul, strength, and mind. The lawyer was also to love thy neighbor as thyself. The lawyer gave a rebuttal, a cleverly disguised opposing argument, to Christ. As lawyers do, he redirected Christ's answer in the form of a question. In redirect, lawyers get the privilege of asking questions again after their witness has been questioned by the opposing attorney. Redirect questions are meant to block the progress of the questioning process. The lawyer asked: "Who really is my neighbor?" Christ responded with the parable of The Good Samaritan.

The Good Samaritan. A certain man went from Jerusalem to Jericho. He fell among thieves, who stripped him of his clothing and wounded him. They departed, leaving him half dead. By chance, a priest passed that way. When he saw him, he passed by on the other side, as did a Levite. A certain Samaritan came where the wounded man lay. When he saw him, he had compassion on him. He went to him and bound his wounds after cleaning them with oil and wine. He set him on his own beast, brought him to an inn, and took care of him. When the Good Samaritan departed, he took out two pence, and gave them to the innkeeper and asked him to take care of him. If his care cost more than the money he gave him, he would repay the innkeeper when the good Samaritan returned. Christ asked: "Out of the priest, the Levite, and the Samaritan, which was neighbor to the man who fell among the thieves?" The lawyer said: "He that shewed mercy on him. Jesus said to him, "Go, and do thou likewise." (Luke 10:25 - 37)

As conflicts escalate in families and step families, biological and step parents are passed by over the slightest disagreements. Children and step children claim this is because they cannot get along with their parent, or their parent will not listen to them. This is not true. Passing by a parent or step parent conveys non acceptance of this marriage or this individual to others, especially their siblings, children, and neighborhood. Their children, neighbors, and siblings are expected to pass by parents and grandparents, too. Neighbors begin to wonder if there really is fire when they see all this smoke. Children, neighbors, and siblings do not want to be passed by, too. Parents and step parents begin passing by their children and step children, beginning with the one they think started the problems in the family. Children and step children know hurt happens. They have been hurt in this manner by peers and family. Naturally, the ones who are passed by are offended. Objection is a synonym for being offended.

Objection. In our present day, Christ could not teach the parable of the Good Samaritan in a court of law. Lawyers from all sides would give a very loud "Objection!" This is exactly what parents and step parents and others hear in the court of family opinion when parents and step parents try to teach mercy, values, and love of family and country and the Savior to their children and step children. "Objection!" This is why we do not have so many Good Samaritans. This is how children create opposition in families and step families. Passing others by, hurting them, and blaming those they hurt as the one who caused the hurt causes many to become offended with family members. The hurt that is caused by you or others turns the good ground the Lord provided you into ground that is by the wayside, a stony place, or full of thorns.

Members of your family, step family, faith, and country have to develop many layers of wax over their hearts to dull the pain of being passed by just for existing. When we hear Christ's parables, our heart strings will be pulled. Hearts who have many layers of wax from despair and iniquity melt. Hearts who are gross soften. We can understand things without being hurt, offended, stonewalled, intimidated, and oppressed. Parables open closed minds and hearts. The Savior's parables keep our minds open with mercy and respect. The Savior's parables reflect other teachings that He taught in the scriptures.

Now, let's see how the soft answers of Christ changes us. This is our maturing process. How we respond to Christ's maturing process determines whether we are depressed or happy. Through understanding of Christ's Parables, we become strong of stature instead of low in spirit and depressed.

We all have rents that hurt. Some rents must come so we can mature. Some rents are through normal wear, tear, and fatigue. Some rents will come from others. Describe the rents that you are having in your life and your family. How would you sort them? Are you putting new material in the Savior's gospel causing your heart to burst?

What do you treasure? If it is your spouse, children, and the Lord, does your actions match your treasure? Have you sold all you have including the blessings that come from the Lord and having a spouse and children to have this treasure plus many more treasures?

Are you treasuring your rents and discarding family and step family members? Are you willing to discard a treasure to make room for a treasure that has a more pressing claim? Have you asked a mother or father to sort and then discard their children?

Are you sorting your treasures according to the natural man's ways or God's ways? God's ways accumulates and inspires people. The natural man's ways sort by hurt feelings and objections. Are you aware that spiritual antonyms are not always objections and opposition?

How do you seek understanding instead of forgiveness when you have committed a sin or a mistake? Are you a scribe of everyone's behavior, but your own? Do you likewise expect an accounting from everyone else about their behavior, but your own behavior you can overlook? You will not have many harvests if you are passed by a lot? Are you hurt and depressed more by being passed by or by a heart that has waxed cold? Can you recognize the time of harvest each year in your family and yourself? There are ways of having harvests with late bloomers.

Chapter Four

The Fig Trees

Jesus Christ taught about fig trees in His Parables. Fig trees are common in Israel. The Savior's parents may have had fig trees on or near their property. Prophets and probably many others were saved from the heat of the day by sitting in the shade of a fig tree and partaking of the figs. *Three stories about fig trees are going to save us from the "frost" of our day.*

The Late-Leafer. Fig trees are odd. The fruit appears first, then the leaves appear on the fig tree. Thus, fig trees are known as "late-leafers," not late bloomers. Fig leaves are large, reaching about one foot in size. Adam and Eve used fig leaves to cover their nakedness because the fig leaf was a large leaf. Fig trees have a spring and a fall crop. The fall crop is the main crop. Figs must ripen on the tree. Once picked, figs will not ripen anymore.

In this day and country, people are use to trees budding out with leaves in the spring. Blossoms appear. Fruit follows if the trees are not exposed to frost. One crop of fruit is obtained at the time of harvest. Fortunately, each type of fruit tree has its own scheduled harvest time.

Trees, bushes, and plants need a certain amount of leaves for photosynthesis to occur. Leaves store the cells which store the nutrients and water needed for photosynthesis. In photosynthesis, chloroplast cells, cells containing chlorophyll, convert nutrients in the soil and water to sugars which plants need for growth. This takes place in the presence of light. In this process, carbon dioxide is needed, but plants produce oxygen. Humans convert energy from the sun, water, and fat soluble vitamins, producing carbon dioxide. It's a give and take process for both which replenishes and restores both.

We may wonder why the fig tree produces figs before the leaves. It could be the latitude and longitude or the heat in Israel. I wonder if it is for this reason. Fig blossoms provide the first foraging blossoms for honeybees. The United States depends on dandelions for the first foraging crop for bees. The queen bee realizes pollen, the protein source for bees, is available. The queen bee begins to lay approximately 1500 eggs a day because there is something to feed her brood.

Every country has a first crop that produces pollen for the bees and pollinating insects to eat and feed their young. If countries eliminate this first crop of foraging plants for bees and insects or contaminate the pollen with insecticide spray, bees cannot produce young. Bee colonies die out. Young bees starve to death or are poisoned when they are fed contaminated pollen. The country has a hard time providing food for itself because other plants are not pollinated. It comes a vicious cycle.

Bees mean industry. Without bees, one must learn to pollinate a large orchard or garden with the wind or a small brush. This is difficult and very time-consuming. Wind pollination requires a minimum of four rows of plants which ties up more land and produces less crops. It seems we are trying to pollinate our families and step families with sports, drugs, alcohol, Hollywood, and the News Media. This is a wind pollination which ties up more land and produces less crop in individuals, families, step families, and countries. We pollinate our spiritual crop with Christ, parents, and step parents, and a spouse, not with manipulation, stonewalling behavior, isolation, and excessive sports and recreation.

The Fig Tree With Potential. The owner of a vineyard looked for figs on a fig tree for three years. Since the fig tree was not producing fruit, the owner felt the fig tree was encumbering that spot of land. He wanted to plant another fig tree or something else there. The gardener in the vineyard asked to dig and dung the fig tree one more year. If the fig tree did not produce, the owner could cut it down. (Luke 13:6 - 9) The gardener, being familiar with the fig tree, knew there was potential fruit production in this tree by the growth of the twigs each year. Fig trees are removed if their branches grow under a certain amount of length per year, usually a foot. We are given parents and step parents so someone is familiar with our rate of growth.

The Story of the Non-Productive Fig Tree. The Savior was hungry and began looking for something to eat. He saw a fig tree with leaves and expected to find figs. There were none. The Savior cursed the fig tree that it would never produce fruit forever. The fig tree immediately withered away. (Matthew 21:18 - 22) This story about a fig tree was surprising even to the Apostles. It is surprising to us. Why did the Savior curse this fig tree? With His power, why didn't He just heal the fig tree and give it some figs? It would be another miracle.

Remember. Fig trees have to grow a certain amount every year, or they are cut down and burned. Jesus probably spent a lot of time where this fig tree grew. He was familiar with the fig tree. He expected to find fruit. He realized it was not growing the normal amount within a year and would not bear fruit. He cursed the tree. It withered immediately.

In Sunday School, we focus on the fact that the Savior cursed the tree, and it withered immediately. Christ was powerful When asked about this power, He told His apostles that if they had faith they could do that to a fig tree. They could also move mountains. This power came from faith and prayer. This power would be needed to protect the apostles and the people they were teaching. Christ was trying to teach them to not be afraid of this kind of power. Sometimes, it is a necessity. You see, if he allowed one fig tree to produce a few figs without effort, the entire vineyard would become a vineyard with poor production.

Notice in these three stories, there is a difference between a fig tree that is a late-leafer, a fig tree that has potential for bearing fruit, and a non-productive tree. One fig tree, the one with potential, bears fruit late. The other fig tree bears leaves late. One fig tree bears no fruit at all.

Parents and step parents can curse a fig tree in the vineyard, their child or step child. They are not getting straight "A's" on their report card and are not a member of the senior varsity sports team in high school. Thus, their children and step children are not producing. Very few parents will have the experience of a child producing this much on their first crop. Your child cannot produce if the parent or step parent does not produce on their first and second crops of fruit. The child produces his first crop from you–the parent or step parents–not siblings.

Siblings in families and step families like to keep their siblings from the ones that will help them produce their first crops. This brings great harm to siblings. Parents, step parents, and siblings have not been given the power or authority or right to deprive their child or sibling of their first and second crops in life.

Parents, step parents, and siblings will notice when they have a child or sibling who is a late-leafer, has potential, or is non-productive. They wonder if their late-leafer will ever produce a first crop of fruit, let alone leaves and a second crop. Parents and step parents and siblings do not have to reward children and siblings in laziness and drug and alcohol addiction. This takes their potential from them. The child withers away. Hopefully, their children and step children will become tired of being withered and decide to do the things that will bring a first and second crop in their lives. This kind of management of children is difficult. Late-leafers are as frustrated by being a late-leafer as parents are in dealing with late-leafers. Psychiatrists call it "tough love." Your children will need love, shelter, food, and clothing.

Trees are known to be supported by other trees' root systems. I do not know of any plant that can obtain the chemicals, nutrients, and water needed for growth from another plant's root system or leaves. A stem is required which connects the root with branches and leaves. *Isaiah called Jesus Christ the stem of Jesse.* Families are the branches and individuals are the leaves.

The fig tree and its fruit are excellent ways to teach spiritual synonyms and antonyms to everyone, not just Israel. Figs are wild or cultivated. Like the fig tree, every country, every organization, and every family has wild or cultivated individuals growing in their midst. They produce fruit of their kind first, they are late-leafers, or they bear no fruit at all. Their leaves come with experience.

Look at any piece of fruit. It has to have a stem for leaves and fruit to grow. Christ is the first fruits of them that slept. Those who will resurrect or be quickened after His Second Coming will be the second fruits, the fall crop. (Doctrine and Covenants 88:96 - 99) The first fruits of repentance are baptism and faith. (Moroni 8:25, The Book of Mormon) The second crop or fall crop comes from the Gift of the Holy Ghost. A family works more smoothly if the husbandman or father is the first partaker of the fruits for the family. (2 Timothy 2:6)

> *32 Now learn a parable of the fig tree; When his branch is yet tender,*
> *and putteth forth leaves, ye know that summer is nigh:*
> *33 So likewise ye, when ye shall see all these things, know that it is near,*
> *even at the doors.*
> *34 Verily I say unto you, This generation shall not pass, till all these*
> *things be fulfilled.*
> *35 Heaven and earth shall pass away, but my words shall not pass away.*
> *Matthew 24:32 - 35, The Holy Bible*

In latter days, Christ again told the parable of the fig tree–in the United States where fig trees are not common. What does Christ want us to learn by stories of fig trees? I suspect that answer is found in verse thirty-seven of this scripture.

> *36 And when the light shall begin to break forth, it shall be with them*
> *like unto a parable which I will show you—*
> *37 Ye look and behold the fig–trees, and ye see them with your eyes,*
> *and ye say when they begin to shoot forth, and their leaves are yet tender,*
> *that summer is now nigh at hand;*
> *38 Even so it shall be in that day when they shall see all these things,*
> *then shall they know that the hour is nigh.*
> *Doctrine and Covenants 45:36 - 38*

Tenderness. The Savior told us that He would come again. All of us are anxiously awaiting His return. The number of people, Earthly governments, and family relationships are encumbering us. We would like to live under His form of government again. However, there is a certain tenderness that the Savior is waiting for us to achieve individually, as a family, and as a group of children of our Heavenly Father before He comes. Otherwise, the whole Earth would utterly be wasted at His coming. (Doctrine and Covenants 2:1 - 3)

The signs of His Second Coming achieve a tenderness in us, but this compels us to be humble. Those who are compelled to be humble are not as blessed as those who truly humble themselves with mercy and endurance. (Alma 32:13 - 16, The Book of Mormon) This is why death bed repentance does not give us the blessings of a repentant life. We may be sorry for our mistakes, but we have not had time to humble ourselves from the hardness caused by our mistakes.

While we are waiting for Christ's return, families and nations are becoming harder and harder over the love of money, sports, alcohol, and drugs. The pressures of providing for many people and a few people's big dreams and big mouths are difficult. We are losing the tender shoots that come with our leaves due to the frost in sports, politics in any organization, alcohol and drugs. Families are partaking of the frost of the world and wonder why they have bitter, small fruit which does not mature and which fall prematurely to the ground.

Fig Trees and Families. A man and woman marry and form a family. The mother gives birth to a normal child, raises them as best as she and her husband can, loves them, but anything that parents do is not enough. Children become poor-achievers, alcoholics, drug addicts, thieves, murders, etc., and participate in all kinds of things which take those tender leaves from them that you once knew when they were children. They give up their ability to be productive. Children and step children wither and die before your eyes. They cause others to wither and die immediately with harsh criticisms, mocking, accusations, and their behavior.

When these individuals die, this is an infirmity that will not be loosed from them. This is an infirmity given up through repentance and restitution. A choice has to be made to give up this kind of behavior. A choice has to be made to have a first crop which determines the kind of fall crop the child has.

Many parents and step parents have handicapped children who will have a small first crop. They will not have a second crop in this life. Parents are forced to sign over guardianship to provide medical services. As parents age, parents have to place them with people who claim to have their best interests at heart, but really do not. One day, your handicapped child will be loosed from his or her infirmity.

Fig Trees and Step Parenting. A woman and man marry. One or both spouses has been married previously. A spouse has fruit from a previous fall crop, their previous husband or wife. This fruit is their children. The quality of your crop in your step family is determined by the problems in this first family. Parents may not realize how hurtful their problems are.

Step parents begin their crop. As they do this, they hear about the many problems in the previous family and the problems that will occur in a step family. Many decide to just add leaves to their tree. Some may add fruit to their blended family. Children expect parents and siblings to live in a child's shadow to make up for these problems. A step mother soon discovers she also has to live in the shadow of her step children, especially step daughters, to make up for these problems–till death parts she and her husband. There is only frost for her in this shadow. Biological daughters expect mothers to live in their shadow, too. Step mother is of course expected to live somewhat in the shadow of her husband. It is difficult to have so many masters who are callous and inexperienced. As expected, she will hate the one, and despise the other instead of becoming tender. (Matthew 6:24)

A step father is expecting to be a spouse, provider, and protector of the family. When he marries, he knows there will be difficulties. He does not realize how much he has to live in the shadow of his wife's biological children and his own children. The children should be living in the shadow of their parents and step parents, especially the father. This is how the fruit of the family is ripened and protected.

This discovery of this unending shadow is worse than being hit with repeated bolts of lightening. This type of shadow causes severe depression. This depression can consume you. When you are depressed, there is not much to consume. Your choices seem to be divorce or suicide. *Divorce, addictions, and suicide are not the only leaves that are left on your family tree.*

My husband did not ask me to live in the shadow of his children. Therefore, I did not ask him to live in the shadow of my child. We still had difficulties to overcome. We had to learn how to add leaves to our family tree, increase the potential of our family tree, and recognize what had no potential in our lives. We have had many second crops in our marriage. The Savior provided a way for us to develop tender shoots and fulfill His words in our generation.

We each have a time of death appointed unto us. It probably is the time when we have developed those tender shoots within us that fulfills all things of Christ in us. It is a time when we are able to rest from the opposition in the world. It definitely is not for us to decide our time of death because our children, step children, or spouse does not have the tender shoots which we want them to have. Children and step children have not been given the authority to decide for parents and step parents what tender shoots their family members can develop. If children and step children persist, they will wither away, usually in the same manner they caused their parents, step parents, siblings, and step siblings to wither.

List your first crop in your family. What is the second crop in your family? List the late-leafers in your life. Are they late-leafers physically, emotionally, socially, morally, intellectually, financially, spiritually, in work, in service, in sacrifice, in persistence, and in obedience? Do they have potential? Who is withering away in your family? Under the best of circumstances, this is quite a drain on parents and step parents. How can you help wayward individuals in your family or step family without causing depression in you?

List the tender shoots that you have and do not have. What tender shoots do you want to develop in yourself and your children? How will you develop more shoots? How are you blocked from developing tender shoots? Can you tell if your shoots have potential, are nonproductive, or are withered? Can you trim the shoots that have turned crisp with tenderness to make room for new shoots? Do you have enough tender shoots to guide your family for an eternity in that kind of environment? Will your tender shoots fulfill the words of Christ in your generation? Parent's tender branches are going to be different than your child's tender branches. However, everyone's tender branches are going to follow a pattern. Pray for the broken heart and contrite spirit that creates tender branches. We have examined your leaves, stems, and fruit. To decrease your depression, let us check your treetop.

Chapter Five

The Allegory of the Tame and Wild Olive Trees

A book about being neither root nor branch would not be complete without The Allegory of the Tame and Wild Olive Trees. This is a story about roots, natural branches, grafted branches, and the decay in the treetops in both tame and wild olive trees. This story is an allegory of mankind from the beginning of time to the end of time. Allegories are stories that have symbolic meaning. Allegories in scripture are ways to learn our spiritual synonyms and antonyms, too.

The Allegory of the Tame and Wild Olive Trees is found in the book of Jacob, Chapter Five in The Book of Mormon. This chapter is about the scattering, grafting, pruning, and gathering of the twelve tribes of Israel and the Gentiles of the World. Jacob quotes Zenos, a prophet who we did not know existed until we received The Book of Mormon. Zenos lived in the period of time before Jacob's parents, Lehi and Sariah, left Jerusalem. Lehi and his family left Jerusalem approximately 600 B.C. and traveled to approximately Peru. Jacob is a younger brother to Nephi. Both are sons of Lehi and Sariah. This family is one of the fruitful branches of Joseph of Egypt that went over the wall.[7]

Allegories are not new concepts for us. Allegories were taught to us by our English and literature teachers in high school and college. I had a few teachers begin this in junior high. One of my seventh grade teachers did not get anywhere with allegories in her class. Our class who had been comparing cats and dogs in grades one through six was now asked to compare elephants in seventh grade. We students were use to comparing cats and dogs which were obviously opposite. Our minds had no experience in comparing opposite and similar when it was not so obvious.

We students did not know how to compare elephants with other elephants. We could not think of anything opposite to elephants, other than big and small. Our teacher became as frustrated as we were. She just needed to tell us that there were differences in elephants other than big and small. There are standards for elephants such as age, health, shape of the ears, weight, tusk size, tusk quality, and most of all, temperament. If only she had explained this, many of her students might not have made some big mistakes by trying to "eat" poor quality elephants. Her students may not have always picked the "white elephants" of their life. If you recall, "white elephants" are junk passed off as gifts at parties.

Comparing people with people is like trying to compare elephants with elephants. We tend to judge people by one thing. Are they old or young, rich or poor, skinny or fat, athletic or out of shape, or black or white? Our minds become closed to anything except our first impression, the judgements that we have always relied on in life. The Allegory of the Tame and Wild Olive trees is going to help us see beyond these superficial qualities that humans first notice

---

[7]Genesis 49:22, The Holy Bible, p. 76.

in other humans. This happens in all families as well as step families. Keep in mind the parable of The Wheat and the Tares as you study this allegory. Scattering by grafting is better than pulling tares. There is less grief.

The Allegory of the Tame and the Wild Olive Trees is going to help us with depression. It is a long allegory, and it can become confusing and intense. If you are depressed, it is difficult to stay on task and think intensely. Read this material slowly and a few verses at a time. Depression is intense and confusing also.

Let's study both the allegory and depression by chunks instead of the whole tree. We are not just newborns, toddlers, pre-schoolers, students in elementary, junior high, and high school, and adult stages waiting to be fed and entertained. We are not just members of a certain tribe. We are the Lord's children living in His vineyard. There is a pattern to the growth and development in the Lord's Vineyard, the world.

The pattern in the Lord's vineyard. Most gardeners have a pattern in the way they plant their gardens and vineyards. The slope of the land and access to water determine the pattern. However, gardeners do not plant gardens which need full sun under shady trees. They also plant tall crops such as corn in a manner that the corn patch does not shade the other plants. This is how the sower sows his seed. This is how the Lord plants young trees in His vineyard, families. Many families have been planted, scattered, grafted, gathered, only to be scattered again. They do not know why. Most likely, they are planting their family garden under very shady trees.

Planting, checking, digging, pruning, dunging, scattering, grafting, and gathering are all parts of the pattern in our Heavenly Father's vineyard. Remember. We are seeking the tender branches which the Savior described in the scriptures, not just ripe, delicious fruit. The Savior wants to preserve the root as well as the branches, and He wants to have tame, delicious fruit to preserve. This is why we are instructed to follow the Savior. Now, let us see why Zenos compared mankind to tame and wild olive trees. Families are the structure of mankind.

The Tame Olive Tree. The olive tree is an evergreen tree usually found in Europe and the Middle East. Hence, its biological name, Olea europaea. I have family who have friends that raised olive trees successfully in California and Las Vegas, Nevada. The olive trees' leaves are leathery and its flowers are yellow. Olive trees produce a delicious, edible fruit which can be eaten green or ripe or which can be pressed into olive oil for many uses. The olive tree belongs to Oleaceae family of trees and shrubs as does Ash trees, lilacs, jasmines, and forsythias. They all have a loose four-petal flower.

The branch of the olive tree, traditionally is a symbol of peace. Olive oil is known for its purity and is used in cooking, salad dressings, liniments, cosmetics, and soap. Because of its purity, olive oil is also used to anoint in religious ceremonies. Carvings in olive wood are beautiful. Olive trees date to many hundreds of years of age. Olives and their products are a major source of industry in the Middle East. Like the buffalo in North America, in times of dispute, olive trees are destroyed or burned to prevent the owners from harvesting their crop of olives and olive oil.

The olive tree is another tree that receives its crop on the wood of the previous year. I suspect that all trees are like that. Olive trees have a gnarled trunk with four main branches. The olive tree grows to a height of fifty feet and a spread of thirty feet. It is pruned to about twenty feet to control fruit size and for easier harvesting. Leaves are replaced every two to three years.

The olive tree begins to bear fruit in its fourth to the tenth years. It can bear fruit for thousands of years. A crop of olives requires a long, hot growing season to ripen the olives. The olive tree is very susceptible to frost. Trees grown from seed or suckers from the roots do not have as good of fruit as the fruit on grafted branches. I would suspect that the energy of the tree is consumed in growing a trunk, branches, and leaves. A grafted branch is grafted to a tree that already has leaves, trunk, and branches. Wild branches grafted to tame, productive trees bear the same fruit as the tree to which it is grafted.

The Wild Olive Tree. There are wild olive trees (Olea Africana). These trees have thorny branches. The wild olive tree has more of the bitter glucoside, oleuropein, circulating in its roots. The tame tree does not. A wild olive tree should bear wild fruit even though it is grafted to a tame olive tree. I suspect that it is the bitterness of the chemical, oleuropein that causes wild fruit instead of sweet, tame fruit. Less bitterness produces tame fruit.

It would be interesting if the branch of a tame olive tree was brought back to Noah by a dove. There was a crown of thorns placed on the Savior's head at the time of His Crucifixion. It most likely came from the branches of the wild olive tree, the one with thorny branches and bitterness circulating in its roots, branches, and leaves.

The Similarity Between People and Olive Branches. We are grafted by birth, adoption, or marriage into a family or step family. Humans also have four main branches, called grandparents. Humans are very susceptible to the frost in their lives. We need a long, hot growing season. Humans begin to really show their personality around age four to ten years. We bear fruit off the previous year's growth in our parents,' step parent's, and spouse's growth, and in our education. We will be bearing fruit for thousands of years. Human beings can be wild or tame. If there is no growth, only frost in parents, step parents, and our spouse, there will be no fruit on the branches. Thorns use the energy of the tree. The suckers from the roots of a family or step family do not bear as much fruit as a grafted branch. As humans age in families and step families, we get gnarled bodies with our trials in the hot and cold temperatures of life. The wild olive branch bears the same kind of fruit which the wild olive branch is grafted, too. In step families, this tree usually is not their biological tree. It is their sibling tree. Families and step families begin to produce wild fruit because there is so much bitterness circulating among family and step family members.

Trials are easier to understand and endure if we know how the Master is working in His vineyard. This is something that we learn to recognize by the Holy Ghost, not by becoming depressed. The Master of our Garden is our Heavenly Father. His servant is Jesus Christ. All of us live in a part of His vineyard, the world. We live in families instead of packs or groves. We all came from the same family tree that was scattered and grafted and cultivated and gathered.

*3 For behold, thus saith the Lord, I will liken thee, O house of Israel, [your names]
like unto a tame olive-tree, which a man took and nourished in his vineyard;
and it grew, and waxed old, and began to decay.
4 And it came to pass that the master of the vineyard went forth, and he saw that his
olive-tree began to decay; and he said: I will prune it, and dig about it, and nourish
it, that perhaps it may shoot forth young and tender branches, and it perish not.
5 And it came to pass that he pruned it, and digged about it, and nourished it*

39

according to his word.
6 And it came to pass that after many days it began to put forth somewhat a little, young and tender branches; but behold, the main top thereof began to perish.

Jacob 5: 3-6, The Book of Mormon

The tree waxes old, decays, and the top of the tree dies. A family is formed by marriage. Tame and gentle children (tender shoots) are born to parents. Any new parent, obstetric nurse, or obstetrician can tell you there is nothing like a clean, fresh spirit that has just entered the realm of his and her Earthly existence. They bring their love with them and create a feeling of home. Parents and others nourish these little shoots as best as they can.

Why after so much care, do parents and children wax old? Why did the prophet Zenos use the terms "wax" and "old" when referring to a tree that was growing enough to produce tender shoots? Wax is a term we do not use much any more. When thinking of wax, we most often think of beeswax or sealing wax for floors or letters. There are other meanings for wax. Wax means to gradually increase in size, strength, effort, intensity, and volume, or become more numerous. The opposite of wax is wane. Remember your child or step child's temper tantrums. They waxed old, didn't they. The temper tantrums were bigger, bolder, and angrier as they aged. *Wax also means a state of anger or rage.*

Old, of course, refers to aging or having lived or been in existence for a long period of time. Old also means existing in the same state for long period of time. Symptoms from an illness or temper tantrums get old because things are not changing, progressing, or improving.

The population of the Earth is increasing in strength, intensity, and volume. The lighted portion that began with Adam and his family is becoming gradually full. This increased population is becoming more angrier each day. It would be interesting if the prophet, Zenos, was referring to the temper tantrums and rages that children and adults experience. Temper tantrums and childhood anger waxes old very quickly. Their behavior is tiresome and obsolete. Anger is harmful for the child as well as the child's family, community, and country if they persist in perpetual anger indefinitely. Individuals become angry over little things as much as they are angry over large offenses.

Cultivating. The Master of the Vineyard cultivated the soil of his vineyard many times by digging, pruning, and dunging. Notice, the Master pruned before he applied dung or manure. Pruning determines how much manure the tree receives. Manure or dung provides warmth as well as nourishment. Both are needed in the fertilizing process.

Hopefully, school and the poor school teacher will assist parents in the cultivation of children. Hopefully, children will produce their first crop of tame fruit. This pruning will make harvest time easier. Psychologists, doctors, social workers, ministers, and the justice system may have to do some specialized pruning, digging, and dunging on your children and step children.

Everyone will be checked on to see if the Master's cultivation system of nourishment has an effect on their growth and productivity. The Master knows that when one has waxed old or becomes angry, temper tantrums and rages get bigger, bolder, and stronger as individuals age. The child or the adult accepts no limits and cannot accept constructive criticism. The angry branch overtakes the root. The top of the tree dies.

The Top of the Tree Dies. It spite of all the care, only a few branches come forth, and the top of the tree dies in family members. In this struggle, the top of the family tree, the parents, particularly the father, dies also. Like the Master of the Vineyard, fathers and step fathers wonder what more could they have done to preserve the top of the tree in their wives, children and step children.

Parents of autistic children notice when the top of the tree dies out in their children. Their child may only be one or two years old. Wives notice when the top of the tree dies out in their husbands or their teenage children. Women may choose to marry a man who has a dead tree top. This marriage and family will be a struggle. To preserve the root and the branches of the natural tree, individuals or families need to be scattered.

In a beautiful tree that is producing fruit, it is hard to determine what is the top of the tree. Beautiful leaves cover the trunk and main branches. Drive down your neighborhood or in the mountains. You will see trees where the top of the tree has died. Now transfer this to your family. What is the top of the tree in people? I believe it is spirituality. I also believe that our spiritual treetop develops by our education. We have been given agency to choose how to develop the top of our tree. To save the top of our tree, the Lord scatters His people.

The Scattering. When there are disputations, conflicts, or poor growth and development in the Master's Vineyard, the Lord usually finds a way to scatter individuals, families, and even nations. We may decide to scatter or go in various directions our self. Over the course of normal growth and development, we do go to various places in our community. Scattering is not the same as spreading our wings or enlarging our borders. In scattering, there is a separation.

Who are the ones that are planted, checked on, pruned, nourished, and then scattered? Let's put a name and a face to those pruned and scattered by grafting and cultivation by the Master of the Vineyard. What is your name? What are your ancestors and descendants names? What are your spouse's name? What are your children and step children's names? Throughout time, past, present, and future, these are the individuals who are being planted, scattered, pruned, nourished, grafted, and gathered. These individuals come from many families. These families and step families come from many nations.

Why are we scattered? Families are scattered because some of this scattering occurs in our periods of normal growth and development. Children and step children go away to school, college, marry, or the military. Family members find employment in other cities, states, or countries. Couples like to develop their own space without interference. These things give them experience and an education.

Usually, families and step families are scattered because of rebellion. Rebellious individuals resist full sun. They resist grafting. They refuse to absorb refreshing water. Rebellious individuals prefer contaminated, muddy water. This behavior causes much grief in parents, in their neighborhoods, and in their country. These individuals are scattered somewhere else to see if they can be grafted and produce tame, delicious fruit instead of bitter fruit. Rebellious individuals are scattered to set limits on their behavior and to reduce their bitterness and anger. This protects those which they continually want to harm, including themselves.

To where are we scattered? When rebellious individuals resist the nourishment of parents, teachers, spouse, employers, or the Savior, they are scattered mentally and physically. The Master of the Vineyard scatters us to five kinds of spots.

The Nethermost Part. The natural branches of the tame olive-tree were placed in the nethermost part of the Master's Vineyard. Most people feel this means far away. Nethermost does not just mean far away. It means lowest point or farthest down. Mentally, this could be what the scriptures call outer darkness. It could also mean our time on Earth.

It is depressing to have a child who has scattered himself to outer darkness. Parents may have several children in outer darkness, a depressed and angry state. Parents and step parents may retreat to outer darkness to keep up the pace of outer darkness in their children. Parents become angry and depressed all the time. If parents do this, the child will remain there because parents usually make outer darkness or the nethermost spot too comfortable. Even the Savior and the Holy Ghost withdraws from us when we choose to remain in the Nethermost Spot.

The Poor Spot. In this allegory, the grafted branches are placed in the poorest spot of the Vineyard. As the story continues, the poorest spot is known just as a poor spot to the Lord. The Lord could find worse spots to graft branches. I have seen this in the hospital obstetric ward. I was caring for beautiful parents who were trying to have a baby. At the same time, there were parents who did not seem worthy of the beautiful baby they were ignoring. Every year at the hospital, we nurses, who thought we had seen it all, saw even poorer spots for children to be planted. Of course, I had no right to judge.

The Poorest Spot. Sometimes, we get planted in the poorest spot in the vineyard. We also think others who have been planted in our part of the vineyard are decreasing the value of our space in the Master's Vineyard. The grass always seems greener on the other side. The fruit of other olive trees looks more delicious at a distance.

There are many varieties of olives. Each produces a different flavor, but are very delicious. Keep in mind that the servant of the Master of the Vineyard asked why the Master of the Vineyard grafted the branches in the poorest spot of his ground. The Master of the Vineyard told the servant that it did not matter whether it was in the poorest or in the withersoever I will spots.

The Withersoever I Will Spots. This sounds like the Lord is placing grafted branches where ever He wanted randomly. The Master of the Vineyard is our Heavenly Father. The Servant in the vineyard is Jesus Christ. They do things with order, not randomly. The whithersoever I will spots sounds like our Heavenly Father's will. We are asked to do our Heavenly Father's will in all things in the Master's scriptures.

When the Servant of the Master of the Vineyard had His time to be grafted on Earth, He talked about the withersoever I will spots in a more eloquent manner. In what we call The Lord's Prayer, the Savior stated, "Thy will be done in earth, as *it is* in heaven." In a garden of olive trees, He stated: Father, if thou be willing, remove this cup from me: nevertheless not my will, but thine, be done. (Luke 22:42) If you recall, an angel appeared and immediately strengthened Him. Christ's mission was accomplished in the "withersoever I will spot."

One of the sad things of this life is how much we branches avoid the withersoever I will spots. By doing so, we avoid the angels that strengthen us. The Servant and the Master know our hearts. They know what we want and what we can do and what we need. The Master has His own purposes also. There is enough of us that He can put us in a spot that will accommodate His needs as well as our needs and wants and desires. Our needs, wants, and desires have to be righteous desires.

The Good Spot. Many branches were placed in good spots. They were productive for a time, produced half tame and half wild fruit for a time, and then produced all corrupt fruit. Good spots do not just happen. Good spots take a lot of work to keep a good spot a good spot. Marriage and children are perfect examples of good spots. Without maintenance and sacrifice, good spots become cumbered. When we are cumbered by things, it is usually is by apostasy, either in ourselves or others. We abandon the Master's Plan for His Vineyard and substitute our will for His Vineyard. Forgetting whose vineyard we are living in decreases fruit production even in the best of spots. We do not even know how He created His Vineyard.

Apostasy. The period of decay of the olive tree is seen as a symbolic reference for apostasy in leaders. In apostasy, we abandon or are coerced away from the ones and things that we have believed in such as parents, spouse, our faith, and our creed. Apostasy in leaders can range from leaders of churches, organizations, schools, and countries to families and employers. Unfortunately, there is apostasy in children. Some children are leaders at a young age. Children become the leaders in the home, not their parents. Many young leaders lead their family and friends into some very tragic situations. In the hospitals of Utah and Wyoming, I have cared for children and parents who were injured mentally and physically. They were victims of apostasy. They were also victimizers by apostasy.

Withering Away. The leaders of rebellion and the victimizers by apostasy wither in the vineyard. They do not accept or receive nourishment from the root. Their identity is control, anger, and rebellion. Eventually, they are pruned and burnt. Unfortunately, the victims of apostasy wither away, too. They do not receive nourishment from their roots.

I have seen this withering away in patients and their families. The medical profession calls it atrophy. Body tissue such as leg muscles, organs such as brain and heart fail to grow or develop. One cause is insufficient nutrition. Another cause is lack of use. When our spirit does not receive nutrition and is dysfunctional, our spirit becomes depressed. Depression is atrophy.

Parents and step parents do not be quick to judge yourself as the ones who are always decayed. Parents and step parents who should be learning to lead children and step children do experience decay or atrophy from lack of use. The children who control parents and their parental home will be the ones that will decay the most. Their siblings will decay or experience atrophy, too. This atrophy comes from lack of use or being cumbered by anger in the family.

Checking the Vineyard. The Master of the Vineyard checks on His Vineyard seven times in this allegory. This is why Latter-day Saint authors divide our world history into seven dispensations. There are other servants who came and worked in the vineyard with the first servant of the vineyard. Each wanted to work a little longer to keep the vineyard going in order to save the vineyard which includes the trees, the roots, the branches, and the fruit. These servants are known as prophets. These servants are also known as parents and step parents.

Of course, the Master of the Vineyard checks on us more than seven times in seven thousand years. He is checking to see how cumbered we are. I think he knows this will happen. Cumbering occurs with large numbers of people. Families and step families were created to lesson the cumbering of individuals by many people. Countries and states were created to reduce this encumberment. More servants, ancient and modern-day prophets, were called into the vineyard to tell us what cumbers our families. Excessive fruits, ideas, opinions, and dreams of many individuals cumber the branches and the ground of the vineyard.

Parents and step parents check their personal vineyards frequently, too. Most parents and even a few step parents would like to work longer in their vineyard to prevent cumbering of their vineyard, their families and step families. Like the Master of the Vineyard, parents and step parents would like to save the root, themselves and their ancestors. They want to save their branches, their children and grandchildren. Parents want to enjoy the tame fruits of their children. Parents hope their own branches are tender, merciful, and gentle. All parents and step parents hope there is tame fruit to preserve in their families.

Cumber. Cumber means to obstruct or interfere with something or someone in a distressful way. This is the stonewalling behavior we see in feuding families and step families, etc. Families and step families can be cumbersome or difficult to deal with because of their size, feuds, weight, attitude, burdens, objections, power, anger, and influence. A stubborn adult is more cumbersome than a stubborn child. When something is cumbered, normal progress stops. The olive trees were cumbered in three ways: by withered or broken branches, by excessive fruit, or the ground of the vineyard was cumbered.

> *9 Take thou the branches of the wild olive-tree, and graft them in, in the stead thereof; and these which I have plucked off I will cast into the fire and burn them, that they may not cumber the ground of my vineyard.*

> *Jacob 5:9, The Book of Mormon*

> *30 And it came to pass that the Lord of the vineyard and the servant went down into the vineyard; and they came to the tree whose natural branches had been broken off, and the wild branches had been grafted in; and behold all sorts of fruit did cumber the tree.*
> *Jacob 5:30, The Book of Mormon*

Anyone who has had fruit trees has seen branches with excessive fruit on them. The fruit remains small, green, hard, and immature to the time of harvest. It does not matter how much water the tree receives if the owner of the tree has not thinned the fruit. Some branches break off with the weight of the excess, immature fruit. This cumbers the ground. People cannot walk safely in the area. Weeds grow among the branches on the ground. Water cannot get to the tree. Fruit falls prematurely to the ground. This creates a perfect environment for pests to grow in. These pests kill the tree. These pests can kill all the trees in the vineyard.

The Master of the Vineyard instructed the servant of the Vineyard to keep the top of the tree and the root equal. The root line usually matches the foliage line. Experienced owners of vineyards can see when parts of the tree are going beyond the root line. The leaves are smaller when foliage has gone beyond the root line. The branch is growing faster than the root can provide nourishment. The tree does not look so attractive. This is why teenagers appear so awkward. Their branches are growing beyond the root line. They should not control the family.

How do we prune ourselves so our foliage is equal to root strength? Repentance. This is the beauty of the Savior's gospel and this allegory. The Savior gave free agency to us. We can decide which immature fruit needs pruning and the timing of the pruning. Through faith and repentance, we thin our excess, immature fruit. The Savior chooses the timing of the Harvest. The Servants of the Vineyard and scriptures have told us which branches on ourselves are unfruitful and unbecoming. The Savior gave us scriptures, covenants, and The Holy Ghost so we can dig, dung, prune, and nourish ourselves and our families in private with the Master of the Vineyard. As a result, we have fruit for the various seasons of life, not just the end of the world.

With mercy, our cumbersome branches and immature fruit are thrown in the fire, consumed, and remembered no more. Some have fruit that is spoiled and must be pruned with our church leaders. When this kind of fruit is pruned with one having authority, even this immature, evil fruit is thrown in the fire and remembered no more, except for murder.

Fruits. The Master of the Vineyard grafted branches from the Mother Olive Tree into wild olive trees in the various spots of the vineyard. All spots, except the good spot, began to bear fruit again. In the good spot, only part of the tree bore fruit. After a time, all spots bore evil fruit in spite of much nourishment.

Approximately. fifty percent of children and step children bear fruits worthy of mentioning. Fifty percent of children and step children in a household interfere with everything parents and step parents try to do for all of their children or step children. As this behavior overtakes a family, all begin to produce evil fruits. These wild fruits cumber the ground in step families with very selfish and very hurtful behavior. Parents' and step parents' ability and access to children are completely cut-off. Parents and step parents feel awkward and cumbersome around their own children.

The Last Time. This is the last time that the servants are laboring in the vineyard. This includes the first servant, Jesus Christ. There is an end to time. The Lord of the Vineyard has purposes to fulfill with the roots, branches, and fruit in His Vineyard after time has ended, too. Even He has to make do with what tender shoots has developed in His vineyard. His purposes are not an endless cycle of continuous digging, dunging, and pruning on a vineyard that does not want to produce tame fruit.

Parents and step parents have a last time in their vineyard. They may threaten that it is the last time that they will do something for their family, but eventually there is a last time. The digging, dunging, and pruning from parents and step parents will have to happen on the other side of the veil. We leave this Earth with the same spirits that we had on this Earth. If we resist the digging, dunging, and pruning by parents, step parents, and spiritual leaders, we most likely will resist this care on the other side of the veil.

Grief. The Master of the Vineyard experiences much grief over the possible loss of an olive tree, its roots, grafted branches, withered branches, and the wild fruit that is produced. Like our Heavenly Father, parents and step parents experience grief over the losses in their family vineyard. They grieve for the wild trees, especially the branches that are withering away before their eyes. Most parents and step parents begin to treat their children as if the children were the roots of the family tree. This only causes more grief. Parent and child become neither root nor branch, and both wither. The root of your family or step family is not your children, step children, or siblings. The root are the parents and step parents as long as they are alive.

This a good time to list how you, your spouse, each child or step child, and the environment that your are living in cause grief in your life and in your vineyard. How do you grieve? Compare your grief with the Allegory of the Tame and Wild Olive Trees. Notice. The

Master is greatly grieved, but he is able to control His grief. He is still able to provide a plan for His Vineyard in His grief. He is able to stick to the plan. His plan and sticking to His plan are what parents and step parents are working towards. Otherwise, we are left with large chunks of grief to bear. If you want to change, consider these chunks of grief and depression.

Are you a tame or a wild olive tree? How is your choice of being either a tame or a wild olive tree causing you grief or causing grief in your children and step children or in parents and step parents? Are you married to a tame or a wild olive tree? Are you trying to keep up with children who have become wild olive trees? Are you calling a wild olive tree a tame olive tree to keep peace in the family? Grief will come in both tame and wild olive trees, but the consequences and methods of comfort and cure are different.

Waxing Old and Decaying. List the behavior in each family member that is waxing old. Who is decaying in your family? How is your family decaying physically, emotionally, socially, intellectually, financially, psychologically, morally, or spiritually? Are they able or willing to work, provide service to others, and sacrifice for things that have a more pressing claim? Can they persist with and obey the various authority figures in their life?

Apostasy. Are children leading siblings away from their biological parents, step parent, and the Savior with some very elaborate stories? Are parents and step parents trying to resuscitate a treetop that prefers to decay instead of being pruned? Apostasy hurts. Apostasy stings. Apostasy has consequences. Are you and your family members a victim of apostasy? Is family members victimizing others by apostasy? Do your children blame you for the consequences of their behavior? This is apostasy.

Cumbered. There are three things that are cumbered in this allegory: branches, excessive fruit, and ground. How are the branches (children, siblings, and extended family) cumbering your family? How are parents and step parents cumbered in your family? Branches break off with the weight of excessive fruit. When family branches break off, they seek to become a law unto themselves. Who has become the law of the family instead of parents and step parents? Is crime, ranging from drug addictions and theft to pornography and murder, cumbering the ground in which you are trying to raise your family?

Withering Away. Are parents, step parents, children, and step children withering away from lack of use and lack of nutrition? What are the common denominators for all of these situations in the vineyard? Usually, it is anger. Become acquainted on how everyone responds to anger and how they reciprocate with anger. Depression is anger directed inwardly. Is your depression cumbering you and your family more than the things that you are anguishing over?

Most parents become depressed over their children's efforts and difficulties in school. Homework and school attendance are very distressing power struggles between parent and child. It is heartbreaking when your child makes such a poor effort that he cannot graduate from high school. Part of mother and father has to die out in this power struggle to keep peace in the family. Their child does not want what parents have to offer them except their money. This prevents nourishment to other children who still have healthy treetops. It is depressing to have to choose between healthy children and angry, lazy children.

Cultivation. A cultivation system is needed, not multiple entertainment centers, to save your family tree, its roots and branches, and to produce tame fruit. What cultivation system do you use in your family vineyard? Does your system provide nourishment or just excessive fruit through spending, sports, and recreation? The Lord's cultivation system, repentance, mercy, and forgiveness, prunes excessive fruit and withered branches, clears cumbered ground, and provides nourishment for the vineyard. Do you, your spouse, children, and step children interfere with the Lord's cultivation system?

Power Struggle with the Master of the Vineyard. *We all need some digging, pruning, and dunging. Do family members resist nourishment? Is this a power struggle with parents, step parents, or the Master of the Vineyard? What are you doing to maintain this resistance? Have you eliminated the Lord's cultivation system before family members are able to prune themselves by faith in Jesus Christ, prayer, repentance, and education? Are you now trying to bear the weight of things that should have been pruned long ago? Are you and your children trying to control instead of nourish the various spots of the Lord's Vineyard? Are you trying to dictate the Lord's will, the withersoever I will spot?*

Scattered. *Which part of the vineyard are you and your family members scattered to by their behavior? Who are they grafted to? Are you rescuing your children from the five spots of the Lord's Vineyard? Are parents and step parents being scattered and discarded by scatter-brained adults, peers, children, and siblings? Are children or spouses angry with their parents, spouse, or children because they are not in what you think is the best spot for them? Everyone will be asked to bloom in each type of spot in the Lord's Vineyard. This is called life, education, experience, work, marriage, family, parenting, etc.*

Fruits. *The Savior told us to not run faster than we can walk. This creates excessive fruit which we do not have the ability to manage. Excessive fruit which has not been thinned remains hard, bitter, and falls prematurely to the ground. What excessive fruit needs to be thinned in your family? Are you angry over the type of fruit that your spouse and children and step children are producing? Are children blaming you for their lack of fruit production? Who is the most bitter branch in your step family? Who is grafted to the bitter branch? Are you afraid that your spouse, children, or step children are going to be some of the branches that are burnt? Only the Lord gets to make this decision. Parents and step parents labor until the Master of the Vineyard decides it is time to stop. It is the role of parents to prepare and preserve their children and step children for this final judgement.*

Preserving. *Most cooks prefer to preserve their fruits in a clean vessel rather than a dirty vessel. When I preserve fruit and vegetables for wintertime use, I choose beautiful fruit that is ready to be harvested. I use clean jars, lids, and rings. For my jams, jellies, and juices, I use damaged fruit. I cut out the damaged part and discard it. We have our favorite recipes to preserve and always try some new recipes. We enjoy the things that we have canned and eaten, but really have no thought tomorrow for what we devoured yesterday.*

Our Heavenly Father does not preserve the fruits of His Vineyard in the manner that we preserve our jams, jellies, and fruits. The Master of the Vineyard and the servants work in the vineyard to preserve the roots and good fruit of the season for their purposes. The Master preserves roots, branches, and fruits so they will not be consumed. He knows and remembers every root, branch, and fruit in His Vineyard. Each has a time and a purpose in His Vineyard.

Your Roles. You are parents and step parents. Your role in the Master's Vineyard is a tough one. You work with the Master and His Servants in the Vineyard twenty-four hours a day, seven days a week, three-hundred-sixty-five days a year to cultivate, gather, and preserve your children until your death. Your role is not just to provide and entertain the seed of a new generation. Your role is to care for children and step children when they are scattered or gathered in the "Nethermost Spots," "The Poor spots," "The Poorest spots," "The Good spots," and "The Withersoever I will spots" of their lives.

Naturally, the Lord's Will Spot will do the most gathering. The Nethermost Spot will probably do the most scattering. In each of these spots, children need food, clothing, shelter, love, and encouragement. Children need a purpose as well as adults. Parent and child, step parent and step child need to have purpose, duties, respect, or all will atrophy before each other's eyes. Nothing will stop this withering, but the Lord's purposes. *How are you preserving your family vineyard? Will your ways prevent your children and step children from being consumed by depression, suicidal thoughts, drugs, and alcohol?*

I know that it matters to parents, particularly mothers, what spots or predicaments our children are in. Our children seem to scatter themselves and others to some very scary and worrisome spots. Each generation needs experience in each of these spots as a child and as a parent. This experience will help God's children recognize the withered branches, excessive fruit, and the tares or weeds that cumber the ground of the good spots of their lives and their families. As painful as our experiences are, it does not matter to the Master of the Vineyard what kind of spot we have been scattered or grafted to. It matters if we are gathered under His wing. This is where we will be the most productive. This is where we will have tame fruits to preserve.

Tender Shoots and Tame Fruit. *In the scriptures, the Savior spoke of tender shoots and tame fruit in a different manner. He called them a broken heart and a contrite spirit. A broken heart and a contrite spirit produce tame fruit. A broken heart and a contrite spirt will not happen in children or parents if parents seek to make a child stronger than the parent. The child will take strength only for himself, and he will become a law unto himself. The child, the branch or foliage in your family tree, overcomes the root instead of developing a broken heart and a contrite spirit. All, and this includes parent and child, step parent and step child, become neither root nor branch.*

Are you trying to make your children stronger than the root, their parent and step parent? Are your children developing a broken heart and a contrite spirit? Do you have a broken heart and a contrite spirit? Without an example of a broken heart and contrite spirit, there will be very little tame fruit to preserve for His purposes.

In your depression, I want you to remember this: It is the one who waxes old, decays, and who allows the top of their tree to die that is scattered and grafted, not the root, the parents and step parents. Can you tell the difference between root and branch and ground and fruit? Can your children and step children tell the difference between family and friends? Can you recognize when you are becoming neither root nor branch?

Can you now see this pattern in your life and family? As we accumulate experiences in life, we experience much grief. We grieve over the tame and wild olive trees in our families. When the branches of our tame olive trees wax old and the top of their tree dies, we become angry and grieve over the many years of work ahead. We become depressed when apostasy occurs in our family. We really become angry when branches overcome the root causing other branches to wither away. When we try to dig, prune, dung, gather, and sort our branches, parents and step parents meet resistance.

The Master of the Vineyard then scatters and grafts our tame and wild olive trees into the withersoever I will spots, the nethermost spots, some poor spots, the poorest spots, and a good spot of the Master's vineyard. Branches are also sorted for grafting or burning. Mothers are not usually ready for this. Mothers become angry with the Master when their tame and wild olive trees and their ground become cumbered by excessive fruit and withered branches. The Master of the Vineyard grieves with us for our branches, roots, and fruits. Only the Master and His Servants are able to preserve the tree, the roots, the branches, as well as the fruits. Only the Master and His Servants can help us be root and branch with tame fruits.

Congratulations on being a grafted branch! New grafts expect some opposition to their grafting. They are surprised at how much and how quickly their roots are cumbered by opposition from the branches, the children, step children, and extended family. The adversary is tethering your family through opposition and their behavior. Your reactions to this interference in your marriage can cause your family to be cumbered more. These individuals learn what buttons to push quickly. Through trial and error, I learned as others have, to act, not react, and to act calmly. This is where soft answers work nicely.

Grafted branches usually feel inferior to the natural branches. Natural branches have many ways to create feelings of inferiority in grafted branches. Natural branches go out of their way to seek new ways to shame a grafted branch. Grafted branches become embarrassed and depressed because they feel inferior and tethered by the behavior of natural branches. Do not be embarrassed for yourself, your heritage, or the part of the Master's Vineyard that you or your children and step children have been asked or volunteered to bloom in. Do not be embarrassed and depressed at the many ways natural branches deal with conflict over grafted branches in their lives. The Lord deals with grafted branches all the time. Let the Savior decide who will have shame and inferiority heaped on their shoulders and be tethered. It usually is the one trying to put asunder a grafted branch.

Remember. If you are placed in the poorest ground by a natural branch of your spouse, the poorest spot brought forth more fruit than the best. They had to work the hardest. The Master of the Vineyard had a Son. He was placed in a grafted family in a very difficult spot in the Vineyard. He had many trials. The Son of God did not feel shame, anger, or inferior because he was placed in a grafted family. He did not forget that He had to control His grief and anger. He did not forget His mission in life.

The Savior fulfilled the plan for the problems in the vineyard of the Master. Our success in life does not depend on where we are scattered and who we are grafted to. Our success depends on whether we are grafted to and gathered by the Savior or grafted to and tethered by the Adversary. The adversary's ways will not preserve the root and produce tame fruit and tender branches, the ones that are needed for an eternity on the other side of the veil.

Gardens always have stones. Your family garden will, too. Be aware. Stones and roots help prevent erosion of the soil of the Earth. Stones tossed at human spirits by ourselves and others cause erosion of the human spirit.

Chapter Six

Stones into Bread

In this chapter, we are going to discuss stones. There are many stones tossed at each other in families and step families. The individuals hurt by these stones are often told that it was for their own good or no harm was meant.

There are so many stones passing back and forth in step families that I am reminded of a verse in 2 Kings 3:19. These were instructions given to the Israelites by the Lord. He told them how to deliver themselves from their present enemy, the Moabites. After the Israelites were delivered, they passed these instructions from the Lord to each generation. Each generation used this method to defend themselves against major and minor offenses. Families defended themselves from other families in this manner, too. If family members disagree in step families, this is how family and step family members are treated. Naturally, they became enemies forever. This was all done with stones.

> *19 And ye shall smite every fenced city, and every choice city, and shall*
> *fell every good tree, and stop all wells of water, and mar every good piece*
> *of land with stones.*
>
>

2 Kings 3:19, <u>The Holy Bible</u>

>

Stones have many uses. Altars, temples, tabernacles, foundations, doors, walls of homes, pavement, dishes, water pots, graves or sepulchers, and idols were made or hewn out of stone. This is where the term stonemason came from. Their cutting tools and knives were made out of stone. There are seer stones, stone boxes, memorial stones, and millstones. Gardens were protected from animals with stone fences. Precious stones were used in crowns and other jewelry to denote power and authority and for adornment. When someone died, a heap of stones was placed over their body to keep the wolves out. Stones were used to block the path of water so families could water their sheep. When this task was completed, the stones were removed. The first weapons of war (David and Goliath) were stones and a slingshot. In ancient times, highways were blocked by large stones to keep horses and chariots from settlements.

The Lord gave the Ten Commandments on tablets of stone to Moses. When someone committed an offense such as murder or adultery, they were stoned. The slingers, as they were called in the Old Testament of <u>The Holy Bible</u>, probably used cutting stones about the size of a baseball or softball. I doubt they used the small, irregular, smooth stones that children find in steams or along the road and toss at other children and cars. Animals which gored other humans were stoned. A man gathering firewood on the Sabbath was stoned. People were stoned for minor offenses. We will never know how many people were stoned over contrived offenses.

Christ is known as the Stone of Israel. (Genesis 49:24) The Savior's Kingdom is a stone cut out of a mountain that will roll forth and will not perish from the Earth. In the Savior's

Sermon on the Mount, Christ asks "...what man is there of you, whom if his son ask bread, will he give him a stone?" (Matthew 7:9) This verse is applicable to families and step families. However, the roles have reversed in step families. Children and step children have stolen the role of parents and step parents. It is now...What man is there of you, when your father or step father asks for bread, will you give him a stone?"

Smite Every Fenced City. Smite means to bring harm, suffering, or hit. Families and step families are small cities within a city. If they own their own property and home, they usually fence their little city. They have their power structure, rules for government, ways to communicate, and ways of providing food, clothing, and shelter. Unlike our large cities, families are suppose to provide these things for each other on a personal nature with love.

When children and step children are cumbered in the branches of their government, their personality and identity tree, they immediately feel that it is those in power that are at fault. They are right. *Children are in power!* The branches of their government which have become cumbered are as follows: their physical branch, emotional branch, social branch, intellectual branch, financial branch, psychological branch, moral branch, spiritual branch (their top of the tree), work branch, service branch, sacrificial branch, persistent branch, and obedient branch.

When cumbered in each branch of personality and identity, children and step children become demanding in each branch. Parents and step parents have one crisis after another to solve. Parents and step parents do not mind helping with the logical crisis' in a family. It does not matter whether it is a natural branch or a grafted branch. Most crisis in a step family are the result of illogical behavior. It is amazing what children and step children will do to get out of a few minutes of work. A parent or step parent, particularly the mother, cannot keep up the pace of all the illogical demands in a divided family with many children.

Failure and fatigue will not stir any compassion for the mother or step mother. This increases the demands. Children claim they are bored, but the parents, especially the step parent become more in their power as parents try to fulfill all the demands of demanding children.

Children and step children demand that parents and step parents cast stones into bread. These stones that children call bread are better than the bread that parents and step parents want for the children or can provide for the family. The stones that children want instead of homework and education will provide more for them. When parents and step parents feel guilty and are intimidated, they do try to cast stones into bread for their children and step children to make them happy. Happiness never comes because the child wants more stones for bread. An example of casting stones into bread is sports. Sports will now make leaders of our children or make our children rich instead of an education and work.

Smite Every Choice City. Many townships and cities have developed from one man. Others came and worked to build the city. Christ would be considered the choicest of cities. Others are helping Him build His Kingdom. This gives us experience. Others smite these choice cities with drugs, sports, and alcohol, etc. This has made them rich at our expense.

When Christ was beginning His ministry which would build His Kingdom on Earth, Christ fasted for forty days. Naturally, Satan picked this time to tempt Christ to turn stones into bread for Christ to eat. Christ told Satan, "It is written, Man shall not live by bread alone, but by every word that proceedeth out of the mouth of God."[8] Satan forgot that fasting strengthens individuals.

In each temptation, Satan tempts Christ to prove that He is the Son of God. Christ's hungry appetite, a pinnacle that He should not be on, and worshiping Satan were going to prove that Jesus Christ is the Son of God. Christ possesses special powers that Satan cannot have. This cannot be changed. Nothing had to be proved. Actually, Satan was taunting Christ over His powers. By giving in to Satan, Christ would have given these powers up. Parents and step parents have powers that Satan cannot have unless they give them up. Satan taunts parents and step parents about the powers which they have to raise children and step children, too.

When parents and step parents are beginning their life and ministry with their children and step children, they are still developing. Skills are scarce in parents and step parents. Parents and step parents have dreams and hopes. They desire many things for themselves and their families. Satan chooses the time when parents and step parents are inexperienced and desirous of many things to tempt parents and step parents. Satan tempts parents and step parents to cast stones into bread to satisfy their various appetites. He tempts parents and step parents with pinnacles that they should not be on and by the people they bow down and worship instead of Jesus Christ.

When children and step children are beginning their lives and are too young to know what their ministry will be about or even if there is a ministry to life, skills are even more scarce in children than their parents and step parents. This is natural. Your children and step children are beginning to develop. Children desire many things. They have dreams and hopes, but they have some gluttonous appetites. They manage to get on pinnacles they should not be on. They bow down to people who do not have their best interests at heart.

Parents and step parents do not have all the powers that Christ has. They will not be able to rescue children and step children from a lack of skills, pinnacles, and idols. Christ has shared some of His powers with parents and step parents. The power and lineage of a parent and step parent cannot be changed and is to be honored. Fathers and step fathers can hold the priesthood. If parents and step parents fall victim to their own temptations as well as their children's temptations, parents and step parents will always be trying to prove they are the parent or step parent. Their ministry is forgotten. It will not matter that Christ is The Son of God.

Children and step children receive their blessings through the powers their parents and step parents possess. The powers parents receive depends on how well they follow Christ and how faithful they are in prayer. If children choose to follow others rather than parents, step parents, and Christ, they will always have to prove something that may or may not be true.

Until of age, children and step children are to live by the words that proceed from their parents, step parents, Christ, and the laws of their land. This is where the bread of life is found for them. There is no bread or power in proving that parents and step parents are terrible, make mistakes, are inept, and cruel. This is trying to turn stones into bread.

Christ could not turn stones into bread. Parents and step parents cannot turn stones into bread. Children cannot turn stones into bread either. Children cannot avoid the same double binds that Satan puts us in over passions, status and power, and idolatry.

---

[8]Matthew 4:4, The Holy Bible, p. 1191.

Fell Every Good Tree. Every couple prepares for their retirement in some way. If not they should be preparing for their retirement. Unfortunately, parents and step parents have to prepare for their premature retirement when they marry. The parents and step parents may only be in their forties, but they are retired. Parents and step parents have to be retired to maintain the power struggles in biological families and step families. It happens quite unexpectedly and expertly. In other words, every good tree is felled in the homes of the world. I suspect premature retirement of parents and step parents is the goal of many movies and television programs. Children seek many things to replace parents. Naturally, the media and entertainment industry controls the things that children choose

Many children who live in step families have several families that they can choose to live with in times of dispute and correction. Your children try to meet their needs of food, clothing, shelter, personal space, money, and love by family-hopping. This family-hopping requires elaborate stories that pit family against family which fells every good tree. Other family members resent caring for a wayward child that parents should be caring for. They resent family members who may have caused children to be wayward.

Step parents expected to assist their spouse in meeting the needs of their new family. Biological parents expected to continue to care for their children. This situation is not a result of poor grafting. This is a situation where parents and step parents were retired prematurely by children and step children and extended family. Many families interfering with a step family encumbers a step family and paralyzes the parent and step parent.

Children will be accountable for the premature retirement of their parents and step parents. Your children and step children will be scattered to the Nethermost part of the Vineyard. They may scatter themselves to the Nethermost part of the Vineyard to avoid pruning and repenting. Children who need repenting and have options of many homes to live in and a social security income are not going to choose to live with parents and step parents who preach and teach repentance and prayer to them. Do it anyway. This will give your dignity back to you.

As a parent and a step parent, you have to decide if you are going to retire prematurely. Underage children in the Nethermost part of the Vineyard with a Social Security Check are very attractive to siblings, friends, boyfriends, girlfriends, coaches, drug dealers, etc. They are more interested in the Social Security Check than the wayward child. Parents who have handicapped children also get prematurely retired. The individuals who do this want your child's unending Social Security checks and Disability checks, and they have the schemes to get them.

If parents and step parents retire prematurely, parents and step parents will atrophy from lack of use. Your children and step children will atrophy, too, especially when the Social Security Check stops coming. Your children and step children will experience the opposition that parents and step parents would have received. Children will not have the support systems that normal grafts receive. Parents and step parents cannot teach children how to overcome opposition by giving into opposition.

Parents and step parents grieve and are easily embarrassed when children leave home prematurely. Parents grieve over the lack of authority and parenting in their home. Those who refuse to reconcile have stolen this authority. The Master of the Vineyard will return to parents and step parents their authority during the Millennium. (Isaiah 40:31) It would be nice to have this authority returned to parents and step parents before they die. I cannot guarantee that you will get the authority back in your home in this lifetime. You will receive your dignity back if you do all you can according to the Master of the Vineyard's plan, the withersoever I will spot.

Do not fell every good tree and cut your losses because you are angry over disagreements or depressed over your losses and mistakes in life. This is why parents and step parents need to do things according to the Master of the Vineyard's plan. *In your premature retirements, step children want to retire your estates. If a couple retires their assets at age forty to make a child happy, the child is never going to be happy to keep your assets retired. Your child will never let you come out of retirement to keep your assets retired. When you are retired prematurely, retire your estates with yourselves. A young adult child does not have the maturity to deal with the stress of million-dollar assets.*

Stop All Wells of Water. The stones of intimidation, manipulation, secret combinations, and isolation of parents and step parents cap the wells in families and step families. Parents and step parents try to remove gracefully the stones of intimidation, manipulation, secrets, and isolation. Parents and step parents dig other wells which are immediately capped with more secrets, intimidation, manipulation, and isolation. For times when parents and step parents are thirsty, they decide to have a secret well.

Children become cumbered as they intimidate, manipulate, and isolate parents and step parents with the stones in which they have capped everyone's well. When children become cumbered, children and step children become more demanding. Children and step children demand that parents and step parents cast stones into bread for children. Parents and step parents are to remain the size of a Banzai Tree with restrictive wires, but they are to cast stones into bread. If parents and step parents decide to remain the size of a banzai tree, the family will have to settle for stones instead of bread.

Demanding individuals have forgotten who they are dealing with. Their demands are so important to them that they have forgotten they are starving their own family tree. They are a part of that family tree. Only the Lord can prevent the loss of these family trees.

The Stones That Limit Access. In disputes and times of correction by parents and step parents, children's and step children's favorite response is: "Whatever." Children ignore parents' and step parents' refusals, advice, and corrections by saying, "Whatever." Parents' and step parents' minds go blank, and they cannot think of a thing to say. Parents and step parents become so frustrated that they put themselves in "timeout" to control their temper. Children and step children again are limiting parents and step parents.

Parents and step parents, the appropriate word is not "whatever." Perhaps a better word is "Enough." Parents and step parents, stop your isolation by saying "Enough." Isolate the child in his room, not yourself. Fathers or step fathers may have to escort their children to their rooms. Remember. "Enough" puts the monkey back on the child or step child's shoulders. To try to remove this monkey, children do not make peace with their parent or step parent, they mar every good piece of land that step parents and parents might find some peace and comfort.

Mar Every Good Piece of Land. Many families and step families are marred and destroyed by gossip. Idle talk and innuendos become truth. Vengeful talk becomes truth. No one knows who and what to believe. Sports, drugs, and alcohol are now their source of ignition and strength instead of parents and step parents. Many families, step families, and spouses are marred by excessive sports and drugs and alcohol. They have given themselves chemical autism.

In power struggles with step parents, step children often give drugs and alcohol to biological children of a step parent. They give drugs and alcohol to their siblings. Families and step families are marred by this kind of betrayal of a parent. This kind of betrayal and pace is very distressing and depressing to parents and step parents. Families and step families may try to plant other things around the family tree to hide the marring of their family tree trunk. There is nothing that will hide this kind of marring. The Lord knows about the marring anyway.

We will never know how many children and step children, young and old, have died because of drugs and alcohol. We will never know how many gifts were never developed because drugs and alcohol were a source of strength instead of talents. We will never admit how many illnesses are caused by excessive sports, drugs, and alcohol. Parents and grandparents grieve for what might have been in their children and grandchildren. No one really wants to admit that excessive sports, drugs, and alcohol are a problem. Sports, drugs, and alcohol are their ignition source, identity, source of strength, their employment, and their entertainment. Sports, drugs, and alcohol are their weapons of rebellion and their weapons of battle.

The Savior has keys which help us instead of stones which hurt, harm, and smite. He shares His keys with the husbands and fathers of the Earth. This includes step fathers. He has keys that He is willing to share with parents and step parents, including mothers and step mothers. This is one of the reasons we are to honor our parents and step parents. What are these keys–the key to a broken heart and a contrite spirit, the key to finances, the key to your education, the key to your physical, psychological, emotional, social, and moral growth. Parents have keys to charity which teaches children how to work, serve, persist, obey, and sacrifice. It takes cooperation and obedience for the Savior's keys to work in your ignition system.

Everyone has locked their keys in their car. Locking keys in a car comes with ownership of a car. Helping a spouse out when she has locked the keys in the car and saying nothing is part of that small print in your marriage license. The key that starts your car is so small. Yet, keys ignite a large engine. The engine can take us where we want to go or where we should be.

When I have locked my keys in the car, they have been in the ignition, on the dashboard, in my purse on the seat, or on the floor by my groceries. I could not bear to smash my car window with a stone. The emergency hanger was on the floor by the keys. So I have waited for hours sitting on floors in stores for my husband or daughter to retrieve my spare set which was at home. I had to wait in the hot sun to guard my purse. I have paid money to locksmiths because I got tired of waiting for busy family members. Finally, I learned that I never lay those keys down in the car. It does not matter what car I am in, my keys stay in my hand or in my pocket. I also had to learn to never lay the keys down which the Savior has shared with me as a child, as a parent, and as a wife of a man holding the Melchizedek Priesthood.

The Savior's keys are how we serve bread instead of stones. Fathers and mothers must continue to serve bread to their children even though their sons and daughters and others serve parents and step parents stones for bread. A good quality loaf of bread has enough yeast and water to turn the flour into gluten, salt for flavor, and eggs for texture. There is nothing like a warm loaf of bread. Learn to bake bread for your family.

The Parables of the Leaven Bread. There are two parables about leaven in bread. In one parable, Christ talks about a woman hiding three measures of leaven into flour until the whole mixture is leavened. (Matthew 13:33) Bakers knead bread until this change takes place. A good baker can feel when the wheat flour has turned to gluten. Inexperienced bakers over knead their bread, and the dough becomes tough. If they under knead the bread, the bread has large holes in the middle of the loaf. Good leaven brings about a desirable change and a good product to consume. Bakers know if they omit the salt, the bread will not have a good flavor.

In the second parable, Christ warns: "Beware of the leaven of the Pharisees and of the Sadducees." He meant their doctrine. (Matthew 16:11 - 12) Leaven is the same as yeast. Yeast works by a fermentation process such as in Sourdough bread. A baker mixes flour, salt, water, and sugar with a sourdough start. This fermentation process does not produce poison. The end result is a delicious loaf of sourdough bread. However, if the baker uses a metal spoon to stir the sourdough start or a metal container to store the sourdough start, the start becomes poisonous. The fermentation process leaches metals out of the spoon or metal container. This is why cooks are very protective of their sourdough starts and keep them in ceramic or glass jars.

Christ's mother probably used a Sourdough start. On occasion, her sourdough start probably became poisonous. A child may have stirred the start with a metal spoon. She could tell by the color. The sourdough start turns orange. Sourdough starts may not be poisonous to cause death. It depends on the type of metals in the spoon and containers. Sourdough starts become ineffective with too much liquid or lack of use. Sourdough starts need to be rejuvenated at least once a week.

These parables of the kinds of leaven in bread has many similarities to our present day life and to our depressions and suicidal thoughts. The three measures of leaven that are hidden within us until we are changed can be: God, family, country; or parents, spouse, and children, or faith, hope, and charity. No matter what we choose, our leaven has to be rejuvenated at least once every seven days. This rejuvenation comes from assembling together to worship and honor God and Jesus Christ. Those who assemble in worship regularly can tell when they have not been rejuvenated.

Anger, lack of forgiveness and mercy, jealousy, etc. leaches out of us things we cannot control, creating poisonous leaven within us and within others. Poisonous leaven is always going to be poisonous leaven. It does not matter what name you decide to call poisonous leaven. It does not matter who tries to use the poisonous leaven. Poisonous leaven will make you sick. Individuals waste a lot of money and time trying to deal with poisonous or ineffective leavens.

Ineffective leaven will always be ineffective leaven. Drugs and alcohol are poisonous, ineffective leaven. Parents and step parents will spend a lifetime trying to get children to understand this. In order for children to understand, parents and step parents must consume bread that has good leaven. This leaven must make a change in parents and step parents. We must remove the stones from our bread to make room for the leaven. We do this with the steps of repentance, mercy, and forgiveness.

How are you and your family members trying to cast stones into bread? Do you smite every fenced city, every choice city, fell every good tree, stop all wells of water, and mar every good piece of land with stones for your family and community? What conflicts occur when these stones are served?

What appetite, pinnacle, power struggle, or form of idolatry do you have to be rescued from all the time? This is asking parents, step parents, children and step children to cast stones into bread. Do you feel the keys given to parents and step parents cumber you? Would you rather be cumbered by the stones passing back and forth in your family tree? Would you rather be cumbered by the stones of others who are caught in the temptations of Satan?

Do you smite every fenced city in your family or step family to force them to side with you? What do you do when they disagree with you?

How are the wells of water prevented from reaching your family? Are you, your spouse, and children demanding? Are these demands a realistic need, or are they demands to control parents and step parents and their estates?

Have you felled any good trees? Were you affected by the crack of the tree as it fell? Did you notice the silence after it fell. These sounds will haunt you all of your life if you have? There is no one that you can place blame. Your countenance will be affected by the loss of the tree. The Comforter, the Holy Ghost, will leave you, and you will become depressed.

Do you smite every choice city? Are you asking others to help you retire your parents and step parents prematurely by tossing stones at your parents and step parents? Are you asking others to support you after you have retired your parents and step parents prematurely?

Have you marred the good land that you are trying to develop in and in which others are trying to develop? The anger that causes you to mar the land that all are living in will consume you—not others. In the history of time, people are consumed by the way they consumed others? It is not Murphy's law. It the way our Heavenly Father allows you to experience the effects of what you have done to others.

Have you marred the ignition of your family or step family so badly that it does not matter to them that there is a Son of God who can help them? Have you encouraged family members to break commandments that will affect their eternal life? If we try to caste stones into bread, or if we use poisonous leaven in our bread, we will live in outer darkness.

Chapter Seven

Outer Darkness

There is a place where depressed individuals live. Depressed individuals do not have to die to live in this space. In this space, depressed individuals are beyond the reach and capacities of the best of parents, siblings, spouses, counselors, spiritual leaders, and even our city, state, and federal governments. This space is beyond the help of the Holy Ghost. The best that the above individuals can offer is medication for the depressed individual.

The Savior called this area Outer Darkness. Other names for Outer Darkness are spiritual darkness, hell, and prison. Outer Darkness, spiritual darkness, hell, and prison, describe depression and suicidal thoughts very well. The Savior has even said that He would cast us in Outer Darkness if we did certain behaviors. We would lose what progress we had even though we were adults. This is maddening and disheartening. One would think that the Savior, if He truly was a Savior, would let us use the Holy Ghost, the Comforter, when we need him the most.

If the Holy Ghost cannot work through you, you cannot work through the Holy Ghost. Depressed individuals, no matter how hurt and just their cause, cannot abuse the Holy Ghost. Families have been held hostage by sinful and depressive behavior. The Holy Ghost will never be held hostage. The sin against the Holy Ghost or denying the Holy Ghost after one has a testimony of the Holy Ghost is very grave. These individuals become Sons of Perdition.[9] Why? Their behaviors remove agency from the Holy Ghost. The Holy Ghost cannot help others.

The behaviors of depressed individuals remove agency from our Heavenly Father and Jesus Christ also. The behaviors of depressed individuals remove free agency from themselves, too. No one can function in the capacities they have been called. Others seem to have more freedom than depressed individuals do, causing resentment. This begins the suicidal chase.

The Suicidal Chase. Depressed individuals have suicidal thoughts. Suicidal thoughts or tendencies are like the childhood game of chase. Remember. *Children do not play chase with someone who can run faster than them or who will not chase them.*

The suicidal chase begins with anger over the misfortunes in someone's life. Depressed individuals blame others for these misfortunes, usually their parents and/or spouse. Depressed individuals make burdensome demands to parents and spouse. Instead of receiving gratitude and closeness, parents and spouse receive personal attacks. Naturally, they become angry and withdraw from the depressed individual. To keep them coming back for more, the depressed individual tells spouse and parents that the depressed individual is suicidal. The family becomes concerned and tries to do everything possible for the depressed individual and his family.

The depressed individual can feel the power he or she now has over family and spouse in the suicidal chase. He or she feels free to take verbal shots at any individual, especially family, who offends them. After all, their family and step family members are the ones chasing them.

---

[9]Doctrine and Covenants 76:30-35, p. 139.

Depressed individuals create the need for the suicidal chase by shooting themselves over and over psychologically. They point out to others that parents and spouse will not help them. Soon others are drawn into this chase of anger, blame, attack, withdrawal, return, and power struggle. This abuse shakes the faith which friends and family have in others and themselves. Friendships of parents and spouse are destroyed. It does not matter if their friends and family are depressed, too. Depressed individuals run out of everyone's reach. They may really commit suicide if confronted. Depressed individuals do not have as little as it appears.

Everyone walks on egg shells with depressed people. At the same time, they provide their meals, pay their bills, provide new clothing, games, travel, and recreation to ease their pain. Children are tended to ease their parent's situation and the tension in children. Individuals find jobs for them which depressed individuals will not accept or will not make any effort to keep. As the bills start coming in, depressed individuals become more depressed. They sense opposition and anger to their needs. Depressed individuals need more meals, more bills paid, more clothing, and more babysitting, etc. They need more travel because of the pain they are experiencing. They need more pills to control their anxieties.

Depressed individuals can say or do anything they want because they are depressed and are being chased. It does not matter if they hurt the feelings of those they come in contact with. They know people are afraid of pushing them over the edge. They accuse family and friends of not loving them if they do not provide their every want, need, and desire by chasing them. Depressed individuals have become addicted to receiving his or her wants, needs, and desires in this manner.

There are consequences for being addicted to this kind of opposition. The money for this kind of addiction has to come from somewhere. Soon others are suffering more than the one who was first depressed and suicidal. These individuals are paying the consequences for the one who was depressed and suicidal and who would not give up depressive and suicidal behaviors.

The first depressed individual has had every need provided for many years. The caretakers have not. They most likely are working two or more jobs to pay for these consequences. They must provide the needs, wants, and desires for their families. Caretakers feel intimidated, manipulated, stonewalled, and they are. They have less than the depressed individual. They feel used when they notice their depressed family member seems to function okay when others are not providing for them. Depressed individuals may even laugh and make fun at those who cared for them for so many years. When their caretakers are sick, they are nowhere to be found. They do not have the money to help their caretakers, but they do have the money to have new clothes, cars, vacations, sports tickets.

Years pass. Families realize they have been "bled from every pore." They wonder, what's wrong with me that my family members care so little for me? Why do they not understand that money does not grow on trees? Caretakers have to work in the heat or cold of the day in a field or an office to obtain this money for which depressed individuals are spending on junk. Relationships are severed.

The first depressed individual becomes angry at not getting what they have had for many years. They are offended at any advice given because they want cash. Depressed individuals are angry that they have to make an effort. They have to give up their spending habits and recreation. They wonder what is wrong with the caretakers of the family. Depressed individuals deny that they are related to their spiteful family. Spouses, children, parents, extended family are betrayed over items barely costing about the price of thirty pieces of silver.

Why are individuals depressed? Are depressed individuals afraid to work and make an effort? Do they just not want to work? Have they been severely traumatized in their youth? Are they experiencing panic attacks? Depressed individuals have to keep parents and family at a distance to keep the giving-behavior of parents and family going. This distance is maintained by picking at others. The chase is on.

The kinds of oaths that we live by determine if we have depression. Frequently, depressed individuals have sworn an oath to destroy the people who have offended them. It does not matter if these people are family who have needs, hurts, and traumas, too. Depressed individuals feel they have the right to tell others how people really are. Depressed individuals feel they have a right to tell others what other people have been saying or doing behind someone's back. They warn that others will do to them what they have done to the depressed individual. This may not be true, but depressed individuals have heard or seen family doing hurtful things to others.

Depressed individuals may only want to "fix someone's little red wagon" or they want to destroy every bit of happiness that comes into others' lives. Individuals are depressed because they have sworn an oath to destroy others, but have bound their own soul. When the spotlight turns to them, or they can feel that they are bound, they become a suicide bomber.

The Suicidal Bomber. We live in an age of the suicidal bomber. Many countries have learned to deal with this kind of behavior. They live without many loved ones who have perished, or they live with ones who have been maimed by the suicidal bomber. The suicidal bomber is prevalent in every society. It is the number one scam for the world. It is most prevalent in a society that is trusting, gullible, and likes to help people by giving.

Everyone has forgotten one thing about depression. Depressed people do not enjoy travel, new clothes, meals, large homes, etc. Depressed individuals do not have the energy to get out of bed and get dressed. They do not have the energy to eat, ski, turn on the television, etc. They are in a period of famine spiritually. The area or space which they live in is small, dark, and cold. Spiritually, these individuals are anorexic.

Remember. If you commit suicide, you will be suicidal on the other side of the veil. What ever principle that you have learned will rise with you in your resurrection. You will be suicidal in a kingdom where there is no death! You are suicidal in a Kingdom where there is no opposition! There will be no desire to change.

The treatment for famine and cold is meat.[10] In this scripture which I have just footnoted, the Lord gives us a Word of Wisdom. We are to eat meat in times of winter, cold, and famine. When we are in the winter of our lives, we do not have to exist in the cold and in a famine. We eat meat. What meat will we be eating? The meat of the prophets. Depression cannot be cured without the meat of the prophets.

Which prophet do you start with? Pick any prophet in The Holy Bible and The Book of Mormon. Begin with the Bible verses that your mothers and grandmothers taught you when you were on their laps. They felt inspired to teach them to you. Add to this.

---

[10]Doctrine and Covenants 89:12-13, p.176

Prophets have meat that we know not of.[11] This meat comes from their testimony of Christ and their desire to live eternal truths taught by Him. Open your scriptures, copy some eternal truths from each prophet on a 3x5 inch card. Add more eternal truths to your pile. When you are angry, hurting, and depressed, sort through this meat. Your mind will be able to focus on something that will help. This meat will defragment your spiritual system.

Low Energy. If you are depressed, you lack energy. Depressed people seek energy boosters that are harmful to your health and are expensive to buy. There is an alternative. Try Brewer's Yeast. Brewer's Yeast comes in powder or tablets. This is not the type of yeast that rises dough. Nursing mothers were told to take Brewer's Yeast, but they were not told why. Most mothers stopped taking Brewer's Yeast because it is bitter. Sweeten it with honey or fruit. Beekeepers who use Brewer's Yeast in pollen substitute patties have healthier bees. The bees have more energy to forage for honey. Brewer's Yeast is full of vitamins and proteins which are needed to complete the energy cycle. Our body's energy cycle includes recognizing glucose, storing glucose as glycogen, and retrieving the stored glycogen. The B Vitamins do this. Most of us take vitamins in pills on an empty stomach. There is nothing to retrieve.

The Suicidal Watch. At some time, for a depressed individual to be happy and functional, the person who has suicidal thoughts must do his own suicidal watch. Others have been sitting with, cooking, calling, babysitting, chauffeuring, begging, and providing a very comfortable suicidal watch. In other words, the only person that can resurrect you is you. This is the work that you will do that is greater than the Savior. Your keys or answers to your resurrection of your best self are found in The Books of the Prophets, the Holy Scriptures.

Am I telling you to drop your counselor? No! Am I telling you to cut out all of your medications immediately? No! This is between you, your counselor, and the Lord. I am not so naive' that I do not know there are patients who will need anti-depressants. There are families and step families that are safer if their depressed and angry family member is on anti-depressants. Just do not add an additional anti-depressant, mood-elevator, anti-anxiety, anti-meanness pill, and pain pill for every problem in your life. In my youth, women had a swear word for each child. In this day, they have an anti-depressant, a pain pill, and a physician who is willing to multi-medicate for every inconvenience, every trial, and every child in the household. Do not ask your family to tolerate behavior that is difficult for staff at a mental hospital to tolerate.

Repent and Refrain. While discussing things with a counselor, discuss your behavior with the Lord. Each depressive behavior that you repent of and refrain from, eases your burdens and the burdens of your family. This behavior does not have to greet you in the neighborhood. Your sincerity will be tested. The Adversary will continue to work through individuals who try your patience. Opposition always seems to come when you do good for yourself and others. For every positive reaction in your life, there is an opposite, equal reaction. *Repentance is your birthright. Do not despise repentance.*[12]

Repenting is hard for depressed individuals who are addicted to a depressed way of life. Depressed individuals do not accept what the Savior has done for us and the words of the

---

[11]John 4:32:34, The Holy Bible, p. 1331.

[12]Genesis 25:28-34, The Holy Bible, p. 38.

prophets. They do not use their Gift of the Holy Ghost. Depressed individuals are tempted to do things which they should not do. They do not have much charity. They need medication for the anxieties caused by this behavior. There is nothing that will be more satisfying than the Atonement of Christ and the sacrifice of the prophets and the parents and step parents of the world, His servants.

Depressed individuals "hang on to" depression and suicidal thoughts to keep their needs fulfilled and to keep from getting excommunicated from a church they love. Let your bishop decide if your behavior warrants excommunication.

Make a covenant between you and the Lord. There are saving ordinances, other than christenings and baptism, which help us out of the pits that we are in. These ordinances are called covenants. In prayer at home, raise your right arm as you would in a court of law. Promise that you will no longer use depressive behavior and thoughts of suicide as a stress reducer and a way to solve your problems. Seek solutions out of the best books. The best books are the words of Christ and the books by the prophets. These words teach us about three important, separate Beings in our life.

God, The Father, His Son, Jesus Christ, and the Holy Ghost. Current popular opinion views the Father, His Son, Jesus Christ, and the Holy Ghost as One Supreme Being with three individuals in one body. This is how the Godhead is omniscient, omnipotent, and omnipresent– knowing all things, all powerful, and being everywhere at the same time. God, the Father, and His Son, Jesus Christ, do know all things. Jesus, the Son of God, is Creator of this world. He was taught by His Father. They are the authorities of this world. Since they are united in purpose with the Holy Ghost, I suspect the Holy Ghost knows what they know. (John 16:13) I do not understand how they can answer all our prayers and be in the midst of all of us. One day we will. This understanding will come when we learn to enlarge our borders peacefully.

I do understand that God, the Father, Jesus Christ, the Son, and the Holy Ghost are not conjoined triplets physically or spiritually. We have seen the problems which conjoined twins have. If the Godhead was a Conjoined Being, the one in the center, Jesus Christ, would be the most paralyzed. Christ could not accomplish His mission of being crucified for the sins of the world. God and the Holy Ghost would be crucified with Him.

Just before the Savior gave His great Intercessory Prayer, He told his Apostles about His approaching Death and Resurrection. They became upset. He told them that it was necessary for Him to go away so He could send the Comforter to us. The Comforter would reprove the world of sin, righteousness, and judgement. (John 16:7 - 10). As we know from scripture and experience, The Holy Ghost reproves betimes with sharpness and then shows forth afterwards an increase of love. (Doctrine and Covenants 121:43) This is a great example for us to follow in disciplining ourselves as well as our children.

The Intercessory Prayer. In the Intercessory Prayer, the Savior prays to the Holy Father for these that are in the world, that they may be one, as *we* are. *(*John 17:11) This means united in purpose. With our house divided, the Savior's Intercessory Prayer for us cannot be fulfilled. The Intercessory Prayer is the prayer where the Savior requests that those who believe in Him are joint heirs with Christ. We show that we believe in Him through our word. The Savior requests that we who believe in Him are to be with Him where He is. This is where our dignity and happiness comes from. Notice. The Savior prayed like He taught us to pray in The Lord's

Prayer. In the Intercessory Prayer are the things that the Apostles, such as the Apostle Paul, are teaching us.

Are you willing to give up these things in the Intercessory Prayer for us for depression, suicidal behavior, drugs, and alcohol, etc.? Do you want to learn that there really is a Heavenly Father, a Savior, and a Comforter without the comfort of the Holy Ghost, without the words of Christ, and without the words of all of His servants? How much agency are you giving up if you give up the two prayers for us by the Savior?

1 THESE words spake Jesus, and lifted up his eyes to heaven, and said, Father, the hour is come; glorify thy Son, that thy Son also may glorify thee:
2 As thou hast given him power over all flesh, that he should give eternal life to as many as thou hast given him.
3 And this is life eternal, that they might know thee the only true God, and Jesus Christ, whom thou hast sent.
4 I have glorified thee on the earth: I have finished the work which thou gavest me to do.

John 17, 1-4, The Holy Bible

20 Neither pray I for these alone, but for them also which shall believe on me through their word;
21 That they all may be one; as thou, Father, art in me, and I in thee, that they also may be one in us: that the world may believe that thou hast sent me.
22 And the glory which thou gavest me I have given them; that they may be one, even as we are one:
23 I in them, and thou in me, that they may be made perfect in one; and that the world may know that thou hast sent me, and hast loved them, as thou hast loved me.
24 Father, I will that they also, whom thou hast given me, be with me where I am; that they may behold my glory, which thou hast given me: for thou lovedst me before the foundation of the world.

John 17:20 - 24, The Holy Bible

How is your family scattered by depression? Are you chasing depression and suicidal thoughts until you are snared into a power struggle which divides your family? Are you and other family members addicted to causing opposition in your family? Are you addicted to accepting the blame for the opposition in the family? Can you only fulfill your needs by becoming a suicidal Bomber? What oaths has family members sworn in anger to each other?
The lean years of depression will devour the fat years of health for anyone.[13] Your house becomes divided, and it is very difficult to gather your house again. It becomes difficult to understand and do the ways of God, Jesus Christ, and the Holy Ghost.

---

[13]Genesis 41:19-21, The Holy Bible, pp. 62-63.

Chapter Eight

A House Divided Against Itself

In previous chapters, we have compared the house of Israel and your house and your depressions to fig and olive trees. Depressions are caused by trying to caste stones into bread with various appetites, pinnacles, and idols. We are left in outer darkness. Apostles point out the stones which we try to cast into bread and the bread that we cast into stone with anger.

In this chapter, the Apostle Paul is going to teach us how branches overcome the root causing other branches to wither away by depression. The Apostle Paul is also going to teach us how our tame olive trees wax old, the top of our tree dies, and apostasy occurs in our families and step families. These things divided the House of Israel. They divide your house and your family or step family. The lean years of anger, rebellion, and depression really do devour the fat years of health and happiness for everyone by encumbering the words of Christ and parents and step parents.

Remember. A burden from Christ gives us rest. Burdens from Christ take us forward. The Adversary places burdens which are heavy and which block our progress. The Adversary takes us backward, and we lose skills. This is the Adversary's curse.

> *28 ¶ Come unto me, all ye that labor and are heavy laden, and I will give you rest.*
> *29 Take my yoke upon you, and learn of me; for I am meek and lowly in heart:*
> *and ye shall find rest unto your souls.*
> *30 For my yoke is easy, and my burden is light.   Matthew 11:28 - 30, The Holy Bible*

Weapons of Mass Construction.   Before we go on, this is a good time to evaluate if you are keeping up and learning by adding precept to precept. This may sound like I am trying to rewrite scripture. I am not. I want to benefit from scripture. I call this type of learning "Weapons of Mass Construction." I am tired of learning with our "Weapons of Mass Destruction." I am hoping you are, too.

As you combine several verses in the Old and New Testament of The Holy Bible with The Book of Mormon, you get an idea of what all the prophets have tried to teach us by adding precept by precept. It may be a matter of semantics, but the Savior and the prophets teach the same things over the years. They are working on the same plan of Salvation and Construction for a very large group of our Heavenly Father's children. We just need to learn our spiritual synonyms and antonyms to be able to recognize similar precepts in language which has changed or in scripture that has been translated by many different people.[14]

In the first verses of the following scripture, the Apostle Paul shows us how to sort withered branches and graft tender shoots. We can also determine how our behavior waxes old

---

[14]Isaiah 28:10, The Holy Bible, pp. 893 - 894.

and the top of our tree dies in our life. I am going to list the ways. There is room for you to write comments that will be appropriate for you and your family. As you see my list, you can recognize the withersoever I will spots, the nethermost spots, some poor spots, the poorest spots, and the good spots of the Master's vineyard.

The Apostle Paul is frank in telling us what cumbers us. These are the stones which we are trying to cast into bread. These verses reveal the appetites that we should not partake or must control, the pinnacles that we should not be on or limit, and the idols that we should not worship.

1 THIS know also, that in the last days perilous times shall come.
2 For men shall be lovers of their own selves, covetous, boasters,
proud, blasphemers, disobedient to parents, unthankful, unholy,
3 Without natural affection, trucebreakers, false accusers, incontinent, fierce,
despisers of those that are good,
4 Traitors, heady, highminded, lovers of pleasures more than lovers of God;
5 Having a form of godliness, but denying the power thereof: from such turn away.
6 For of this sort are they which creep into houses, and lead captive silly women
laden with sins, led away with divers lusts,
7 Ever learning, and never able to come to the knowledge of the truth.

2 Timothy 3:1 - 7, The Holy Bible

We do not need an ancient or modern-day prophet to tell us that we live in perilous times. All we have to do is turn on the television news or read a newspaper. The media shows us many examples of people in many countries who are polarized. Many try to cumber our Constitution in America. They are always in the news. Their ideas, crimes, and wars are outrageous. Those defending themselves are always to blame. When the aggressors run out of money, they lay down their weapons briefly, and receive a peace prize. They do not allow their own children to destroy their home with these behaviors. It is okay to use these behaviors when you want to destroy other's homes, families, reputations, and lives.

People may get rich off their schemes, but they also have polarized large groups of people. This polarizes or separates nations as well as families and step families. This polarization is beyond personal opinion. Polarized individuals live on opposite sides of "the fence of life," forming cliques, communes, gangs, exclusive friendships, etc., which are antagonistic to anyone that disagrees with their opinions or causes or another's existence.

In the medical community, we hear the term "bi-polar disorder." In the old days, this disorder was known as manic-depressive behavior or melancholia. Bi-polar individuals have many highs and many lows in their life. Bi-polar individuals are depressed. They often claim they could not produce an early crop in their life because of abusive parents or step parents. Since they did not produce an early crop, they cannot produce a late crop. This justifies chasing crimes, their uncontrolled appetites, their useless pinnacles, their behavior, and their idols.

Individuals will have many peaks and valleys in their lives if they do not turn away from the behaviors that the Apostle Paul advised us to avoid. The Prophet, Isaiah, states in the last days our valleys would be exalted, and our peaks made low. The Apostle Luke records the

Savior repeating the words of Isaiah in Luke 3: 5- 6. Most people think this will happen in The Big Earthquake which we have been expecting. This nurse is hoping this will not happen by "The Big Earthquake." This will occur in people—like it has in latter-day prophets and many other individuals who serve the Lord.

> 3 ¶ *The voice of him that crieth in the wilderness, Prepare ye the way of the LORD,*
> *make straight in the desert a highway for our God.*
> *4 Every valley shall be exalted, and every mountain and hill shall be made low:*
> *and the crooked shall be made straight, and the rough places plain:*
> *5 And the glory of the LORD shall be revealed, and all flesh shall see it together:*
> *for the mouth of the LORD hath spoken it. Isaiah 40:3 - 5, The Holy Bible*

Isaiah was given the privilege to see all of us till the end of time. Thus, Isaiah could record what John the Baptist preached. This verse sounds like John the Baptist is giving instructions to all of us. It appears that we all are to prepare the way of the Lord, not just John the Baptist. We are to make straight in the desert a highway for our God. How do each of us prepare the way of the Lord? There can only be one head of The Church of Jesus Christ. How does one make a highway for our God in the desert of our lives? Like John the Baptist, we are forerunners of Jesus Christ for our children and step children.

We prepare the way of the Lord by exalting our valleys and making low our mountains. We will increase and then have a decrease so our children and step children can prepare the way of the Lord for their children. Sadly, parents and step parents will be "beheaded spiritually" by our children and step children because children are being overcome by the Adversary.

How does one exalt our personal valleys and make low our personal peaks, especially when there is so much opposition in the world? We do it like the Apostle Paul eliminated his peaks and valleys. I do not know what scriptures Paul began with to develop the saving graces in his life. I do know this. I suspect when the Apostle Paul was without form and in void, he divided the Darkness from the Light, like the Creator of this World did in the beginning. The Apostle Paul separated the Night (the Adversary) from the Day—Jesus Christ. This is how we ease our depression and find that firmament that is so strong that we can rise and take up our beds, and walk. We do not have to sit and cry. If we have not provided a highway for ourselves, we will not be able to provide a highway for the Lord and our children and step children and for those we need to serve.

The firmament is not the base of the Earth. Firmament is from the word firm which gives strength and support. Firmament also gives brightness. (Daniel 12:3) In poems and scripture, firmament is described as the sky or the heavens. I suspect the scriptures about firmament are not just referring to the sky, but literally means the heavens. If you recall in Genesis 1:8, after the firmament which was called Heaven was formed, the water was divided, and the land appeared. Heaven's firmament or principles will always be our strength and support as well as our highway.

I have wondered if the Apostle Paul had bi-polar disorder. It is hard to think of an apostle having manic-depressive disorder or bi-polar disorder. If Paul did have this disorder, how would Paul get bi-polar disorder? From accounts in scripture, he seems educated. Paul got this disorder by persecuting the Christians, followers of Christ. He was a despiser of those that were good. When he stopped persecuting the Christians because of the miraculous vision which he received, he persecuted himself. After all he had done to the Christians, there was still something good in him. However, he was still a despiser of those that were good–himself. His repentance was not complete until he forgave himself.

The Lord's Highway is for all ages. Paul mentions the behavior of all age groups. Notice the patterns of behavior in yourself and all of your children, regardless of age. There is a gate for you to leave the wayside, the stony places, and the thorny places of life. You do not have to live by just charity or the dole. You, too, can harness the powers of heaven for yourself and your family. When you do, not only do you receive great blessings from the Lord, it is an interesting experience.

26 And when I had said this, the Lord spake unto me, saying: Fools mock, but they shall mourn; and my grace is sufficient for the meek, that they shall take no advantage of your weakness;
27 And if men come unto me I will show unto them their weakness. I give unto men weakness that they may be humble; and my grace is sufficient for all men that humble themselves before me; for if they humble themselves before me, and have faith in me, then will I make weak things become strong unto them.

Ether 12:26 - 27, The Book of Mormon

The things which the Apostle Paul told us to turn away from are weaknesses. These weaknesses cause depression in ourselves and others. These weaknesses are the stones that can not be caste into bread. We may achieve some high, dangerous pinnacles. We may become idols, but we are not idols. We are children of God. As we eliminate these weaknesses, and this is a life long process, we eliminate depression.

There is a highway that leads us back to our Heavenly Father's loving arms. We can walk this highway with our parents and step parents until we reach the age of accountability for our own sins. Latter-day revelation tells us the age of accountability is eight years of age. The Lord and parents and step parents know there are many years of work ahead in an eight year old. They are uneducated and inexperienced. They are growing and developing fast and need to take responsibility for their mistakes. They also need to learn direction. This begins at the age of eight, the age of accountability.

At the age of accountability, we must choose to walk this highway. His highway is straight as is the gate. (Matthew 7:14) Many people never walk this highway, or they wait until they are old. Straight is boring. *At what age, are you willing to walk the Highway of the Lord?*

Are you living by the wayside, the stony places, and in the thorny places of life? This is where you will plant your seeds. This is where you will walk. This is where you will grow. If you cannot walk or grow, this is where you will sit. You have your agency to choose where you want to walk or sit. What can you harness where you are walking or sitting? What seeds will grow where you are walking? Are you trying to obtain a hundred fold crop in a thorny place or without even planting seed anywhere?

PEAKS OF DESPAIR

He loveth transgression that loveth strife: and he that exalteth his gate seeketh destruction.
Proverbs 17:19

AGE OF ACCOUNTABILITY

1. *LOVERS OF THEIR OWN SELVES*
   a. *Person is able to provide for their needs/wants/desires.*
   b. *Parents or spouse able to provide for your needs, wants, and desires.*
   c. *Person has bullimic appearance and attitude.*
   d. *Individuals obsess over what others have.*

2. *COVETOUS*
   a. *They are greedy.*
   b. *They have a strong desire for wealth and things, but work too much.*

GATE IS: REPENTANCE AND BAPTISM

Harness the powers of Heaven–righteous principles and ordinances beginning with: faith in Christ, repentance, and the Gift of the Holy Ghost

AGE OF ACCOUNTABILITY

1. *LOVE GOD WITH ALL THY MIGHT, MIND, AND STRENGTH.*
2. *LOVE THY NEIGHBOR AS THYSELF.*
   a. *Do this when angry with your neighbor/ self/spouse/family/ the neighbor's kids, and the neighbor's cats and dogs, etc.*

2. *DO NOT COVET OR ENVY.*
   a. *Share.*
   b. *Fast.*
   c. *Give to the poor and needy–even if it is family.*
      (a) *There are limits to giving.*
      (b) *Do not give so much that you become poor.*

VALLEYS OF DEPRESSION

He loveth transgression that loveth strife: and he that exalteth his gate seeketh destruction.
Proverbs 17:19

AGE OF ACCOUNTABILITY

1. *LOVERS OF THEIR OWN SELVES*
   a. *They are unable to provide for their needs/wants/desires.*
   b. *Parents will not provide for the needs of family.*
   c. *They expect others to provide when they cannot provide. Has:*
      (1) *broken wing*
      (2) *broken wing act*
      (3) *broken wing act deluxe*

2. *COVETOUS*
   a. *They are greedy.*
   b. *They have a strong desire for wealth and things, but work too little.*

PEAKS OF DESPAIR	FIRMAMENT	VALLEYS OF DEPRESSION

PEAKS OF DESPAIR

3. BOASTERS
   a. They brag.
   b. They are arrogant.
   c. They are superior to others because of:
      (1) ancestry/family
      (2) friends
      (3) wealth/job
      (4) efforts
      (5) appearance
      (6) positions
      (7) talents
      (8) anger

4. PROUD
   a. They made a better effort than others.
   b. They have a better station in life.
   c. They have more honors which are deserved.
   d. Their election is made sure.
   e. They are domineering when they do not get their own way.
   f. They disdain those who are beneath them.
      (1) Parents
      (2) Step parents
      (3) Siblings
      (4) Employees
      (5) Poor

FIRMAMENT

3. TESTIMONY OF WHAT WORKS AND WHAT DOES NOT WORK
   a. Some can be shared.
   b. Some are to be kept silent.
   c. Be fair.

4. SERVANT OF ALL

VALLEYS OF DEPRESSION

3. BOASTERS
   a. Individuals brag they have no strengths or resources.
   b. They brag their family won't help them.
   c. They deliberately anger parents/family so they will not help them.

4. PROUD
   a. They are proud of no effort.
   b. They are proud of no station in life.
   c. They are a born loser and proud of it.
   d. They are proud of anarchy–their civil disorder.
      (a) with parents and step parents
      (b) with community
      (c) with country
      (d) with God

PEAKS OF DESPAIR	**FIRMAMENT**	**VALLEYS OF DEPRESSION**

5. BLASPHEMERS
   a. They curse God.
   b. They curse sacred things.
   c. They curse others:
     (1) parents
     (2) step parents
     (3) children
     (4) siblings
     (5) employers
     (6) strangers
	5. ABRAHAMIC COVENANT
	   a. Lord blesses the families of the Earth.
	   b. He blesses those that bless them.
	   c. He curses those that curse them.
	   d. Our communications are to be:
	     (1) Yeah-Yeah
	     (2) Nay-Nay
	     (3) Silent
		5. BLASPHEMERS
		   a. They curse God.
		   b. They curse sacred things.
		     (1) self
		   c. They write letters to others.
		   d. They use filthy, irreverent remarks.
		   e. They are sarcastic.
		   f. They swear oaths to destroy others.

6. DISOBEDIENT TO PARENTS
   a. They refuse to follow simple commands or requests of parents.
   b. They won't obey rules of family.
   c. They ask parents to harness things that are impossible to harness.
	6. OBEY PARENTS
	   a. They honor parents.
	   b. They honor forefathers.
	   c. They honor our Heavenly Father and Jesus Christ.
	   d. They allow parents to have free agency.
	   e. They allow parents to fulfill their patriarchal blessing.
	   f. They don't ask their Heavenly and Earthly parents to harness things that Christ would not harness.
		6. DISOBEDIENT TO PARENTS
		   a. They want parents to harness things that cannot be harnessed.
		   b. They follow just enough rules to get out of trouble at parents' or others' expense.

PEAKS OF DESPAIR	**FIRMAMENT**	**VALLEY OF DEPRESSION**

7. UNTHANKFUL
   a. They have food, cars, clothes, shelter, but have nothing to be thankful for.
   b. They have nothing to wear or to do.
   c. They have no soft answers.

7. KEEP THE SABBATH DAY HOLY
   a. Thank Heavenly Father and Jesus Christ daily.
   b. Thank parents.
   c. Use soft answers.
   d. Pay tithing.
   e. Assemble on the Sabbath to worship God and Jesus Christ.

7. UNTHANKFUL
   a. They are ungrateful when others help them. They should have done more.
   b. They are unappreciative.
   c. They do not use soft answers with others.

8. UNHOLY
   a. They are wicked.
      (1) They break most of Ten Commandments.
   b. They have outrageous behavior.
   c. They have dreadful behavior.
   d. They do not get enough sleep which lowers threshold of anger/hostility.
   e. They need energy boosters.
   f. They need sleeping pills to compensate for the energy boosters.
   g. They need pain pills to counter the effects of energy boosters on heart, joints, and muscles.

8. KEEP THE WHOLE WEEK HOLY
   a. Work
   b. Pray
   c. Get adequate sleep.
   d. Don't run faster than we can walk.
   e. Do not abuse music or television.
   f. Don't allow music and television to abuse us.
   g. Eat nourishing food.

8. UNHOLY
   a. Live in dark rooms.
   b. They watch R-rated movies over and over.
   c. They sleep too much.
   d. They listen to Heavy Metal music.
   e. It is now easier to justify breaking a commandment.
   f. They need energy boosters.
   g. They need energy pills to compensate for sleeping pills.
   h. They need pain pills to counter the effects of energy boosters on heart, joints, and muscles.

PEAKS OF DESPAIR	FIRMAMENT	VALLEYS OF DEPRESSION
9. WITHOUT NATURAL AFFECTION a. The workaholic is gone all the time. b. They buy many things which they cannot afford to buy. c. They are miserly. d. They are controlling. e. Spouse works for junk. f. Husband refuses to give paycheck for support of family. g. When wife works to meet others' needs, who meets her needs? h. Sports-aholic is gone all the time. i. Excessive recreation j. Many pets k. They do more for others than family. l. Excessive competition m. They hate God.	9. TEMPLE MARRIAGE FOR ETERNITY a. Tender thoughts b. Tender feelings c. Tender care d. Spend time together. e. Date night f. Family Home Evening g. Eat at table together. h. They do more for spouse, children, and others than SELF. i. Love letters j. Educate children and self. k. They have love for God. l. They have love for Jesus Christ. m. They have love for family. n. They have love for country. o. They have natural affection for others and self.	9. WITHOUT NATURAL AFFECTION a. They hate self. b. They hate everything. c. They hate everybody. d. They cannot buy self anything. e. They are not affectionate with spouse. (1) They have no desire for intimacy with spouse. f. They have flat affect. Their emotion does not fit the occasion. g. Children are angry with parents for not meeting their needs and not loving them like they should. h. They hate God.

PEAKS OF DESPAIR	FIRMAMENT	VALLEYS OF DEPRESSION

10. TRUCE BREAKERS
  a. They do what have promised not to do.
  b. They pick a fight.
  c. They feign an attack on self.
  d. They attack others, but appear innocent.
  e. They give the silent treatment.
  f. They gossip to let others know how someone really is.
  g. Truce breaking is the tension breaker when the spotlight is on you and your behavior.
  h. Truce breaking flips one from the peaks of despair to the valleys of depression.
	10. PEACEMAKERS
	  a. Chasten fallowed by love.
	  b. Work is a tension-breaker.
	  c. Acknowledge the various authority figures in your life.
		10. TRUCE BREAKERS
		  a. They fall off the bandwagon.
		  b. They pick a fight.
		  c. They attack self to appear innocent.
		  d. It feels better to be apart.
		  e. They give the silent treatment.
		  f. Relationships are severed.
		    (1) Divorce
		    (2) Friends
		    (3) Parents
		    (4) Wars
		  g. They feel forced to make a truce when the spotlight is on them.
		  h. False truces flips one from valleys of depression to peaks of despair.

11. FALSE ACCUSERS
  a. They find fault with others.
  b. They point the finger.
  c. They participate in lawsuits.
  d. They blame others for poor performance.
  e. They lie.
  f. They refuse to be accountable.
	11. RECONCILE WITH THY BROTHER, CHILD SPOUSE, PARENT.
	  a. Do not lie.
		11. FALSE ACCUSERS
		  a. They find fault with self.
		  b. They point the finger at self.
		  c. They lie.
		  d. Person blames self falsely to appease others.

PEAKS OF DESPAIR	FIRMAMENT	VALLEYS OF DEPRESSION

12. INCONTINENT
  a. They do not have any restraint with others.
  b. They have uncontrolled anger.
  c. They have an uncontrolled tongue.
  d. They have uncontrolled sexual activity.
    (1) Adultery
    (2) Fornication
    (3) Homosexuality
  e. They are incapable of holding or keeping covenants.
	12. MEEK
	Keep your dignity by:
	  a. Keeping the Commandments.
	  b. Word of Wisdom
	  c. Keep Chastity
	  d. When in conflict:
	    (1) Say nothing
	    (2) Soft answers
	    (3) Agreement with thine adversary– kind thoughts
		12. INCONTINENT
		  a. They have emotional outbursts.
		    (1) yelling
		    (2) screaming
		    (3) swearing
		  b. They have uncontrolled imaginations.
		  c. They have uncontrolled curiosity.
		  d. They have uncontrolled sexual activity.

13. FIERCE
  a. They rely on knife-stabbing behavior.
  b. They are violently cruel or abusive to others.
  c. They are cruel to anyone who gets in their way.
  d. They are intensely eager to succeed at all costs.
	13. LOVE ONE ANOTHER
	  a. Bear one another's burdens.
	  b. Service
	  c. Listen
	  d. Judge situations, not people
		13. FIERCE
		  a. They are their own worse enemy.
		  b. They have temper tantrums all their life.
		  c. They are cruel to self.
		  d. They intensely do not want to succeed at all costs.

14. DESPISERS OF THOSE THAT ARE GOOD
  a. Parents, spouse, children, family, friends, country
  b. Dig a pit for them.
	14. PRAY FOR WHO PERSECUTES, DESPITEFULLY USES, & REVILES AGAINST YOU.
	  a. Inspired how to act or help others
		14. DESPISERS OF THOSE THAT ARE GOOD
		  a. Self
		  b. They fall into the same pits they dug for others.

PEAKS OF DESPAIR	FIRMAMENT	VALLEYS OF DEPRESSION

15. TRAITORS
   a. Betray parents.
   b. Betray spouse.
   c. Betray children.
   d. Betray friends.
   e. They steal friends, spouses, boy or girl friends.
   f. They gossip about others.
   g. They refuse to serve.
	15. SUPPORT LEADERS
	   a. Keep Confidences.
	   b. Do not speak evil against the Lord's Anointed.
		15. TRAITORS
		   a. They betray self with gossip about self.
		   b. They betray one's cause for money.

16. HEADY
   a. They are impetuous or lacking thought.
   b. They are bold.
   c. They make hasty decisions.
   d. They are intoxicated.
     (1) Alcohol/Drugs
     (2) Grief
     (3) Anger
   e. They take or do anything for acceptance or popularity.
	16. SHARPEN SENSES
	   a. Read and study scriptures.
	   b. Pray often.
	   c. Enjoy blessings.
	   d. Keep Word of Wisdom
		16. HEADY
		   a. They take anything to dull the senses.
		   b. They take anything for energy.
		   c. They are always intoxicated.
		     (1) Alcoholism
		     (2) Drug abuse
		     (3) Depression

17. HIGHMINDED
   a. Are proud of fame/popularity.
   b. Are arrogant about successes.
   c. Proud of honors
   d. Disdain for those without honors.
   e. Do not take any criticisms.
	17. SEEK YE FIRST THE KINGDOM OF GOD.
	   a. Charity to:
	     (1) God and Christ
	     (2) Family
	     (3) Employer and Employee
	     (4) Country
		17. HIGHMINDED
		   a. Are too proud to admit failure.
		   b. Too proud to ask for directions.
		   c. Slightest criticism is like a bullet.
		   d. Disdain for those who have honors.
		   e. Wants no advice.

PEAKS OF DESPAIR	FIRMAMENT	VALLEYS OF DEPRESSION

PEAKS OF DESPAIR

18. *LOVERS OF PLEASURE MORE THAN LOVERS OF GOD*
    a. *Movies/dance*
    b. *Sports/recreation*
    c. *Hobbies*
    d. *Parties*
    e. *Travel*
    f. *Large homes*
    g. *Multiple, big cars*
    h. *Clothes*

19. *HAVING A FORM OF GODLINESS, BUT DENYING THE POWER THEREOF*
    a. *Declare there are no idols in my life.*
    b. *Idolatry does not have power over them.*
    c. *Devoted to God, but has no faith.*
    d. *Is pious, but does not repent daily.*
    e. *Believes in Christ, but does things the prophets warn us not to do.*
    f. *They believe in God, but cannot or will not keep the commandments.*

FIRMAMENT

18. *DELIGHT IN THINGS THAT GOD DELIGHTS IN*
    a. *Anxiously engaged*
    b. *Kingdom of our Father in Heaven*
        (1) *Redeem the dead*
        (2) *Preaching the gospel*
        (3) *Perfecting the Saints*
        (4) *Start with*
            (a) *Self*
            (b) *Families*

19. *THOU SHALT HAVE NO OTHER IDOLS BEFORE GOD.*
    a. *Spiritual gifts*
    b. *Patriarchal blessing*
    c. *Temple endowment*
    d. *Temple Marriage*

VALLEYS OF DEPRESSION

18. *LOVERS OF PLEASURE MORE THAN LOVERS OF GOD*
    a. *They delight in being alone.*
    b. *Television*
    c. *Loner hobbies*
    d. *Loner sports*
    e. *Costly apparel*

19. *HAVING A FORM OF GODLINESS, BUT DENYING THE POWER THEREOF*
    a. *They compare self to idols.*
    b. *They hate self when they do not have what idols have.*
    c. *They hate self when idols fail–and they will.*
    d. *They become religious, but nothing soothes.*
    e. *They hate the leaders of our country because idols hate these leaders.*

PEAKS OF DESPAIR	FIRMAMENT	VALLEYS OF DEPRESSION
20. EVER LEARNING BUT NOT ABLE TO COME TO THE KNOWLEDGE OF THE TRUTH a. They have experiences in good and evil, but do not learn from their mistakes. b. They read scriptures, but are too busy and too tired to apply them to their life. c. They cursed others and are without the Holy Ghost. d. They acquired degrees of learning, but don't work. e. Busy acquiring habits and things. f. Demand justice for others.	20. OBTAIN AN EDUCATION a. WORK–NO HONEST TASK IS MENIAL IN THE SIGHT OF OUR HEAVENLY FATHER. b. Janitors are saved as well as the rich man. c. Seek wisdom and knowledge out of the best books d. Discuss criticisms with the Lord in prayer. e. Have mercy for others and mercy for self.	20. EVER LEARNING BUT NOT ABLE TO COME TO THE KNOWLEDGE OF THE TRUTH a. Resist parents. b. Resist spouse. c. Resist counselors. d. Divide God from life and curse God. e. Counselors don't or cannot include God because of the rules of Psychiatry f. No mental space for real learning is left. g. Sins repeat. h. All repented sins return to bear. i. These sins demand justice for self.

PEAKS OF DESPAIR	FIRMAMENT	VALLEYS OF DEPRESSION

21. RESIST TRUTH
  a. Evil called good. Good called evil.
  b. Dark called light. Light called dark.
  c. Bitter called sweet. Sweet called bitter.
  d. They want the burdens of their life-style more than they want their burdens eased by repentance.
  e. Don't know who to believe.
  f. They are deceived.
	21. RESIST NOT EVIL
	  a. Ask and it will be given to you.
	  b. Seek and ye shall find.
	  c. Knock and it shall be opened unto you.
	  d. Truth given to all men liberally.
	  e. Lord upbraideth not.
	  f. Do not be cumbered by evil.
	  g. Overcome evil with good.
	  h. Give to no man evil for evil to make up for damages and losses.
		21. RESIST TRUTH
		  a. Evil called good. Good called evil.
		  b. Dark called light. Light called dark.
		  c. Bitter called sweet. Sweet called bitter.
		  d. Are unable to admit guilt. They are in denial.
		  e. Depression has become addicting.
		  f. They will listen when they feel better.
		  g. They never feel better.
		  h. They are deceived.

"Vengeance is mine. I will repay." A house divided creates much hatred and vengeance among family members. I know there are many parents and step parents who are suffering terribly because they have a child, step child, or a spouse who becomes vengeful and sadistic at the slightest provocation. When biological parents held their child or a spouse in their arms for the first time at their birth or marriage, they had many dreams. Parents had many dreams about what they wanted to accomplish in employment and life. Parents never dreamed they would have to protect their own life, the life of their spouse, their other children, others outside their family, and their job from this beautiful baby they are now holding or an ex spouse. Their child or spouse meanders or runs along the highway which the Adversary has prepared for us and that Hollywood and peers have made so attractive. When mishaps occur, parents are blamed. Parents and step parents may be running along this highway, too.

Life with their baby has become a nightmare. Parents are called every filthy name in Satan's book in spite of the care and hours parents and step parents worked to provide for their child. The top of the tree and all of the branches has died in their child, except one–life. Parents and step parents cannot correct or prune this child even for the child's safety. The child over eighteen is their own person. It does not matter if they are handicapped in some way. Parents and step parents are powerless to change things in their child's life. People will not let them, especially if their child is receiving a Social Security Check. Children are powerless to change things in their life on their own with the few skills they have. These children are not powerless to exercise control or dominion over parents and step parents.

These children need counseling. Yes, they have behavior disorders and personality disorders. However, they are not going to listen to a counselor anymore than they would their parents. Adults and children who are vengeful and sadistic with parents and animals are not going to take an inventory of their life to see how they can improve their life. They will not take medication recommended by counselors. They sell the medication.

Adults and children who are vengeful and sadistic and who make abnormal efforts in life and are proud of this behavior are usually on drugs. They need money for more drugs. They obtain this money by making parents and step parents and others powerless. Parents and step parents count the days until the child reaches eighteen. The child leaves home bitterly, or he or she is escorted out of their parents' home. Now, parents, particularly mother, is thinking this is going to be forever. The child insists this separation is forever.

First, stop the "forever" mode. When parental energies are consumed by years of vengeance, hostility, and anger in a teenager, parents begin thinking this is forever. They state that counselors have no idea what it is like to live with this child. A year seems long, two even longer. When the child leaves, it seems like forever, too. Parents and step parent wonder if their child is safe, warm, and has food. Your separation may be for along time. Usually, angry children with few skills return home. Parents and step parents now must endure illogical behavior from an adult child. Fathers may have to say "no" to your child when he or she wants to come back home. Mothers and step mothers have to let "no" mean "no."

Second, parents wonder if any thing exists of that precious baby you carried for nine months and committed to provide for an eternity for. You wonder: Who is this stranger standing before me, cursing me in front of his or her friends? The voice sounds like your child, but it does not look anything like your beautiful child. They are pale, with dark circles under their eyes, rotten teeth, and a hair-trigger temper. Vengeful children gave up their identity, and now want to crush your identity.

You long for the child you once knew and who does not seem to exist anymore. Humans do a pretty good job at destroying their spirit and the top of their own tree. In the end, the spirit can never be destroyed. Parents and even step parents will have another chance. It may be in the next life. It may be when the child is compelled to be humble by the justice system. This is why God created families. Families are the second chance the Savior died for us to have.

Everyone may avoid each other, but parents still need protection. You may need to move away. However, a future spouse and your future grandchildren need protection. Society needs protection. If the police become involved, let them be involved. Police usually keep an eye on these offenders. Abusive children do not keep civic laws either.

Each state usually has a home for incorrigible children. They usually are known as Boys' or Girls' Ranches. I recommend that you contact these agencies. I know they are expensive. Some children and step children have social security income. See if they will make arrangements for this money. Brothers and sisters, aunts and uncles cannot control these children any more than parents could. Placement in one of these facilities may salvage something of your child. He will never have the confidence that he would have had if he or she was not an ungovernable child who participated in drugs and all that goes with drugs. Do not expect it.

When one has tossed stones all of his life at his family and step family and himself, he eventually discovers all he has in his life are stones. He also discovers that he has to do more ducking than the ones he has been throwing stones at. To preserve their estate and their retirement, parents and step parents often let children run free of limits. Do not try to preserve your estate and retirement by throwing these kinds of stones. This does not help your depression and distress. It does not help your child. This is why the increase in their family tales. This is the reason why we have so much hate in our lives.

16 Be of the same mind one toward another. Mind not high things, but
condescend to men of low estate. Be not wise in your own conceits.
17Recompense to no man evil for evil. Provide things honest in the sight of all men.
18 If it be possible, as much as lieth. in you, live peaceably with all men.
19 Dearly beloved, avenge not yourselves, but rather give place unto wrath:
for it is written, Vengeance is mine; I will repay, saith the Lord.
20 Therefore if thine enemy hunger, feed him; if he thirst, give him drink:
for in so doing thou shalt heap coals of fire on his head.
21 Be not overcome of evil, but overcome evil with good.

Romans 12:16 - 21, The Holy Bible

Parents and step parents in the next chapters we are going to discuss some ways of dealing with ungovernable children and step children while you are depressed. You may not be able to decrease the ungovernable behavior in your children and step children. They have their agency. Hopefully, you will find some ways to decrease your depression. It take practice to not be depressed. First, we must learn how to deal with enmity.

Chapter Nine

Enmity, Part I

We have been learning our spiritual synonyms. It is now time to learn our spiritual antonyms. It is just as important to distinguish opposites as it is to recognize the things that are the same in our life. We learn our opposites by learning some things about enmity. We do not hear of the word, enmity, anymore. Nonetheless, if we want to decrease our depressions, enmity is something important for us to learn.

We first heard of enmity in the Garden of Eden. Let's return to the story of Adam and Eve in the Garden of Eden to see what we can find out about enmity. First, we must find out what happened in the Garden of Eden. Eve was created after Adam as a helpmeet for him. The Lord told them to be fruitful and multiply and replenish the Earth. Adam and Eve were then placed in the Garden of Eden. Adam and Eve were told they could eat of every tree, but they could not eat fruit from the Tree of Knowledge of Good and Evil. All animals and fowl were brought to Adam, and he categorized them and named them. Adam was to have dominion over them. He was also head of Eve. Eve wanted more knowledge and was beguiled by Satan. She ate of the forbidden fruit of the Tree of Knowledge of Good and Evil. She commanded Adam to remain with her so they could have children. He ate the forbidden fruit, too. The Lord God visited them and discovered what they had done. For their actions, the Lord God cast them out of the Garden of Eden. Adam had to till the soil, and Eve had to bear children in sorrow.

The Forbidden Fruit. To counter the effects of Satan beguiling Eve, the Lord God placed enmity between Satan and the woman and her seed (Genesis 3:15) So what is enmity? Does the story of Adam and Eve and enmity apply to us in our day? The Lord God commanded Adam and Eve to not eat of the fruit of the Tree of Knowledge of Good and Evil. Adam and Eve also could not touch it, or they would surely die. (Genesis 3:3) Eve ate the forbidden fruit from the Tree of Knowledge of Good and Evil. Adam ate the fruit to stay with Eve.

Why would the Lord God be upset over a piece of fruit? Some have thought Adam and Eve's bodies were not really mortal yet though they lived on Earth. They must not have had the kind of blood like we have now. Yet, they could eat and digest other fruit in the Garden of Eden. The blood which they had enabled them to do many things in the Garden of Eden.

Why would the Lord God be upset over Eve wanting more knowledge? I suspect that Eve did not exactly want more knowledge. She was beguiled by curiosity. In an old wives' tale, pioneers tell us that curiosity kills the cat. Education requires a straight path of fulfillment of requirements. Then we obtain experience. Knowledge is not an instantaneous thing.

I suspect the forbidden fruit is Satan's Plan, the one which was discarded in the pre-existence. Satan's plan was that we could do anything we wanted no matter the consequences. He would force us to be saved. He would receive the glory. Eve was not the head of household. She should have told Adam what was happening before she ate the apple. After all, she was to cleave to Adam not to her desire for more knowledge.

Cherubims and a Sword. Our Heavenly Father, the Lord God, was concerned that Adam and Eve would eat of the fruit of the Tree of life since they were now familiar with good and evil. Both sexes have a tendency to seek more evil than good after eating of the Tree of Knowledge of Good and Evil. *The way of the Tree of Life was protected by Cherubims and a flaming sword so Adam and Eve would not live forever in their sins.* (Genesis *3:24)* This sword turned all directions.

> *24 So he drove out the man; and he placed at the east of the garden of Eden Cherubims, and a flaming sword which turned every way, to keep the way of the tree of life.* Genesis 3:24, *The Holy Bible*

Notice, in this scripture, "the way" is protected by Cherubims and a flaming sword. I have heard many times the thoughts in this verse shortened to the Tree of Life being guarded. This makes the verse have a different meaning. There is a great difference in "the way" and "the tree." *It never made sense to me that the love of God would be guarded and not the tree of knowledge of good and evil?* Keep in mind. The Tree of Knowledge of Good and Evil is in opposition to the Tree of Life. (2 Nephi 2:15) The Tree of Life is the Love of God which is manifested in the Gospel of Jesus Christ. (1 Nephi 11:22)

I suspect that our depressions come from clashing with the flaming sword which still protects the way of the love of God. In our day, we call it bumping our heads against a brick wall continually. I suspect this is the sword that will not be sheathed until the Second Coming of Christ to protect "the way" from being corrupted. Over time, many of God's children felt it was easier to change "the way" of the love of God instead of repenting. Scriptures tell us that we learn wisdom so that we may learn "there is no other way or means whereby man can be saved, only in and through Christ." (Alma 38:9, The Book of Mormon) Jesus stated, "I am the way, the truth, and the life: no man cometh unto the Father, but by me." (John 14:6) Even Satan knew the way was protected when he tempted Christ. (Matthew 4:6)

When we realize it is "the way" that is guarded, we discover that the scriptures make more sense, especially the scriptures in the New Testament when Christ instructs His Apostles and future disciples. This way will be the same, yesterday, today, and forever because Christ stays the same yesterday, today and forever. Since Jesus is the only way, the way cannot be corrupted by: resisting evil with evil, not agreeing with our adversary, not reconciling with our brother, hiding our lights under a bushel of anger, shame, and guilt, by not keeping or eliminating commandments, principles, and ordinances, and by destroying the prophets and their words. This is why the Savior asked us to not lay up treasures that will corrupt, rust, or attract thieves.

Cherubims and the sword is how we reap what we sow. There is nothing more depressing than to get rid of the beams in our eyes only to have some one deliberately place them there again with their ungovernable behavior. These individuals are comfortable with their beams and motes and the pits in which they live. They think they will ease their suffering by forcing others to be in the pits of life. It takes the spotlight off them. Many good people have been injured on the way by others' beams and motes.

> *7 And if thou shouldst be cast into the pit, or into the hands of murderers, and the sentence of death passed upon thee; if thou be cast into the deep;*

if the billowing surge conspire against thee; if fierce winds become thine enemy;
if the heavens gather blackness, and all the elements combine to hedge up the way;
and above all, if the very jaws of hell shall gape open the mouth wide after thee,
know thou, my son, that all these things shall give thee experience,
and shall be for thy good.
8 The Son of Man hath descended below them all. Art thou greater than he?
9 Therefore, hold on thy way, and the priesthood shall remain with thee;
for their bounds are set, they cannot pass. Thy days are known,
and thy years shall not be numbered less; therefore, fear not what man can do,
for God shall be with you forever and ever.

Doctrine and Covenants 122:7 - 9

Agency. From the beginning of time, the Lord God and Jesus Christ knew that we could not serve two masters. Our Heavenly Father gave us agency, the freedom to choose for ourselves which master to serve and which way to follow. Heavenly Father allowed opposition into the world so we could have a choice between good and evil not just good and good or evil and evil. Without the bitter, we could not discern between bitter and sweet.

If you recall, Satan did not want us to have agency. He would force us all to salvation. Satan would take all the glory. Our Heavenly Father knew that we developed by making choices and learning from our mistakes. I suspect that Satan did not want us, especially Adam, to have this kind of knowledge. Adam, who is known as Michael, fought Satan in the pre-existence. (Revelation 12:7) Adam will most likely be head of the forces that fight Satan again when he is bound and then loosed again. (Revelation 20:1-2) We were given agency to discern between the righteous and the wicked, and between those that serve God and those who do not serve God. Hopefully, we will be on the right side. (3 Nephi 24:18, The Book of Mormon)

Preparatory State. Other scriptures tell us that if our first parents would have partaken of the tree of life, they would have been forever miserable because they would have no preparatory state. The plan of redemption would have been frustrated, and the word of God would have been void, taking none effect. (Alma 5:62, The Book of Mormon) We need a preparatory state to learn the principles of the Plan of Salvation if we are going to live in, teach, or fight for God's Plan of Salvation. Everyone needs a preparatory state for their life's work.

Consequences. The Lord God gave consequences to Satan, Adam, Eve, and their seed in the story of the Garden of Eden. These consequences were given because Adam and Eve tried to change "the way" and God's Plan of Salvation. Satan adds temptation after temptation to us to give us more consequences than him. Satan has given us very heavy loads so that we fall short of "the way." He drives us from "the way" into Satan's way or plan of salvation.

Notice. The Lord God did not give consequences to Himself. The Lord God did not do wrong. Adam, Eve, their seed, and Satan are the ones doing wrong. The Lord God lost one-third of His children in the war in Heaven. (Revelation 12) The Lord God is not going to come down to Earth and sow the same seeds by which He can lose the rest of His children?

The story of Adam and Eve and their consequences reminds me of the following verses, found in Matthew 12: 24 - 28. The Savior was accused of casting out devils by Beelzebub, the prince of devils. The Savior told His accusers that Satan would be casting out Satan. His kingdom would be divided and could not stand. (Matthew 12:24 - 28) Satan would not bruise Satan nor would Satan cast out Satan. Heavenly Father would not cast out Himself or His Son. Heavenly Father did not divide His Kingdom by casting out Eve. He restored order by restoring opposition. Our agency was maintained because we had a choice between good and evil–not evil and more evil. When parents and step parents discipline children, they must be careful to not cast themselves out or give parents more consequences than the child they are disciplining.

In God's Plan of Salvation, everyone was given "the way,"agency, a preparatory state, and consequences for not following "the way." The Lord God still needed to overcome the effects of Satan beguiling Eve. Adam and Eve broke a commandment. *Notice. The Lord God did not ask Adam and Eve to eat dust all the days of their lives.* The Lord God placed enmity between Satan and Eve. *So what really is enmity?*

> 14 *And the LORD God said unto the serpent, Because thou hast done this,*
> *thou art cursed above all cattle, and above every beast of the field; upon*
> *thy belly shalt thou go, and dust shalt thou eat all the days of thy life:*
> 15 *And I will put enmity between thee and the woman, and between thy seed*
> *and her seed; it shall bruise thy head, and thou shalt bruise his heel.*

Genesis 3:14 - 15, The Holy Bible

Enmity. Dictionaries define enmity as settled hatred, animosity, and hostility. We can see and feel the settled hatred and hostility in step families, biological families, between ex-spouses, in communities, and nations. The animosity is so deep-seated that families hate their own blood. To make others suffer and eat dust all the days of their lives, family members have taken others' agency and their preparatory state. They have affected how they feel about God and themselves. There is no way family would accept "the way." They have made it almost impossible for family to repent and recognize the Savior. This is the kind of hatred and animosity that Satan brought to the Earth and maintains over the Earth in his jealousy over Jesus Christ.

I suspect that we have come to associate enmity with hatred because of the consequences we receive in God's enmity. Our consequences are why we blame God and our parents and step parents for our choices that went wrong in our life. We ate the Forbidden Fruit which even our Constitution has laws for, but our misery is God's fault or our parents' and step parents' fault. We want God and our parents to suffer the consequences. If God or our parents and step parents really loved us, they would remove the consequences of their children's actions. Parents and step parents do continually try to remove consequences from their children and step children. Our children are not learning and go from one crisis after another. Parents and step parents are fighting a losing battle and are adding consequences on their shoulders.

I do not believe that the Lord God, our Heavenly Father, placed more evil on the Earth and to Adam and Eve. If the Lord God placed more evil on the Earth, the Lord God would be casting out himself after Satan tried casting the Lord God out as the Father of the Human Family. The Lord God would not find joy in causing more problems for His children. The Great Plan of Salvation would have been abandoned if the Lord God allowed his anger to get away from him.

His children would not have a Shepherd to succor them if the great Plan of Salvation did not remain the same yesterday, today, and forever–even when the Lord God and his children were upset and angry with someone. When Satan beguiled Eve, this became a great test of the Plan of Salvation. The Lord God passed. We can pass, too, if we restore the enmity that the Lord God placed on the Earth. We start in families and step families. If we do, this will spread.

Opposition. God placed enmity on the Earth so His children, beginning with Adam and Eve, would not live forever in their sins. God's enmity is different from the hatred and hostility which we have come to associate with the word enmity. (Doctrine and Covenants 101:26) God's enmity restored Adam and Eve after their fall. So the enmity that God placed between Eve and Satan must be opposite of what Satan tried to accomplish. Satan tried to split Adam and Eve and prevent the population of the Earth which would prevent the birth of the Savior of mankind. God's enmity includes all of Adam and Eve's seed. The opposite of Satan's hatred is: forgiveness, love, repentance, and mercy. The Savior would not be able to teach us to not retaliate or resist evil if the Lord God retaliated against our first parents, Adam and Eve.

Prophets of All Time. Our Heavenly Father taught Adam and Eve how to restore things by placing enmity upon the Earth. This is how other prophets have taught us about enmity. My favorite is from Apostle Paul when he was teaching in Romans. By placing enmity on the earth, this is what the Lord God restored to Adam and Eve and their seed.

16 Be of the same mind one toward another. Mind not high things, but condescend to men of low estate. Be not wise in your own conceits.
17Recompense to no man evil for evil. Provide things honest in the sight of all men.
18 If it be possible, as much as lieth. in you, live peaceably with all men.
19 Dearly beloved, avenge not yourselves, but rather give place unto wrath: for it is written, Vengeance is mine; I will repay, saith the Lord.
20 Therefore if thine enemy hunger, feed him; if he thirst, give him drink: for in so doing thou shalt heap coals of fire on his head.
21 Be not overcome of evil, but overcome evil with good.

Romans 12:16 - 21, The Holy Bible

Fast Forward to Present Day. Children and step children do things which parents and step parents have requested or warned them not to do. They refuse to listen to parents and step parents. Children and step children partake of that tree of knowledge of good and evil because they are curious, bored, and want to be popular. They discovered more evil by which to relax or to obtain more money for more evil ways. Your children and step children will not repent. They blame parents and step parents for their problems. In their love for their children, parents and step parents could not punish them. In some things that children and step children have done, there is no way for an honest parent or step parent to give consequences. Your children, God's children, live forever in their sins. Their time of probation is wasted. They waste the probation of their parents and step parents. This affects many generations, and each generation becomes angrier and angrier. Many families try to solve their problems by avoiding each other and by committing crimes. Our Constitution has laws for forbidden fruits to protect the way of its citizens. (Matthew 7:16) Families and step families are happier when all members of the family or step family keep the laws of our land and the laws of God.

Many step children do the same thing as Eve. They take authority from their fathers and mothers and their step parents in order to preserve their family and the rights of children. This takes God's enmity from their family as well as their agency and preparatory state from each member of the family. The removal of authority of father in the home removes the consequences which soften us and create a desire for repentance and a more meaningful life. The weightier matters of the law which Christ taught us restores God's enmity to the Earth.

List the kind of enmity which you have in your family or step family and how this enmity is expressed by each family member. This enmity will be either Satan's enmity, the forbidden fruits, or God's enmity, authority.

Decide whose dominion and authority you will live under. The dominion which you decide to live under will show your children how to live with or hate the authority of God. Whose dominion has more to offer families and step families? If you are trying to live under God's authority, are you living by righteous dominion? Decide how to respond to opposition.

Are you and your family members seeking the mysteries of the world like Eve? Has God withdrawn Himself from you to let you rely on your own strength in your experiences with good and evil? Is this the cause of your depression? Can you take His word that there is evil and good in the world? Do you and your family members prefer to find out for yourselves?

Are you depressed and miserable because you and family members are wasting your preparatory state with excessive sports, television, movies, video games, and addictions? Can you keep up this pace? Are parents and step parents giving themselves more consequences than children and step children?

Mankind has encumbered God's enmity, but God's enmity is not bad. God obeys the same laws which he is trying to teach us. Remember. Others are learning how to live under God's dominion and authority as well as you. All are going to make mistakes. All are entitled to repentance with the exception of those who commit murder or deny the Holy Ghost.

How is enmity, the authority given to you by God as parent and step parent, taken from your home? Is it by a forbidden fruit or living without The Plan of Salvation? Does the authority of your family lie with children because parents and step parents are too busy? Are family members trying to change "the way" that the Cherubims guard? Are any family members clashing with that sword that will not be sheathed till Christ comes?

If you cannot decide what the enmity in your home is, list the opposite of their behavior. Now, you should know the source, who the enmity is directed towards, and have an idea how to deal with the enmity in your home. It will be found in scripture.

Do you have family members refusing to live in families and step families? Is a child or step child casting him or her self out of the family and blaming parents and step parents? Are you trying to cast your self out with anger, fear, depression, and suicidal thoughts? The Savior asked us to love our neighbor as we love our self, not hate our neighbor as we hate our self. Hating our self is not a cure for hating our neighbor and God.

What would happen if God's enmity was removed from the Earth again? Could there be benefits for us if we are willing to live under God's enmity upon the Earth? What would these benefits be? Is there a way to restore God's enmity upon the Earth?

Chapter Ten

Enmity of the Earth, Part II

The Savior stated in Jonah 4:11, in the great city of Nineveh, there were more than six score thousand persons who could not discern between their right hand and their left hand. (Jonah 4:11) More cities than Nineveh have trouble discerning their right hand from their left hand. (Matthew 26:63 - 64) If we or our children and step children do not know our right hand from our left hand, we probably are going to have many problems and suffer with depression. If we do not know how to discern our right hand from our left hand, we will not be able to discern the difference between Satan's enmity for us and God's enmity, His love, for us.

After so much mothering, education, and training, why is it that we and our children still cannot discern our right hand from our left hand? Right and left are opposites. I suspect that we have not learned our spiritual opposites. We know that opposites exist in the world. Latter-day prophets have told us that not only is there opposition in all things, but opposition is needed to bring to pass righteousness and the Lord's purposes. Learning how to deal with opposition is going to bring about the goodness in children and step children that parents and step parents are seeking. Learning how to deal with opposition will bring about the righteous purposes that parents and step parents want to and are supposed to fulfill in their families and step families.

11 For it must needs be, that there is an opposition in all things. If not so, my first–born in the wilderness, righteousness could not be brought to pass, neither wickedness, neither holiness nor misery, neither good nor bad. Wherefore, all things must needs be a compound in one; wherefore, if it should be one body it must needs remain as dead, having no life neither death, nor corruption nor incorruption, happiness nor misery, neither sense nor insensibility.
12 Wherefore, it must needs have been created for a thing of naught; wherefore there would have been no purpose in the end of its creation. Wherefore, this thing must needs destroy the wisdom of God and his eternal purposes, and also the power, and the mercy, and the justice of God.
13 And if ye shall say there is no law, ye shall also say there is no sin. If ye shall say there is no sin, ye shall also say there is no righteousness. And if there be no righteousness there be no happiness. And if there be no righteousness nor happiness there be no punishment nor misery. And if these things are not there is no God. And if there is no God we are not, neither the earth; for there could have been no creation of things, neither to act nor to be acted upon; wherefore, all things must have vanished away.
14 And now, my sons, I speak unto you these things for your profit and learning; for there is a God, and he hath created all things, both the heavens and the earth, and all things that in them are, both things to act and things to be acted upon.

15 And to bring about his eternal purposes in the end of man, after he had created our first parents, and the beasts of the field and the fowls of the air, and in fine, all things which are created, it must needs be that there was an opposition; even the forbidden fruit in opposition to the tree of life; the one being sweet and the other bitter.

16 Wherefore, the Lord God gave unto man that he should act for himself. Wherefore, man could not act for himself save it should be that he was enticed by the one or the other.

2 Nephi 2:11 - 16, The Book of Mormon

Fast Forward to Present Day. Just like in 2 Nephi 2:11-16, parents and step parents have children who feel the laws of their family and their land are not just. Thus, they do not obey the law of the family and the land. The laws do not apply to them anyway. Therefore, there is no sin when they break family rules or the laws of the land. Since children do not recognize sin, there is no righteousness in their life. Without righteousness, there is no happiness or holiness for them or their parents and step parents. Since there is no righteousness and happiness in their life, parents and step parents and even lawyers and the courts feel that we cannot punish them according to the laws that exist in families, good sense, or the laws of the land. There is no misery over their sins because it is not a sin, and they were not punished. These individuals claim there is no God. They feel that all men, including themselves, are nothing and so is the Earth. Life is neither to act nor to be acted upon. They just exist, but they have their rights.

In short, this is a long painful process because we want to victimize someone (our parents, step parents, any authority figure) who has asked us to take out the trash in our homes and our lives. There are many people teaching our children to retire parents and step parents prematurely to keep the trash in their lives. These individuals are making a lot of money off the trash that we have incorporated into our life. These individuals do not want to take the trash out of their homes and lives either. They have many soap boxes from which to preach their form of indignation to stir up nation against nation and children against parents and step parents.

Being a soap box victimizer or a soapbox victim does not work. This destroys the purposes of a family and the purposes of a nation. Parents and step parents have much to teach their children while providing for themselves and their families. Parents and step parents have been given some of the keys of the gospel to bring about change in their children and step children. No one else has these keys. I suspect this is why the Savior has told us to honor our parents–which includes our step parents.

Parents and step parents cannot teach their children and step children until parents and step parents can communicate with their children and step children. While children were learning to walk, talk, read, and write, etc., parents could communicate love to their children by providing food, clothing, shelter, and encouragement. When parents and step parents tried to teach their teenagers how to sit in good places, walk uprightly, and talk spiritually, parents and step parent could not or were not allowed to communicate these good things to their children. We call this a generation gap. It is not that simple.

Our children and step children could not recognize their right hand from their left hand. However, many adults and children always choose the left hand. With the law of averages, one would think there was a fifty-fifty chance of getting some good in his or her life. We forget this is a preparatory state, and we have agency to choose the right hand over the left hand.

The blessings of the right hand do not come to us accidently, by right or by osmosis. We have to choose the way of eternal life to receive the blessings of the right hand. The right hand is Jesus Christ. The left hand is Satan. There are benefits or gifts from God for choosing the right hand and choosing to maintain God's enmity on the Earth. There are consequences for choosing the way of the left hand or Satan. Forbidden fruits always have consequences.

THE GIFTS IN GOD'S ENMITY

Functioning Chain of Command. Each family or step family needs a functioning Chain of Command to succeed. This Chain of Command is God, Jesus Christ, and father or step father. The father or step father may hold the priesthood of our Heavenly Father and Jesus Christ now or in the future. The priesthood is the power to act in God's name.

God does not hate his children. God loves His children. Because of this love, he has provided numerous blessings for us. Some of these blessings come automatically, and others come after requirements are fulfilled and a lot of work is completed. The blessings and requirements of our Heavenly Father require a functioning Chain-of-Command or administrator to present these blessings, to give these blessings value, and to acknowledge that requirements are fulfilled.

Satan tried to wrestle the Chain-of-Command from Heavenly Father, Jesus Christ, and Adam through Eve. Satan continues to try to take the functioning chain-of-command from fathers on Earth to this day. Thus, this functioning chain of command has value or Satan would not bother. Heavenly Father did not relinquish His Chain of Command over the Earth to Adam and Eve. Neither will Jesus Christ. God and Jesus Christ will not relinquish control to us. Remember. A functioning Chain of Command is a blessing for us, not a curse.

Many families and step families do not have a functioning chain of command in their homes and extended family. Wives, children, and step children are not the Chain of Command in your home. Nannies, coaches, peers are not either. The Lord, the Administrator in His Chain of Command, will limit this kind of chain of command in some way. Our Heavenly Father will not replace the authority of the father or step father with commands from a wife, child, step child, babysitter, nanny, or house parent. This may be why many of our prayers are not answered.

Wives may get more things done faster. It may be easier to avoid conflict by letting children and step children take over the Chain of Command. Parents and step parents may not have any choice. If parents want to see their children and grand children, they have to allow children to be the chain of command. Naturally, parents and step parents become depressed when the Chain of Command for their family or step family is not functioning or is bypassed.

Barker–Parent, Step Parent. Adam and Eve formed the first family. When Eve ate the forbidden fruit, this split the family. God's enmity united and established the boundaries for families. Parents and step parents do not have to be barkers instead of parents. A barker stands out in front of a show at a carnival and tries to attract customers. When parents are "barkers," parents and step parents receive more consequences than their children and step children. Parents and step parents often become "barkers" instead of a functioning chain of command in their home to relieve their depression. To soothe children, parents and step parents become "barkers" for many carnivals. This will not build social skills in their children and step children. Entertainment does not build social skills nor does it build men and women. There is not much interaction in which to build social skills when entertainment is the basis of our life.

God's Enmity Restores Families and Step Families. When the Lord God, our Heavenly Father, placed enmity upon the earth at the time of Adam and Eve, the Lord God's mercy, forgiveness, and love restored Adam's family to Adam. God's enmity gave value to the families and step families which we form. This same mercy provided a method to restore future families in conflict. Notice. This is the opposite of what Satan tried to put on the Earth.

Hatred–Authority. Adam and Eve had to decide quickly whose authority they preferred to live under–Satan's hatred or God's love and authority. God's authority includes many blessings for His children because God loves His children. Satan gives us everything we want, especially the things that will hurt us and our families and step families the most.

Mankind has always had difficulty with authority. Today, we call this difficulty an authority complex. Mankind could be afraid of the paths which various authority figures in their life have taken them down and the cost of the trip. Mankind simply does not like to be told what to do. They develop a hatred for those telling them what to do. It does not matter that mankind is walking a more difficult and costly path than the path the authority figures in their life would have taken them.

Recognizing and following certain authority figures in our live has blessings. Many of us have college educations and a better life because we were willing to walk the extra mile with parents and teachers, employers, and employees. It is a blessing to able to turn problems that we cannot handle over to the authority in charge or to have an authority figure support you in your decisions. There is a special confidence that comes to you when working with authorities instead of working against authority figures. We cannot ignore or isolate authority. It does not help to manipulate or keep secrets from authority figures. Retiring a functioning chain-of-command prematurely is harmful and such a waste.

In spite of the various authority figures in our lives, there are two authority figures for this world. We all have them in our life. Those authority figures are God and Satan. We have to learn how to deal with both of these authorities in this world. One Authority, the Lord God, transferred authority from Himself to Jesus Christ to Adam so Adam could begin the dominion of man over the Earth and his family. Adam became the first prophet of the First Dispensation of time. If Adam was going to be the head of the First Dispensation of Time, Adam's sons or Eve could not take over his authority when they felt like it or disagreed with Adam. Eve could not talk Adam out of making sacrifices in remembrance of Savior's Sacrifice.

The second Authority, Satan, obtains his power with temptations and acts which separate us from the powers which God gave Adam and Eve and the seed of Adam and Eve. This includes us. The forbidden fruits of Satan's plan, the ones which were suppose to be so knowledgeable, fun, sweet, and satisfying are now bitter and insatiable.

Smorgasbord–Agency. The Lord God gave us the power to choose for ourselves and to rule over our personal space, physically and mentally. God's enmity gives value and authority to our personal spaces and choices. There are twelve aspects to this personal space: physically, socially, intellectually, financially, emotionally, morally, or spiritually, work, service, sacrifice, persistence, and obedience. We call this power agency. Agency is choice. Our Heavenly Father and His Son, Jesus Christ, accomplished their purposes in this world with freedom of choice. The opposite of agency would of course be no choice. This is how Satan wanted to accomplish his purposes.

When God created this world, he created a variety of plants, trees, shrubs, flowers, animals, textures, colors, climates, landscapes, etc. However, the Lord God did not give us a body which could provide and use all of the benefits of all of the plant and animal life and the sources of stimulation in this world. We have to learn to not run faster than we can walk and what is healthy to eat. We can learn how to choose inspiration over stimulation and inspiration over desperation and depression. God gave us a sense of taste to develop our agency.

Satan has cleverly disguised "no choice" with a smorgasbord of choices. Smorgasbord consists of so many choices that we cannot make a choice. We partake of a little of everything. We may go back for our favorites. Smorgasbords make it hard to choose favorites. Satan knows that it is difficult to give up a variety of unimportant choices for a few important choices. He also knows that a variety of choices brings more burdens instead of satisfaction.

I use to think that agency is the right to choose between right and wrong. I have discovered agency is the power to choose between right and wrong: physically, emotionally, socially, intellectually, financially, morally, or spiritually, in work, in service, in sacrifice, persistence, and obedience. There is a difference between power and right in enmity. Everyone can have the power. Only a few get the rights.

Not Judge–Judge. When we were given agency to choose right from wrong, we were also given the power to judge. We can evaluate, make conclusions, make decisions, and decide the worth of things. It is not a sin to judge the situations that we are in and change if needed.

The Angel Moroni wrote this scripture about 400 years after the Savior was born. The Savior also told us in scripture that we will be judged by the same judgements we make. To make sure that we make peaceable judgements that we and our families can live with, our Heavenly Father and the Savior has asked prophets to record scripture for us to follow.

18 And now, my brethren, seeing that ye know the light by which ye may judge, which light is the light of Christ, see that ye do not judge wrongfully; for with that same judgment which ye judge ye shall also be judged.

Moroni 7:18, The Book of Mormon

1 JUDGE not, that ye be not judged.
2 For with what judgment ye judge, ye shall be judged: and with what measure ye mete, it shall be measured to you again.

Matthew 7:1 - 2, The Holy Bible

Each of us have varying degrees of the light of Christ within us. This is a gift that we received that will carry us to the point that we receive the gift of the Holy Ghost after baptism. This light of Christ is known as our conscience. Since it is the light of Christ, the light of Christ is not going to work against the Holy Ghost. The Holy Ghost is not going to work against the light of Christ. The development of the light of Christ within us will not come from public opinion and passing fancies. The light of Christ is the same yesterday, today, and forever and will work on the same principles or precepts found in scripture. This is a great spiritual muscle to develop. Protect this gift as this gift will eventually develop into charity–the pure love of Christ. God's love or enmity has provided a way to develop charity so that things will go well with us. We do not want to be judged by people who are really not making a decision in our best interests, but they are categorizing us quickly so they can go play eighteen holes of golf and then go to their favorite sports teams. When we do not make righteous judgements or do not judge at all, impulsive behavior brings us consequences.

No Consequence–Consequences. When Adam and Eve ate the forbidden fruit, the Lord God gave Adam and Eve consequences. Adam and Eve had to leave the Garden of Eden. They could not just say, "I am sorry" and chalk this up to a learning experience. Other than records of prophets such as Moses, there is no record of how Adam and Eve viewed their consequences. Apparently, they accepted their consequences because Adam remained head of the first dispensation of time.

When we make mistakes, we receive consequences, too. Most people view consequences as punishment. There are gifts in consequences. Our consequences soften us and lead us to repentance. We do not make the same mistakes over and over. We do not want to live in our sins forever. Thus, everyone receives consequences. We, as well as Adam and Eve, need to know what behavior is contrary to the Authority and enmity of the Lord God and that our behavior and feelings have an effect on ourselves and others for time and eternity.

Satan has led many people astray by beguiling them with what is called a no-consequence–no-rule lifestyle. Satan also gives consequences. Satan's choices for us are called temptations. Our temptations leave us with fears, anger, shame, stress, hate, diseases, divorce, betrayal, discouragement, depression, oppression, suicidal thoughts, and death. Everyone who has been born on Earth voted for Jesus Christ and His Plan of Salvation. I suspect that Satan gives us these kinds of consequences because Satan is angry with us for voting in favor of Jesus Christ. Satan will not let up on those who voted for Jesus Christ's Plan.

It would be interesting to know how Adam and Eve gave their children consequences for their actions. As Cain, we do not get to just say "I am sorry" without consequences either. How to give blessings and consequences to children and step children is a life-long learning process for parents and step parents. How to recognize and accept blessings and consequences is a life-long learning process for children and step children of all ages.

The Lord God has given us an example of giving blessings and consequences which we can follow. The kind of consequences which the Lord God gave to Adam and Eve and their seed brought seed and life to the Earth. Adam was the father of us all. Adam began tilling the ground for us. Satan's consequences take seed and life from the Earth. Satan leads us to believe the Earth does not need to be tilled now or ever. Satan leads us to believe that we can escape the authority of God. We will not be able to escape the authority of God.

Like Adam and Eve, consequences bring us a lot of extra, heavy work for us, but consequences awaken us. We do not want to live forever in our sins. We will not live forever in our sins if we learn from our consequences and follow the rules of authority of God. Individuals can also learn from the consequences of others. The Lord God has given powers to parents and step parents so our families and step families will not live forever in their sins.

Most parents and step parents give their children and step children consequences because parents and step parents do not want children and step children to hurt themselves more or to hurt others. Parents and step parents also want their children and step children to understand who has control or dominion over a parent's and step parent's home–father and mother. It does not matter if one is a step parent. I suspect this is what our Heavenly Father was trying to teach Adam and Eve with their consequences. Unfortunately, many parents and step parents, children and step children think if an individual lives forever in his sins. It does not matter. It was his choice.

No-Rules–Rules. Adam and Eve discovered there were rules to follow in God's enmity, His authority on the Earth. Like Adam and Eve, mankind has also discovered there are rules in the Lord's Kingdom. God's rules are called commandments. Covenants with God help us keep the commandments. There are blessings attached to each covenant that we keep in His kingdom.

There are rules for our choices which work against God's Authority and His Chains-of-Command, individuals, fathers, families, step families, step father, communities, and nations. There are rules when we want to work with all these individuals, including God and Jesus Christ. We learn these rules in families and step families. Naturally, everyone is not happy about following rules which they really do not understand. Many wonder why things must be done God's way. They want His grace to save them. Man's idea of grace is the same as a "no rules" environment. Man's idea of grace cannot save us because we are judged by our works. (3 Nephi 27:14, 27, The Book of Mormon)

When mankind does not like to obey the rules of God, they usually create a no-rule society in varying degrees to keep everyone happy. A no rule-society has standards, too. They call their standard of measurement hot and cold, not right or wrong. Hot and cold can change like seasonal temperatures with each passing fancy. The ways of Satan always change. His rules are never the same for one individual or group of people, even for safety reasons. This is to take from us, not to give to us. Satan has no powers to bless the Earth.

I am an American. Our country has a Bill of Rights. Our forefathers gave us the choice between rules with agency and a no-rules with a smorgasbord of things to choose from. Enmity gave our forefathers and our present leaders the right to protect and defend our borders from those who live by no-rules. There are rules for both leader and follower. Each country should have a Bill of Rights for its citizens. Some citizens need to be reminded that all members of the country have the same Bill of Rights. The same Bill of Rights does not consume me to provide for you and to calm your angers and fears and cravings. You and I are accountable.

Manipulate–Accountability. Adam and Eve discovered they were accountable for their actions. They could not manipulate their Father in Heaven with excuses or that it was Heavenly Father's fault because He created something for us. God kept His authority intact. This was a good example for Adam and all parents and step parents to follow.

When the Lord God placed enmity upon the Earth, all mankind became accountable for their personal actions and the effects of those actions on their home, not just Adam and Eve. Adam and Eve were willing to be accountable. We can have the same blessings that come from accountability and performance as Adam and Eve. One blessing is that children and step children are accountable as well as parents and step parents. Cain was. Our children and step children are, too. Agency without accountability for everyone is force. At best, your choices become only suggestions.

Shame–Repentance. Before the Lord God visited Adam and Eve and placed enmity on the Earth, Adam and Eve were already experiencing shame. They noticed they were naked and sewed fig leaves together. (Genesis 3:7) They were experiencing their first consequence–shame. Submitting to their consequences took away the shame which they would have had to live with the rest of their life. Their shame would have accumulated in layers, like it has in us, if the Lord God did not give consequences for Adam and Eve and their seed to over come. Relieving shame is a gift of our consequences. We do not have a body to carry the burdens of many layers of shame. Remember. Repentance is a sign of being able to handle agency and relieve shame.

No Opposition–Opposition. The Savior asked us to be as perfect as our Father in Heaven is perfect–not to be like Satan. *We cannot be perfect without opposition.* We do this by loving our enemies, blessing those that curse us, doing good to them that hate us, and praying for them which despitefully use us, and persecute us. (Matthew 5:43 - 48) These are the ones who need our prayers. Notice. We do not become perfect by just loving more those we already love, blessing those we are blessing, doing good to those who love us, praying only for those who do not use us despitefully and do not persecute us. We do not have positive results by cursing those we have already cursed or hating more those we hate or cursing those who love us and who are there to help us. No wonder nothing has changed in our world for a long time. We do not learn from same and same, we learn from opposites. First, we must recognize an opposite.

Many parents or step parents have had a child or step child tell them "I hate you" many times. Children and step children have the actions that seem to prove it. Parents and step parents are still to teach their families and step families about recognizing and handling the enmity in this world and the enmity in God's Kingdom. We will not be perfect in this school of life. Parents, step parents, siblings, and grandparents are not the Great Sacrifice that was needed for mankind. Our lives involve other purposes of God such as maintaining God's authority on earth till the end of time. To do this, we learn our spiritual opposites and teach them to our children. The Lord God prepared a foundation for us to recognize and travel in the opposition we receive in this life.

Satan–The Lord God. There are two foundations in which we can choose from: The Lord God's foundation or Satan's foundation. Because of the enmity that God placed on the Earth, God's foundation is a sure foundation which is built upon a rock. Satan's foundation is built upon the sand. God's foundation has a cornerstone, Jesus Christ. Satan's foundation does not have a cornerstone. His foundation keeps shifting with the sands and the winds.

God will not persuade us to come to His foundation. We may have tried to live on Satan's foundation on Earth. We need to remember this. When we die, we will not be returning to Satan. Satan does not have a dominion or Kingdom or foundation in which to return. We will return to Heavenly Father and Jesus Christ.

Christ employs no other servant at the Gate–Jesus Christ. The authority of this world was given to Jesus Christ by His Heavenly Father. Jesus Christ offered to and did die for our sins so we may return to our Heavenly Father and Heavenly Home. We did not lose an elder brother. We reaped the benefits of an elder brother who was willing to die for us and share with us His testimony of our Heavenly Father's love for us. In other words, Christ received many gifts to achieve His mission. We are joint-heirs with him for the same gifts. We do not have to die or fight over these gifts. To receive these blessings, there is a gate that we must walk through. The keeper of the gate is the Holy One of Israel. He employs no other servant there. (2 Nephi 9:41, The Book of Mormon) If you are trying to live under another servant by only grace or are trying to put another servant at Christ's gate, you are living in Satan's enmity. Our parents, step parents, siblings, idols, etc. cannot help us on this choice. They can teach, beg, and persuade, but we must make the choice. Scriptures help us find this gate and return to Heavenly Father's authority.

Movies, Television, Video Games–Scriptures. Authority figures keep records. Jesus Christ is the Authority and Creator of this world. I cannot change that, and you cannot change it. Jesus Christ left records for us. He has records for Himself. Christ's records for us are known as the scriptures. There are four of them. Eventually, there will be more. I do not know when.

Christ's record for Himself is known as The Book of Life. His Book of Life began with Adam and Eve. Adam has a page that is nine hundred and thirty years long. (Genesis 5:5) The page of man dropped to one-hundred-and-twenty years at the time of Noah. (Genesis 6:3) In this day, our page is about seventy two years long. Some generations have been shorter. We have to learn the same things that Adam did in his long life span in a short life span. Some individuals have even shorter life spans than the normal life span.

Every two-celled embryo as well as the oldest people on Earth has a page in Christ's Book of Life. Christ died for them. Christ is going to notice what we do to ourselves and others, even to two-celled individuals. This will be recorded in His Book of Life. How we respond to Christ's blessings, covenants, consequences, God's Authority, Christ's Authority, the chains-of-command in our life, parents and step parents, and children and step children will be recorded.

However, if you and I were to speak at a function, we would not be allowed to mention the name of God and Jesus Christ, the verses from His scriptures which have inspired us, or even our favorite verses or hymns. We can talk all we want about a movie or television situation. We can sing a song from the movie as long as we do not make money off the song. It does not matter that this movie has objectionable material. Movies, Television, Video Games, and their stars are now the authority of this World, not God, Christ, their scriptures, or parents and step parents, or our national leaders. Movies have web sites from which schools have been given permission, probably for a fee, to educate our children. Movies and television are now the record keepers and educators of this world. This is called Freedom of Speech.

This free advertizement of a movie in our churches and schools is suppose to inspire us Can you imagine a nurse walking into a room and finding a patient who is crying because they are suffering and going to die from cancer, diabetes, heart disease, etc. They may also be shouldering the burden of a divorce and family members on drugs. This nurse tells them to cheer up and remember what the fictional, insubordinate characters in the current movies did when they were discouraged. These characters usually resorted to immoral sex, smoking, drugs, and alcohol. Can you imagine a teacher trying to comfort a child who is failing in this manner? If we want more inspiration, we buy or rent the movie. Movies do not inspire us when we suffer from cancer, diabetes, heart attacks, divorce, depression, addictions, etc. Movies will not stimulate us, when we are failing. They depress us, causing more failure, creating the need for more movies.

There is a record of God's enmity or authority on Earth. It is called scripture. His scriptures are found in The Holy Bible, The Book of Mormon, Doctrine and Covenants, and The

Pearl of Great Price. Scriptures contain the forms of Satan's enmity prepared for us. Christ has left records of His Birth, Ministry, Death, and Resurrection through prophets. He left records of the things which draw us closer to him or lead us away from him. These records are the records which comfort, inform, and instruct us. Scriptures provide a record of the covenants and principles of Heaven which the Savior has prepared for us.

Through scriptures, prophets teach us correct principles, and we govern ourselves. I am referring to our selves, not just a group of people who are organized into families, communities, states, and nations. We learn how to govern ourselves in happiness and sorrow by learning how to discern between our right hand and our left hand. Jesus Christ is on the Right hand of God.

Void–Structure and Function. After Adam and Eve's transgression, a functioning Chain of Command, Authority on the Earth (God's enmity), rules, agency, power to judge, a conscience, accountability, consequences, and a firm foundation gave Adam and Eve and their seed structure and function. God does not want His Children to be tossed to and fro by living forever in their sins and the sins of others. This is why He shared structure and function, the blessings of the priesthood, with His sons and their families. Each individual has been given talents according to the structure and function needed and followed in their life. When we are lukewarm about God's authority, much can be taken from us. The first thing that is taken from us is our ability to recognize our opposites. This manipulates the kinds of choices we make.

Void–Pattern. Can you see the pattern developing? Opposites are not always clear. Opposite is not always what we think it is. Spiritual opposites are not a matter of doing and not doing. Opposite is not just an opinion or belief. Opposites do not begin with the prefixes "non" or "dis," or "un," etc. Opposite is an action or state of being verb that is opposing something or someone. There are actions that go along with our opposing opinions and opposing beliefs. It is not possible to know another's heart to know when they are with us or against us. We learn this by their fruits. This is why standards of measurement were created. Opposites oppose standards, creating Satan's enmity or hatred on the Earth. In a no-rules society, we have no-rules opposing no-rules. Someone always gets caught in the middle of this polarization.

Christ is the pattern. He came to Earth to ransom us from Satan and so he would know how to succor his children. He taught us the difference between *prey–pray, lukewarm–hot and cold, dreams–anxiously engaged in a good cause.* What a gift prayer has been in our lives! Without prayer, we would not have the many miracles of God bestowed on us. A life of preying is a life of requests to Satan. Satan cannot bless. He destroys. If we prey instead of pray, we lose the ability to recognize who is the fish, who is the fisherman, who is the hunter, and who is the hunted. (Jeremiah 16.16) We have the fish chasing the fisherman, and the deer chasing the hunter. The fish even try to chase the hunter. Instead of being fishers of men, we have hatred and fear of man, worldly enmity.

Anger/Dissension–Soft Answers. One of the roles of parents and step parents is to teach their children to avoid dissension. Dissension begins early between siblings and parents and step parents. Dissension is contagious. Once learned, dissension will transfer to their school, work environment, and future family. It is important for our children to respect Authority. If they do not, they will not learn from authority. The Savior told us that soft answers turn away wrath. Soft answers can only turn away anger in the one using soft answers. Anger and dissension increases wrath. Anger and wrath are the same, but differ in intensity.

Physical–Spiritual. The Apostle Paul teaches us that the carnal mind *is* enmity [a settled hatred] against God: for it is not subject to the law of God, neither indeed can be. (Romans 8:5 - 10) Carnal refers to the appetites of flesh. The seed of Adam and Eve have to decide if their spiritual mind controls their physical body or their physical body is subject to the spiritual mind. *As you make this decision, keep in mind what you are rises with you. If your physical body controls your mind, what is your mind going to do while it is separated from your body for perhaps hundreds or thousands of years?*

The Manipulation Process–The Tree of Life. I have written three books, one on step parenting, one on attention deficit disorders, and now this book on depression. In these books, I discuss how parents and step parents are intimidated, manipulated, and isolated by power struggles with their children and step children. Manipulation by secrets and dissension have become the foundation of our way of life, including marriage, families, and step families. Manipulation by secrets, powers struggles, and dissension have become the foundation of businesses, organizations, states, and countries. If you do not believe me, look at the many ways that your stock accounts are manipulated. "They" say this manipulation is for your own good, or you are the one at fault because you were the one who chose the various companies that your stock company invested in. We had no choice in the matter. In most cases, we did not even know who the companies were which our stock investor was investing in. Our fault was having money and wishing to make more money. The formula for interest is so confusing we are easily manipulated out of our money. Again, we are told it is our fault.

Manipulation began in the Garden of Eden after Eve instructed Adam to eat of the forbidden fruit, and they became afraid. When the Lord God discovered Adam and Eve in fig leaves, He asked Adam if He had eaten of the tree of knowledge of good and evil which God had told him not to eat. Adam said, "The woman whom thou gavest to be with me, she gave me of the tree, and I did eat." (Genesis 3:12) It sounds like Adam was trying to shift blame to The Lord God as well as Eve. Adam listening to Eve and eating of the forbidden fruit was the Lord God's fault because the Lord God gave this woman to him. This attempt to manipulate the Lord God may have been why The Lord God seems to be more angry with Adam.

Parents and step parents, you have been in similar situations with your children and step children. Your child or step child does something wrong. You ask what they have done. They reply: "Well, yes, I did do this, but I would not have not done it if you were not married to this step parent." "I did not ask to be born or be a part of this marriage." "I did not want you to marry this spouse." Parents and step parents forget why they were disciplining their child or step child and begin disciplining them over the confrontation instead of their behavior. Parents become angry because the child is disciplining parents over things that cannot be changed.

It may help your depression to know that our Heavenly Father was treated this way, too. We can follow His example. The Lord God, our Heavenly Father, acted, not reacted with His Authority. He placed enmity on the Earth. The Lord God gave both Adam and Eve consequences which encourages and allows repentance to change their behavior. When you are manipulated this way, give consequences that encourage repentance. The consequences for your children and step children should fit their "crime," not match your sorrow and anger at being manipulated and betrayed by children and spouse. Parents and step parents really do raise their children in sorrow. You must learn to control your sorrow, or sorrow will control you.

Neither Root Nor Branch–Root and Branch. Jesus Christ has taught us how to trim our leaves of pride, anger, and hatred so we can become root and branch with our families, step families, and Jesus Christ. We begin with respect for authority and the chains of commands which will appear in our life. During the Savior's ministry, He recognized when we did not have respect for the enmity which God had placed on the Earth. I have wonder if this is what the Savior meant when He told us that we were like salt who had lost its savor. (Matthew 5:13) We restore our savor with the Patriarchal Order.

Void–The Patriarchal Order. The synonym for God's enmity is the Patriarchal Order. The Church of Jesus Christ is founded upon principles of The Patriarchal Order. The Patriarchal Order travels from God, the Father, His Son, Jesus Christ, to prophets, local high priests, and the fathers or step fathers of the families or step families of the world. If a father or step father does not hold the priesthood, The Church of Jesus Christ recognizes and will not interfere with the Patriarchal Order of this father's family or step family. God's authority or enmity, the Patriarchal Order, establishes families with father as the patriarch or head of household. There is an orderly way to bless us and an orderly way to curse us. Our blessings and curses are based upon established principles which never change. The gifts in God's enmity or authority teaches us how to recognize our Right Hand from our Left Hand and establishes the words of Christ in each generation. Opposition to the Patriarchal Order teaches us some overwhelming lessons, too.

A sign that we are willing to live within the Patriarchal Order of God as a follower is obedience to parents and step parents. When men are married to women for time and eternity, both enter the Patriarchal Order of God. It is a learning process. A sign that we are willing to live within the Patriarchal Order of God is faithfulness and mercy to your spouse. There are blessings for living within the Patriarchal Order or enmity of God. They are called Patriarchal Blessings. We bury our talents, the gifts given by God to us in our Patriarchal Blessing when we are disobedient to parents and step parents, and are unfaithful to our spouse.

Blind Obedience–Obedience. In life, there will be many times when we obey or follow instructions. There will be times when we conform. We hear of the term "blind obedience" accompanying acts of obedience to the Patriarchal Order of God which includes church leaders, parents, step parents, or a spouse. Faith is not "blind obedience!" Leaders in the Patriarchal order usually have the Gift of the Holy Ghost which gives them immediate access to inspiration on how to lead others. Some individuals which we choose to obey may have the Gift of the Holy Ghost all the time or a sporadic influence of the Holy Ghost. We were given the Gift of the Holy Ghost to know how to keep the pace with our Church leaders, parents, step parents, spouse siblings, step siblings, teachers, employers, or community leaders.

I suspect that Blind Obedience is in opposition to obedience. Blind obedience is following power hungry individuals, suggestions in movies, cartoons, rock groups, FYI programs, talk show programs, idols, a jealous friend, a doctor or psychologist–all who may or may not know what they are talking about. It is a matter of "the blind leading the blind." Blind obedience is obedience to commandments of men who do not have any authority. Drug addicts and alcoholics take medication blindly and expect blind obedience to help them though they have done nothing to help themselves. Obedience to God's ordinances and commandments which are administered by one having authority, the priesthood, develop faith in us. Faith in Jesus Christ, our parents, step parents, and ourselves does not come with blind obedience.

Who is entitled to those gifts that came with the enmity that God placed on the Earth? Everyone who has been born on this Earth is entitled to the gifts in God's enmity. It does not matter if you are a boss or a hireling. There are gifts which have prerequisites that both boss and hireling must fulfill to obtain or use. If you have held a position of authority, you have discovered the boss has a lot of work and responsibility. Bosses have more choices and a larger salary in the program, but ultimately the boss has to keep the organization running even over his own preferences. A good boss also likes to bless the organization of which they are in charge.

Those not entitled to the gifts in God's enmity. Satan is not entitled to the gifts given by our Heavenly Father. When Satan rebelled against God and Christ, he was cast out of Heaven. Satan is the one that is cursed. Satan does not have a body that can benefit from God's blessings. Satan is the one that is forced to crawl and eat the dust the rest of his life. We are not the ones that were cursed or forced to "crawl" the rest of our life. Others may force us for awhile. However, anyone who follows Satan will be forced to crawl the rest of their life. They get to find out how many blessings Satan really has for them and the limits of their own strength, too.

Forbidden Fruits–Plan of Salvation. The natural man in us thinks less enmity or authority in our life is going to benefit us. Every parent has had a child say to them that there is no law about what they are doing wrong so there is no sin. Thus, parents and step parents should not interfere or try to do anything about their behavior. When their child believes there is no sin, parents and step parents notice there is little or no righteousness in their child or step child. They have lost their identity. They are not happy so we cannot punish. Children feel if there is no righteousness in the world, there can be no happiness. If there is no righteousness, there is no God. This is Satan's kind of enmity. This attitude says it is okay to live with Satan's enmity, the forbidden fruits of the world. We do not need God's enmity, His Plan of Salvation and authority.

Everyone has their war stories with authority. We also have many blessings which we take for granted because of authority. However, mankind has always felt that more land and possessions with less enmity or authority will benefit them. Mankind takes dominion over families, things, communities, states, and countries which they do not have the right or experience to claim dominion. We become encumbered, and we encumber others. We do not know why. We thought we were acting for our selves. We were enticed against the authority within us to govern ourselves. We began controlling others, instead of controlling ourselves. This begins with disobedience to parents and step parents. Where will it end? Your land and your possessions are not going to rise with you when you die. There is a Plan of Salvation prepared for us by a functioning Chain-of-Command. Our mortal life is the time given to us to learn how to live under the Plan of Salvation that we will be living with for an eternity. The Savior died to give this Plan of Salvation value above all other things.

Stop here. Do you understand what God's enmity is? The Lord God did not need to restore hate, anger, envy, pride, manipulation, isolation, etc. to the Earth. Satan did this. God's enmity is expressed in the patriarchal order, charity, work, service, sacrifice, obedience, endurance, laws, sense, happiness, etc. Satan's enmity is expressed in lack of work, selfishness, no obedience to parents, insensibility, corruption, misery, no laws, no sin, no God.

What kind of enmity is prevalent in your family or step family? Is it God's enmity, man's enmity, Satan's enmity, children's enmity, or the enmity of animals? Have you replaced God's love for you with man's enmity or the enmity of animals? Remember. God placed enmity on the earth so his children would not live forever in their sins. With the patterns of behavior in your home, will your children live forever in their sins? If so, how will you change this?

How is the enmity that you live under expressed in your home? Is it anger, jealousy, and hatred or is it love and respect for others and God's authority in their lives? When conflicts and sin occur in your home, how do you restore God's enmity to your home? Consequences alone will not restore God's enmity to your home. It takes a lot of love, mercy, justice, and forgiveness. We build on our choices and their blessings. Are you trying to build on side effects of consequences? If we build on indigestion or pain, we increase our indigestion and pain.

Do you have a functioning Chain-of-command? A functioning chain of command would be God, Jesus Christ, fathers or step fathers. Mothers are head of household when they are single or divorced. Children and step children and grandparents are never head of your household. Does your chain of command allow you to develop your agency, judgement, your conscience, (the light of Christ,) and the use of the Gift of the Holy Ghost? Are you trying to live in a no rule-no rule environment to avoid conflict? In your family, do some children and step children live in a no-rule environment while other children live under a rule environment?

How is God's enmity removed from your home? Satan removes God's enmity from us with many temptations and transgressions which nullifies the many miracles performed on our behalf by those willing to live with God's enmity. We are left with Satan's authority and our own strength. Are you trying to compete with Satan in giving your children and step children many temptations which removes them from the enmity of God? Without the authority of our Heavenly Father, our appetites for evil, bitterness, and darkness cannot be quenched.

Are you neither root nor branch to your children and step children? Is this why you can feel there is a void in your family and step family instead of structure and function? Who are you and your children following? Is this the reason there is a void instead of a good pattern in your home? Have you replaced scripture and the words of the Savior and prophets with the words of coaches, movie stars, and fictitious, insubordinate characters?

Grandparents are often manipulated into giving a grandchild many expensive things with no restrictions to compensate for the trauma of being in a financially-strapped step family. Their grandchild's lack of effort and family rules are ignored. The grandchild will not share or treat others kindly. This drives grandchildren from parents and step parents. When disaster occurs, and it will, it is the parent's or step parent's fault. This is Satan's enmity at its worst and may create an amoral child. This is a very difficult environment to live in. Siblings and grandparents are not better than parents and step parents. This prevents the family from working together.

Our experiences with both kinds of enmity are not always going to appear with labels which list all ingredients and the manufacturer. The ingredients and manufacturers will be both good and bad. We are going to have opposition that is not so obvious. We will have opposition that is obvious. We are going to do things thinking we are making things better, and things become worse. I suspect the Lord God placed enmity, His Authority, on the Earth so we could recognize the covert (hidden) opposition in our lives as well as the overt (open) opposition. After we recognize opposition, there is a correct authority to deal with it. This returns the sunshine to our lives. By submitting to God's enmity and learning spiritual opposites, we can live again under His wing–the one He gathers His children under like a hen gathers her chicks. Are you and your family members willing to develop the faith to live under His wing?

Chapter Eleven

Enmity, Part III

Parents and step parents, children and step children, you have agreed to live in and bless your family. This experience will come as a child, spouse, and parent. When a step family forms, children and step children often want signs that their real parent still loves them and that the step parent is an honest person. Personally, I think children and step children want to prove to the world that their parent does not love them and their step parent is mean and dishonest. They have the stories from movies to prove it. This justifies a child's or step child's actions and disobedience when greed has overtaken them.

Parents and step parent and their finances become encumbered by trying to give signs to prove they are an honest, loving parent or step parent. Parents and step parents, especially mother and step mother cannot keep up the pace of these signs. *Like Christ, your miracles for your children are not a sign that you are a real parent or a good step parent or a real child or a good step child.*

Sign of the Devil–Sign of Christ. Christ states the only sign for the Son of Man is Jonah and the whale. As Jonah was in the whale three days and three nights, so shall He be in the heart of the Earth. This of course is referring to the period of time between Christ's Death and Christ's Resurrection. We all wish that our problems would only last three days. Most problems in step families last longer than three days and three nights, especially without a prayer to God for help. It takes about three days and three nights for our adrenalin to return to a normal level. By then, we can be swallowed by many more irritations from others which raises and keeps our adrenalin and other stress hormones at stress level.

Serpent–Whale. The sign for belief in Christ for all peoples is the story of Jonah and the whale. We are no better than the families of times past. I suspect that the sign for belief in present-day families and step families is found in the story of Jonah and the whale, too. Since this is such an important sign for all of us, let's review the story of Jonah and the Whale. I am paraphrasing to save space.

Jonah and the Whale. The Lord was aware of the wickedness in Nineveh. The Lord asked the prophet Jonah to go to Nineveh, "and cry against it." This sounds like crying repentance. To avoid the Lord, Jonah went to Joppa and found a ship going to Tarshish. The Lord sent a great wind which caused a storm in the sea. The ship was about to be broken. The mariners or sailors were afraid. Every one began praying to his god. They cast things overboard to lighten the ship. Jonah who was tired from his emotional stress of avoiding the Lord and his journey was asleep in the ship. The ship master found him and asked him why he was sleeping instead of praying. The sailors cast lots to know why this evil came upon them. The lot fell upon Jonah. (Jonah 1:1 - 7)

Jonah was asked if he knew why this evil came upon the ship. Jonah received the third degree. The sailors wanted to know his occupation, where he came from, the country he lived in, and his nationality. Jonah told them that he was Hebrew, and he feared the Lord. The men became afraid. They knew he fled from the presence of the Lord. They asked Jonah what they should do to make the sea calm again. Jonah told them that the mariners had to cast him into the sea. The sea was very tempestuous. The men rowed hard to try to bring the ship to land. They prayed they would not die for Jonah's folly. They cast Jonah into the sea. The sea immediately calmed. The men became more scared. They offered a sacrifice unto the Lord and made vows. (Jonah 1:8 - 16)

The Lord prepared a great fish to swallow Jonah. Christ calls that fish a whale in Matthew 12: 40. Jonah was in the belly of the fish three days and three nights. After three days and three nights, Jonah prayed to the Lord to get out of the fish's belly. He told the Lord his afflictions were great. The waters encircled him. He could feel the weeds, probably seaweeds, wrapped around his head. He describes the feelings of going to the bottoms of the mountains of the sea. We know this as an increase in hydrostatic pressure or water pressure in the depths of the ocean. He fainted, but he still remembered God. He promised to do that which he had promised the Lord to do. The Lord spoke to the fish. The fish vomited Jonah out on dry land. (Jonah 1: 17 - Jonah 2: 1 - 10)

The Lord again asked Jonah to go to Nineveh and preach repentance to this city. He called Nineveh that "great city." As Jonah entered the city, he stated that in forty days, Nineveh would be overthrown. The people of Nineveh believed Jonah. They began a fast, put on sackcloth, and sat in ashes. The king stated that he and all young and old, flocks and herds would fast forty days from food and water. God saved the city. (Jonah 3: 1 - 10)

Jonah became angry because God saved the city. The people of Nineveh were very wicked. Jonah would rather die than have the people of Nineveh saved by God. He begged to die. He made himself a booth on the east side of Nineveh. He waited to see what God would do with the city. God grew a gourd over Jonah that it might shadow his head and deliver him from his grief. The next morning, God killed the gourd with a worm. When the sun arose, an east wind caused an increase in temperature. It was so hot that Jonah fainted. Jonah again wished to die. He said: "*It is* better for me to die than to live." (Jonah 4:1 - 8)

God became angry with Jonah. Jonah had pity for a dead gourd which he did not labor over. However, he had no pity for the thousands of people in Nineveh, plus their cattle. The Lord was concerned that the people of Nineveh were not able to discern between their right hand and their left hand. (Jonah 4:10 - 11)

By this time, you are probably wondering what enmity has to do with both step parenting and depression? How is the story of Jonah and the Whale a sign for distressed parents, step parents, children and step children? If you are a step parent or a step child, the story of Jonah and the Whale sounds a lot like parenting and step parenting. Let's take a closer look.

The Lord Is aware of the sins in families and step families. Families and step families are an important part of His Plan of Salvation. He keeps track of them. The Lord is also aware of the wickedness in the communities in which they dwell. God is aware of the resistance to parents and step parents and the care of his children. Like all parents and step parents, God has seven things which he hates to see in His children: a proud look, a lying tongue, hands that shed innocent blood, a heart that devises wicked imaginations, feet that run swiftly to mischief, a false witness *that* speaks lies, and he that sows discord among his brethren. (Proverbs 6:16 - 19)

We have been asked by the Lord to live in biological families which can become blended families on Earth. These families did not begin with Adam. Our spiritual families began with God and Jesus Christ. I suspect living peaceably in families is one of the things which we promised to do when we were given permission to come to Earth to gain experience with a mortal body. Parents and step parents also promised to teach their children and step children about faith in Jesus Christ, repentance, prayer, and to not argue with one another, etc. (Malachi 4:6; <u>Doctrine and Covenants</u> 2:2)

Why did this evil come upon them? God's children are found in places where they are hurt terribly and where they hurt others terribly, especially their parents and step parents. The family ship is about be broken up and sunk. This causes quite a stir in the family and the neighborhood. They want to know the cause of these catastrophes. If children are asked why this evil has come upon them, they give some very classic responses which parents and step parents hear. "I dunno." (don't know) "She (the step mother) is always mad." "I did not do anything wrong." "My friends' mother lets him do this."

Lots are cast to see why this evil came upon this family. In this day, we cast lots by opinion or vote. The lot always falls upon the step parent, especially the step mother. After all, she sets the stage for the family. It does not matter that the children and step children continually destroy the stage which she tries to set for her blended family.

When family waters become boiling like a tempestuous sea, family members become afraid like the ancient mariners or sailors were afraid on tempestuous seas. They begin praying to their gods. This could be to a movie star, sports figure, or a sports ball. The family sailors cast things overboard to lighten the intensity of their predicament. They begin with Christ, parents, step parents, and their teachings. The family now tires easily and are often found asleep at their post. They are not carrying their weight. They expect others to carry their weight. They have much enmity or hatred for each other when this does not happen.

Most individuals in a step family agree on one thing. Divorce or throwing the step parent *overboard will make them feel better.* If their parent and step parent do not divorce, children and step children will torpedo and sink parents and step parents to the bottoms of the family sea. This is done by the pits found in the twelve aspects of personality and conflict. As in some birth defects, parents and step parents, children and step children now have a separate circulation.

The family tries to row the family ship to calm seas. It cannot be done by rowing against each other and against parents and step parents. Half of the rowers or less may be rowing. The family remains in tempestuous seas. When parents and step parents are thrown overboard, the sea does not calm for children and step children. To try to calm their family seas, they make many sacrifices such as going to sports games, shopping, vacations, or drugs and alcohol. It does not matter that family has a house payment due and needs food. They have no respect for your dominion or the bills of your dominion.

The Lord has prepared a fish for families and step families. This is interesting. If you want to be a fisherman, the Lord has to catch the fisherman with a fish, a great fish. The sign of Christ was a fish. Jonah was swallowed by a whale. When we ask for help to get out of the Lord's fish and are repentant, we will be asked to return to our families and step families. We are older now and may be bringing grandchildren with us. This returns that functioning chain of command and structure and function to families and step families. Parents and step parents can care and teach children and step children and grandchildren about themselves and faith in Jesus Christ, repentance, and prayer. Children and step children are asked to listen and return to their families and step families so their children can experience, not just see, a functioning chain of command in their lives. There is that law of two or more witnesses again.

Jonah was in the belly of the fish three days and three nights. It seems unfair that we humans are in the depths of a "whale" longer than three days and three nights. Notice. Jonah gave a poignant prayer to get out of the whale. It was a prayer of repentance and a vow to do what he was asked to do by the Lord. When parents and step parents, children and step children make their poignant prayer of repentance and make vows to go to that "whither so ever I will spot of the Lord," they will be spit out, too. Leave feelings of hatred behind. There are other feelings for you to experience. Someday, we will see the unseen whales that took us to dry land.

The Lord asked Jonah to go to Nineveh and preach repentance to save that "great city, Nineveh." The Lord feels this way about our house or family. God will save our great house like He saved the city of Nineveh. First, we do the Lord's will and listen to the prophets and our parents and step parents–even in our sorrows. I know it is difficult to understand a parent and step parent in their sorrow just as it is difficult to understand a child in their sorrow.

Our families and step families are not responding like the great city of Nineveh. For one thing, they are not praying and fasting. Children and step children are resisting parents and step parents and God's attempts to help them. Parents and step parents receive the third degree and then the silent treatment from their children, step children, neighbors, psychologists, church leaders, and community leaders. Unlike the mariners in the story of Jonah, these individuals do not know or acknowledge that children and step children have fled from the presence of the Lord. People are uncomfortable recognizing God in these days. The individuals who refuse to recognize there is a God over us all may be fleeing the presence of the Lord, too. People forget there is a period of time between their death and resurrection also–to find His presence.

Family members become angry that the Lord has saved the family and step family members with whom they are angry. Parents and step parents fast, pray, work for, and teach their children and step children. When parents, step parents, children or step children make a plea for help to the Lord, not their peers, siblings, the government, etc., and they repent, we become angry that they are saved. We are angry when they are taken to dry land and are also taken out of bondage. Family members fear other family members might have a relapse. They do not feel the Lord is punishing them enough for the trouble they caused you. This attitude brings the relapse.

Both parent and child complain about another's repentance process and wait to see what the Lord will do with their parents, step parents, child, or step child. The family ship masters and sailors become angry and pray they will not be lost because of another mistake by their parents and step parents. They would rather die or have a family member die than to have all of their family saved by cooperation with the family and God. This causes depression.

We are not angry at our family member's wickedness. We are more angry that we cannot control a family member anymore. Siblings who have encouraged a lack of self-control in siblings become angry and distant when they cannot control their siblings. They withdraw from family. They cling to things which have no substance or no life instead of a human being in their family. New cars, sports stadiums, sports parks, golf courses, and possessions seem to have more authority and demands in a child's life than a parent, step parent, child, or step child.

The family becomes swallowed by a large serpent. It does not mention a serpent in the story of Jonah. We avoid the Lord too long to be in His whale. The Lord does not prepare for any family or step family what is happening now in families and step families. This serpent is prepared by the Adversary through vengeful family and step family members and conspiring people outside of the family. This family serpent disgorges family members violently into areas where they can be swallowed by other serpents. The Lord prepares whales which can spit you onto dry land with a prayer of repentance.

Conspiring individuals in and outside of family are more than willing to prepare many things to trap your children and step children, especially if they have a social security check or an inheritance coming. They want parent's money and the money of children and step children. I call this the Social Security Gourd, but the Social Security Gourd dies at age eighteen. In spite of our pleas and our children's pleas, these serpents have no intentions of letting us and our children go. Parents and step parents do not have dominion over their own creations, their family or step family. Conspiring people do. Children and step children even claim what a wonderful ride they are having down to the depths of the seas in these serpents. They need that "weed" that is wrapped around their heads.

Children and step children who refuse to live peaceably in their families or step families will not allow parents and step parents to have righteous dominion over them. They resist parents and step parents when they teach them about faith in Jesus Christ, repentance, prayer, opposition, and how to avoid dissension with others. These things are important. *The same things that ease dissension with others eases dissension within our selves! This kind of dissension is called depression.* Each generation needs these valuable tools. They will not have them if children and step children do not learn them in their childhood.

Families are out of the whale, but not willing to listen to God again. We are angry that God has saved our family or step family. We are angry that others are kind to our step parent and step siblings. Evil is called good. Good is called evil. Light is called darkness, and darkness is called light. Sweetness in our life is exchanged for bitterness.

We do not care or realize our behavior is affecting thousands of descendants and thousands of ancestors as well as ourselves. Our behavior is affecting other people and their ancestors and descendants. As things intensify, we become depressed and wish to die. Because of our lack of pity for family, we are not able to discern between our right hand and our left hand. We do not know who to believe. We do not believe in our selves. We cannot distinguish between love and hatred. The story of Jonah and the whale has become more of a story about the whale than Jonah. We have forgotten this verse.

They that observe lying vanities forsake their own mercy. Jonah 2: 8, *The Holy Bible*

This verse is important in depression. Jonah, in his fear of preaching to the people of Nineveh, forgot to give himself mercy. Where does this mercy come from? By doing the Lord's will and learning the difference between our right hand and our left hand. The whithersoever I will spot in the vineyard includes parents and step parents, chores at home, school work, history, language, writing skills, and spiritual training. A child is merciful to himself if he learns how to read, write, and do arithmetic. He will be merciful to his present family and his or her future family if a child chooses to do the things he should be doing in each year of schooling. There is no mercy for us in setting ourselves above our parents and step parents and others.

Jonah was distressed by his anger for the city of Nineveh. He claims the people of Nineveh were too wicked to save. It sounds like he is saying: "They have not repented enough." He forgot about the degrees of glory and the many mansions of Heaven. I suspect that all prophets were taught similar concepts before these concepts were recorded in scripture.

Jonah and his people, the Israelites, were not friendly with the Assyrians for a long time. Nineveh was the capital of Assyria. The founder of Nineveh was Nimrod, a grandson of Ham. Jonah probably was not concerned over the wickedness of Nineveh. It was their nationality. Many people through out generations of time have felt that it was okay to preach to the descendants of Ham, but not save them or be kind to them.

Parents and step parents, children and step children are angry with each other all the time. This is very distressing to the step family. They claim their anger is the result of the wickedness of each member of the step family. However, they do the same things which they say angers them. They seem to be more angry over everyone's family origin instead of behavior.

Children of all ages set up semi-independent kingdoms to protect themselves and their possessions. These little kingdoms cause much grief to parents and step parents. Family members experience hate for family. All family members want a sign to know if they can trust family and believe in their family members again. The sign would be meaningless. Neither parent nor child, step parent or step child could recognize the sign. They have too much hate for each other. They have not learned their spiritual opposites nor do they understand God's enmity.

Though parents and step parents give signs of love and affection to their children and step children, children and step children hurt parents and step parents over and over. They want a sign that parents and step parents can be trusted. However, children and step children do not bother to give parents and step parents a sign that children and step children can be trusted.

How is the stage that mother wants to set for her family defeated by children and step children, father, mother, and grandparents? What do family members do when others become aware of their behavior? The Lord is aware, too. What evil comes upon your family or step family if family members will not change?

Are parents and step parents encumbered by trying to give signs that they are a good parent or step parent? Do children and step children not bother to prove that they are trustworthy? Are we angry that God has saved certain individuals in our family and step family? Are we delighted that our favorite rock star or sports star is saved?

Do you know the sign of Christ and the sign of the devil? The sign of the devil is not doing what we are asked to do by God, parents, and step parents. The sign of Christ is doing the Lord's will. Are family members swallowed by larger and larger whales or serpents? What family members are feeling the pressures of life as they descend lower and lower in their behavior and attitudes toward authority and God's functioning chain of command?

Are you trying to live with the gifts in Satan's enmity: no functioning chain of command, barker, without family, a smorgasbord of forbidden fruits, no rules, no judgement, voids in large parts of your life, no opposition, manipulation, dissension, blind obedience, shame, guilt, anger and movies? If so, you will be cumbered by depression and seek for signs that someone loves you—signs that even Christ could not fulfill. It is no wonder that ye are of little faith.

Chapter Twelve

Oh Ye Of Little Faith

The Pattern for Faith. In Chapter One, I discussed the pattern that Christ used for the creation of the Earth and everything which dwells on Earth. When it is our turn to learn how our bodies and minds functions together, it is logical that we will use the same steps of creation to form our personalities. This is how body and mind become one in purpose and strong.

Fuel Source. Our first building block or precept must be strong. Thus, we begin with faith. However, we are not just developing faith in anything which can easily be destroyed. Faith in Jesus Christ is the first principle, not blind trust in things which can toss you to and fro. Faith in Jesus Christ gives you and I structure, organization, and strength to build precept upon precept our entire lives. This is why Christ is called our chief cornerstone. (Ephesians 2:20) There are synonyms and antonyms for faith in Jesus Christ.

Eating and Drinking Anything–Word of Wisdom. As long as the body is alive, we will have requirements for fuel. We need energy to accomplish anything in this life. All though we have fruits, grains, vegetables, and meat, humans have made many food concoctions from various plants as a source for fuel, mentally and physically. These foods and energy boosters have become so popular that we have many health issues and new diseases in the world. Many wars and rumors of wars have occurred trying to convince the world who dominates the world and their fuel sources. The quickest things to eat or drink are not going to add physical stature or energy to you. The quickest things usually take more from us than they give even though there is a brief spurt of energy. Many addictions have occurred with these alternative fuel sources.

Dominion. It is a common practice in war for two opposing countries to destroy or steal each other's fuel source. This is the quickest way to take dominion over a country. If they cannot steal your fuel source, both countries charge outrageous prices for a fuel source that has been free or low in price. This makes the citizens of a country so angry and uncomfortable. The citizens switch their allegiance from their leader to a country which is at war with their country.

When citizens of a country switch to other fuel sources, these entities use the same tactics of charging outrageous prices for your new fuel source. For some reason, they claim they have dominion over your fuel source which gives them dominion over you. They call it The Law of Supply and Demand. Only there is more emphasis on the demand. As our wallet empties, we may become aware of the many spiritual alternative fuel sources in our country. Naturally, the countries who are at war with each other wants control of these alternative fuel sources, too. They provide alternatives to spiritual fuel. These sources have no substance, but they are very expensive. Faith in Jesus Christ is free. There is some work involved. This fuel line does not have to be cut or stolen from you, too? It is your choice. Do you want to gather ice all your life when you need to gather light and heat?

Management. There are many ways which we try to manage our lives while facing opposition or when our fuel sources have been stolen from us. We begin with fear and worry, proceed to popularity, and will substitute many devices. Even the things we eat and drink are used for management of opposition in our lives. Worrying is a quick step to discouragement. This is what the Savior taught us about worrying. Remember. We are learning opposites.

Taking Thought–Give Thought. During His Sermon on the Mount, the Savior asked: "Which of you by taking thought can add to his stature, raiment (clothing), or the food we eat and drink? (Matthew 6:24-34) The Savior answered His own questions. He pointed out the lilies of the field and the grasses. The grasses would be destroyed tomorrow, but God had clothed the lilies and grasses more than King Solomon. If God clothed the grasses of the field, then he will clothe you more, O ye of little faith. He told us to take no thought, saying, "What shall we eat? or What shall we drink? or how shall we be clothed?" Your Heavenly Father knows that you need these things. Christ told us to seek first the kingdom of God, and His righteousness; and all these things would be added to us. (Matthew 6:27 - 34)

I suspect that "taking thought" does not mean pondering. It means worrying, the kind of thoughts which take more from people than their thoughts give. We have seen the results of people who do not worry about anything. It is unrealistic to think we will achieve a happy, successful life without pondering and planning for our daily bread and our futures. Our plans should first include prayer. Our Heavenly Father knows what we need and will help us achieve righteous plans if we ask for His assistance. Prayer helps us stay on task with our many thoughts.

Popularity–Stature. We all like to do well, be noticed, be appreciated, valued, and have friends. Children and teenagers will do most anything for this kind of acceptance. This kind of management is called popularity. Popularity is fleeting, especially if you are breaking any of the Ten Commandments to be noticed and accepted or to have a boy or girl friend. Children become bored with friends easily and move onto someone who they think is a better offer. You are left to clean up a mess which several people made. Individuals cannot hide their depression or be valued more by breaking more of the Ten Commandments. You increase depression in yourself and others, especially mothers and step mothers, as the "behavior bills" come in. Count the bills which you have because you did not keep The Ten Commandments. It is no wonder that many people want every mention of the Ten Commandments abolished.

In our quest for popularity, we forget there are other areas of stature to develop besides our physical stature. Popularity is often built upon this aspect of our personality. These things require a fuel source and a cornerstone, too. There is our emotional and psychological stature, social stature, intellectual stature, financial stature, moral stature, spiritual stature, our work stature (ethics), service stature, our sacrifice stature, our persistence stature, and our obedience stature. All are needed to grow in favor with God and man. A physical stature will not develop an intellectual or moral stature or a spiritual stature.

Devices–Talents. We rely on our own devices more than faith in Jesus Christ who blesses us with talents. Many people seek million dollar finances, a financial stature, to make up for what they lack in stature. They travel from one device to another. A great financial portfolio will not make up for the absence of stature in the important areas of your personality. I doubt you will have a million dollar portfolio without stature. You will create a million dollar portfolio for those who have stature. You also may create a million dollar portfolio for those who already have access to money. You will not be able to ease your anxieties and boredom if you have access to money. You will be tempted with more anxieties, boredoms, and more burdens to calm.

A devise is suppose to be for function. If we are not careful, we create devices for non-function instead of function. Some of these devices will be cheap. Most of these devices will be very expensive and time consuming. We always arrive at the same point of wondering what do we do for an encore until we are unable to do an encore.

The Parable of the Talents. I suspect this parable is a story of developing our stature. In the Parable of the Talents, Christ talked of a man traveling into a far country. This man called his own servants and delivered unto them talents. One servant received five talents, one servant received two talents, and another one talent. They were given according to their ability. The first two servants traded and doubled their talents. The one receiving one talent decided to bury his talent because the traveling man was mean. When the traveling man returned, he asked all servants to account for their talents. He took the one talent from the servant who buried his talent, gave the talent to the servant with ten talents, and cast the unprofitable servant into outer darkness. (Matthew 25:14 - 30) I suspect this one talent was faith in Jesus Christ.

Presently, there are a lot of talents being taken from servants who think their parents, step parents, God, neighbors, teachers, employers, countrymen, leaders, etc. are mean. These unprofitable servants are cast into outer darkness. They were unsuccessful in their attempts to manipulate the Lord. Unprofitable servants are experts in manipulating a person with many talents and much stature into outer darkness with them. After all, the ones who are willing to work must come with those who prefer outer darkness. Temptation is manipulation.

A person with ten talents, probably a mother or step mother, has many talents because she will do the work that develops the talent. She also has the chief cornerstone, faith in Jesus Christ, on which to build her talents. Fathers and step fathers are away from their families too much. Mothers are given some of their talents. Children are the ones with one talent.

Subdue. Without the chief cornerstone in our life, faith in Jesus Christ, we have to find other ways of subduing or taming our selves. It may not seem like it, but we are trying to subdue ourselves and our families with pride and the polluted waters of the world. We are trying to subdue ourselves and others without being tame and gentle. As these things become our alternative fuel source, the prices have skyrocketed for their use. The most popular ways which we now use to subdue ourselves are excessive sports and recreation, music, movies, television, and the company we keep. These things were not meant to subdue, but excite and inflame.

Excessive Sports, Recreation, Exercise–Moderate Amount of Sports, Recreation, and Exercise. I have watched communities switch their fuel source to excessive sports and recreation to subdue their depressions and anxieties. Parents want to subdue their children. They feel their children and step children will be more manageable if they are entertained, exercise a lot, and are tired when they get home. Children are entertained, but are irritable from fatigue when they get home. State of the art stadiums are built and rebuilt, named and renamed.

Inventories reveal what you are using for each sport or recreation. Many businesses and governments feel if parents and step parents can afford this kind of entertainment frequently, they can afford higher prices and taxes. Educations are forgotten. The time that you had to teach your family about the chief cornerstone for this life, faith in Jesus Christ, is lost. You and your child are left with pride instead of faith in each other and faith in God and Jesus Christ. Your sports team and favorite recreation will not exist in the eternities. *You tried to subdue yourself and children and ended up being subdued and controlled.*

Controlling Music–Soothing Music. The music which we listen to controls the kind of thoughts, emotions, and actions that we have. Music often determines our ability to carry on. The tunes "Come, Come Ye Saints" and "The Battle Hymn of the Republic" are prime examples. Music controls our amount of faith in Christ and determines whether we are happy or sad. How? Music is a prayer unto thee. We reap what we sowed in prayer–a blessing or a cursing.

12 For my soul delighteth in the song of the heart; yea, the song of the righteous is a prayer unto me, and it shall be answered with a blessing upon their heads.

<u>Doctrine and Covenants</u> *25:12*

"Our songs are a prayer unto Thee." We are all children of God. We were all righteous enough at one time to be born on Earth.[15] All who came to Earth voted in support of the Savior. We were able to come to Earth, obtain a body, be tested, and learn how to control our body with our minds. Body and mind become one in purpose. After some rough testing, we have become lovers of our own selves, unholy, disobedient to parents, and lovers of pleasure because we do not know how to deal with depression. We feel we have the right to do any thing any way we want. As a result, there are many prayers offered to our Father in Heaven to kill cops, kill parents, ruin parents' reputation, justify adultery, fornication, and burglary, etc. because someone likes the lyrics or beat of the music All these prayers were made in the form of music. These things are part of the Ten Commandments. We are praying to break the Ten Commandments. If we abuse music, we will always be depressed. When we meet the Savior, I suspect He will call us, "Oh Ye of little faith," too. (Matthew 8:23 - 27; Matthew 14:22 - 33)

Dr. Michael Ballam has done much research on how music can heal and teach us or control us. I do not need to repeat it. He has audio tapes that will tell you how to reach him to read his research. Dr. Michael Ballam suggests making a musical first aid kit for you or your family to play to overcome depression. This works. Soothing music works for study time, but it has to be the right kind of music. Any music will not replace the Chief Cornerstone in our life, faith in Jesus Christ.

The Fiery Furnace–Faith in Jesus Christ. Everyone now lives in a fiery furnace like the furnace that was prepared for Shadrach, Meshach, and Abed-nego. This furnace was heated seven times hotter because Shadrach, Meshach, and Abed-nego would not worship the golden image which King Nebuchadnezzar set up. Everyone had to fall down and worship this golden image at the sound of the cornet, flute, harp, sackbut, psaltery, dulcimer, and all kinds of music. This furnace was so hot that those who put them into the furnace were killed. (Daniel 3:13-30)

Parents and step parents have taken their children to these hot furnaces for entertainment. This is how your furnace is made seven times hotter. *One,* our children and step children now worship the golden images of Hollywood instead of parents, God, and His Son, Jesus Christ. Hollywood has done nothing for you or your children, but take your money. Yet, parents and step parents, God, and Jesus Christ have sacrificed their all for the children and step children of the world.

---

[15]Revelation 12:1-17, <u>The Holy Bible</u>, p. 1577-1578.

Two, movies with violence have become an acceptable way of expressing violence against those with whom we disagree, dislike, or who do not provide for all our wants, needs, whims, and desires. It is not wise for a step family who is already experiencing extreme bitterness and anger to view movies with violence. Movies show your step family how to create more bitterness and anger in your home with more bitterness and anger. Watching reviling for reviling is as harmful as committing reviling for reviling.

It is very distressing for parents and step parents to deal with children and step children who copy the behavior of the current, cute, insubordinate, bitter, fictitious characters in the movies and who go from crime to crime and immoral act to immoral act to solve their problems. Many parents and step parents are suffering the affects of diabetes, auto-immune disorders, cancers, heart disease, etc. from the stress and heartbreak of worrying over children who also go from one crime and immoral act to another. Parents and step parents provided for children that golden image of Hollywood which is portrayed as better than faith in Jesus Christ, their parents, step parents, spiritual and community leaders, and the President of their country.

Three, your children and step children experience fornication, adultery, rape, murder, homosexuality, bisexuality, alcoholism, drug addictions, burglary, abuse, gambling, and profanity by being a spectator. Your children and step children experiment on the words and actions of stars when they should be experimenting on the words of Christ, school teachers, and parents and step parents. Like Sarah, Lot's wife, parents and children become bitter instead of tender. Through movies, they look back at behavior which they do not really want to give up or which is not popular to condemn. It is impossible to have faith in Jesus Christ while living their life vicariously through the golden images of Hollywood, television, sports, and violent video games.

When children get hurt or caught while experimenting with the words and ideas from the big screen, they do not admit that they were doing wrong nor do children admit that they were experimenting with things they saw in the movies, on television, and X-rated video games. Their parents would not buy movies and games again. Children say: "My friends' parents let them do it." Their parents are taking or sending them to the same movies.

Four, our children and step children become jealous of a fictional, insubordinate, bitter character and covet what these characters have on a multi-million dollar budget. Our children and step children become more and more angry with their parents or spouse because they cannot provide for them the million dollar life-style which they continually see in the movies. Our parents, spouse, or ourselves may be only earning $20,000 - $35,000 a year.

Five, we are trying to learn knowledge from the experiences of fictitious, bitter characters in the mysteries of this world: theft, rape, murder, alcoholism, drug addictions, homosexuality, bisexuality, bestiality, gambling, depression, suicide, etc. For added emphasis, favorite sports stars are in the movies. We are to learn knowledge and wisdom by learning about the mysteries in the scriptures such as faith in Jesus Christ, forgiveness, mercy, repentance, and the Atonement of Jesus Christ, a person who does exist.

Six, one wonders why Hollywood would do these things to their customers. In their case, the customer is not always right, especially when the customers keep coming back for more "stripes." Americans are not their customers. The sports, movie, and music industries are not playing to America. They have not for a long time. The movie industries are playing to other countries who have different standards and qualities of life and more theaters than in America.

There are many complaints about the movies and video games released. At Senate hearings, many parents and leaders have asked and begged for Hollywood and television to stop R-rated movies and X-rated video games. We still have a majority of R-rated movies and X-rated video games. It is our fault that these are the only kind of movies and games to watch or play. The more parents complain, the worse the movies and games become. No one is going to tell Hollywood what they are going to do with their industry. By the power of suggestion, it is okay for Hollywood to determine what parents can do for their children and how children are to treat parents, siblings, their neighbors, the leaders of their country, God, and Jesus Christ.

I suspect the entertainment industry is angry with America as they are other countries. They have portrayed too many characters and countries as bumbling, stupid, inept, angry, evil, etc. They want the world to view each other as they view the world. Hollywood wants the world to change as fast as they can change a script. We have to change as many times as they change their script. People do not change this fast. Their emotions become scrambled instead. People change by having faith in Jesus Christ. This takes time to develop. Christ sacrificed His life for us to have this time to develop faith in Him, repentance, be baptized, and to learn how to use the Gift of the Holy Ghost–the real Comforter of this world.

Seven, when people in foreign countries have problems because they or their children are copying the behavior of fictitious, insubordinate, bitter, characters, they have the same results Americans do. However, America is blamed for these countries' problems and qualities of life because the movies, music, movie stars, and sports starts which these countries watch and emulate come from America. America is not like these movies, music, sports, and music stars. Americans do get bored, restless, and like an action story or a good love story. They would like to take their children out for an evening of benign entertainment, too.

If you want to have faith in Jesus Christ and also do not want to be depressed, you will have to avoid movies and television programs which are inflammatory, portray evil acts as acceptable behavior, and which dull your senses. You will also have to turn off your television. Latter-day prophets have urged us to turn our televisions off. Prophets have asked us to not watch R-rated movies and worse. Is this interfering with our agency? No. Prophets are not allowed to interfere in our agency. Prophets are allowed to warn us of the things that take agency from us. They also warn us of the things which take faith in Jesus Christ and the ability to be accountable for our sins with Jesus Christ from us.

Sin is a sin whether you are a participant or a spectator. The court of our land tells us this. With sin, we are not a spectator. We are in a fiery furnace. If you do not want to be consumed by a life that has become as a tinkling cymbal, turn the television off. The Gospel of Jesus Christ is not according to the television and movie stars. The Lord has said we are not to look upon sin with the least degree of allowance. (Alma 45:16, The Book of Mormon)

Peers–Family. The company we keep affects our level of faith. If your associates do not have any faith in Jesus Christ, most likely, you will not have any faith in Christ either. A child may play with friends after school. Today, parents and step parents are both working, sometimes two and three jobs, to provide for their children's needs, wants, and desires. They do not want other children in their home while they are gone. Movies, television, and video games, the golden images of Hollywood, have become your children's company and friends while you are working. The Holy Ghost will not come around while your children are spectators to sinful behavior. Their ministering angels cannot come around either. This means your children are really unattended in spite of your prayers. Television and movies are not your ministering angels or babysitters.

To develop faith in Jesus Christ in your children, parents must provide at least some of their needs, wants, and desires by faith in Jesus Christ. Children have to trust parents for this kind of faith to develop. Families must discover the difference between family and peers. Family includes step family members. Children must learn that peers are not treated nicer than family. Families must discover who the real standard for this world is. When family members discover the real standard for this world, they can establish the words of Christ in the generations they are raising. This is how you turn the heat down in the furnace in your part of the world.

Failure. Over time, we have made many mistakes. Just when we think we have seen it all on television, the movies, or the Internet, someone commits even more outrageous mistakes or sins. The news has to make sure the world knows about it by making a public example of them. Christ knew that we would make mistakes while learning the pattern of creation and development in our lives. This is why His Plan of Salvation includes repentance. Christ's Death and Resurrection give value to this plan. Instead of repenting, many of God's children prefer the doctrine of grace. Grace will save them in spite of all the immoral acts they did or persuaded others to do. Grace did not save the victim who was murdered, the family from being killed by an alcoholic, or the drug addict from his own addictions. Grace is not going to save you.

Grace–Faith in Jesus Christ. We cannot fight Deity and smooth things over for the Devil and smooth our sins with the doctrine of grace and develop faith in Jesus Christ at the same time. The doctrine of grace is the one reason we cannot discern between our right hand and our left hand. With the doctrine that we will be saved by grace alone in spite of what we do, we act like Christ is the one who needs to develop faith. Jesus Christ already has faith in His Heavenly Father. He does not need to change to fit every one's fancy. It is parents, step parents, children, and step children who need to develop faith in Jesus Christ and repent to change their ways.

The doctrine of grace is a synonym for the plan which Lucifer offered in the pre-existence. Lucifer stirred up a rebellion against our Heavenly Father over our agency. One third of God's children followed Lucifer. Lucifer offered to save the rest of us no matter what we did. He wanted the glory. He did not want us to have agency or faith in Jesus Christ. He is jealous of Jesus Christ. Now, the same plan is taught around the world. We are making a lot of effort trying to force the doctrine of grace, the Doctrine of Lucifer, on our Heavenly Father again–after Heavenly Father lost one third of His spirit children, and He gave His only Begotten Son, Jesus Christ, as a sacrifice for us.

Lucifer was cast out for this plan. We also will be cast into outer darkness if we pursue Lucifer's plan. With the doctrine of grace, we become a law unto ourselves. There is no organization and structure in our Heavenly Father's family. Think about this now. When we were disobedient to our parents, step parents, and their rules of their household, grace did not save us from the anger of our parents and step parents. Grace will not save us from the ire of our Heavenly Father when we are disobedient to him.

Rest. The last part of the pattern is rest. Fatigue is a main reason that we do not have faith in anyone or anything. This can be physical or mental fatigue. Our minds and bodies are too weary to remember that we are building upon the Chief Cornerstone, faith in Jesus Christ.

The Lord gave us the Sabbath Day to rest from the oppositions in our life to decrease our cares and sorrows. On the Sabbath Day, we assemble together to share stories about our faith in Jesus Christ (testimonies) and to partake of the sacrament, a symbol of our remembrance of the suffering of our Lord. We have a chance to settle our minds and remember what faith in Christ has done for us and our family.

Not only has the Lord asked us to Keep the Sabbath Day Holy, the Lord has also given us scripture about sleep. These scriptures warn us to not run faster than we have strength and to not sleep longer than is needful. (Mosiah 4:27; Doctrine and Covenants 88:124)

Notice. I did not start with dividing the Light from the Darkness in our life. Dividing the Light from the Darkness never ends. This pattern is how we choose who has dominion over us and how we manage and subdue ourselves and rest. We gather the living waters and discard the polluted waters. This is how we gather ourselves and our families instead of the ice in this world. This is how we all are cared for and educated, not just the affluent or most intelligent. We do this with the chief cornerstone of this world, Faith in Jesus Christ. We have agency to choose between the pillars of the world or the pillars of our Heavenly Father.

Pillars of the World

O YE OF LITTLE FAITH

1. Philosophies of Men
2. Platitudes of mankind
3. Ethnic jokes
4. Gender jokes
5. Fear of man
6. Honors of men
7. Control of man
8. Wave to and fro
9. Occasional Prayers
10. Occasional church worship
11. Educated by Hollywood and sports.
12. Alcohol and drugs are fuel source.

DENIAL

1. No repentance
2. Occasional Repentance
3. Deathbed Repentance
4. Insincere Repentance
5. Former Sins Return
6. Justice

NO BAPTISM/ BAPTISM WITHOUT AUTHORITY

1. No Baptism
2. Baptism as an infant
3. Baptism of Repentance
4. Grace will save us.

DO NOT HAVE THE GIFT OF THE HOLY GHOST

1. Our fruits fall prematurely to the ground.
2. Our fruits have no substance.
3. We are easily disorganized.
4. We cannot be comforted.
5. We cannot be satisfied.
5. Our actions do not match our beliefs.
6. The things which we have repented of return.
7. We have no fruits or labors.

114

The Pillars of Our Heavenly Father

FAITH

1. **LORD JESUS CHRIST**[16]
2. Prayer
3. Scripture Study
4. Sabbath holy
5. Church Attendance
6. Service
7. Word of Wisdom
8. Tithes and Offerings
9. Honesty
10. Chastity
11. Fasting
12. Food Storage
13. Gardens–a lot of faith
14. Music
15. Journals
16. Family History
17. Church Callings
18. Work
19. Blessings of Priesthood which my husband has
20. Agency

---

[16]John 14:6, _The Holy Bible_, p. 1353.

REPENTANCE

1. Recognize
2. Refrain
3. Remorse
4. Restore
5. Forgiveness as I have forgiven others
6. Mercy

BAPTISM BY AUTHORITY

1. Christ's Atonement applies to my life/my sins as well as others.
2. Renew this covenant weekly with the Sacrament
3. Renew this covenant daily by the Abrahamic Covenant.
   a. Bless Others– will be blessed
   b. Curse Others– will be cursed
4. Follow the Prophets
   a. Too busy to undue curses all the time

GIFT OF THE HOLY GHOST

1. The Comforter
2. Teacher
3. Revelator of Truth
4. Testator of Christ
5. Holy Spirit of Promise
   a. Eternal Marriage
   b. Eternal Family
   c. Blessing of the Sick
6. Office of the Holy Ghost
   a. Prophets
   b. Apostles
   c. Seventies
   d. Area Authorities
   e. Mission Presidents
   f. Temple Presidents
   g. Stake Presidents
   h. Bishop
7. Remember all things.
8. The Great Organizer
   a. Thoughts
   b. Feelings
   c. Actions
   d. Knowledge
   e. Duties
   f. Fruits

Why is faith in Jesus Christ the Chief Cornerstone for our life? Why is not faith in our Heavenly Father the chief cornerstone? After all, we pray to God in the name of Jesus Christ. I believe the Apostle Paul has the answer. Before faith came, we were kept under the law, shut up unto the faith which would afterwards be revealed. The law was our school master to bring us to Christ. By faith in Jesus Christ, we are all the children of God, are Abraham's seed, and are heirs to the promise. (Galatians 3:22 - 29) Christ does not want to be our school master. He wants to be joint-heirs with us. When we realized he would be making an enormous sacrifice for us, it must have been a very worrisome time. Could He really do it? He asked us to have faith in Him.

Remember. Christ died for you, your spouse, and that child who you are worrying and grieving over because they are caught in sins which bring justice, not mercy. We apply the blood of His Atonement to our life by having faith in Jesus Christ. Our biological family and step family does not have to be another family caught between Jesus and Lucifer, never knowing who to believe. We do not have to be a step child for an eternity unless we choose to. If someone died to save my child, spouse, or myself, I would be very grateful. I also would be grateful that I did not have to experience the isolation of a step child caught between Jesus and Lucifer eternally.

Faith in Jesus Christ has another basic benefit. When working as a nurse, I always kept track of my patients' blood pressures. I have had patients with stable blood pressures, patients with extremely low or high blood pressures, and patients with no blood pressures. My patients were often connected to monitors which were connected to computers as well as the patient. These monitors had alarms which set the upper and lower limits of blood pressure for my patients. The alarm sounded when the patient's blood pressure went below or beyond these limits. Patients who had pathologic blood pressures received medication which were titrated to their blood pressure. When my patients went home, I instructed them to continue to monitor their own blood pressures and keep a record of them. Our physical blood pressure is measured in millimeters of Mercury in a blood pressure cuff called a sphygmomanometer.

Likewise, we have a spiritual blood pressure. What is our spiritual blood pressure? Faith in Jesus Christ! Naturally, we prefer an unshaken spiritual blood pressure, (Jacob 4:6, The Book of Mormon), but there are those who have fluctuating spiritual blood pressures. Life is full of stresses which cause fluctuating spiritual blood pressures or a fluctuating faith in Jesus Christ.

Faith in Jesus Christ, our spiritual blood pressure, is the substance of things hoped for, the evidence of things not seen. It is by this faith we earn a good report card. (Hebrews 11:1-2) Spiritual blood pressure has upper limits (pride, rage) and lower limits (addictions, depression, suicidal thoughts) just like our body's physical blood pressure. We can use artificial means to try to raise and lower our spiritual blood pressures. However, we can ask to have a good, nourishing spiritual blood pressure. Our spiritual blood pressure will make us whole.[17] Spiritual blood pressure is measured in millimeters the size of a mustard seed. If we have faith as large as a mustard seed, nothing is impossible, and we are strong and sound.[18]

Faith really is the substance of things hoped for, the evidence of things not seen. (Hebrews 11:1) Your physical blood pressures are also the evidence of things hoped for and not

---

[17]Luke 8:48, The Holy Bible, p. 1290.

[18]Matthew 17:19-20, The Holy Bible, p. 1217; Acts 3:16, The Holy Bible, p. 1370.

seen. Without your physical blood pressure, you can do nothing. Without your spiritual blood pressure or faith, you can do nothing. (Doctrine and Covenants 8:10) Our prayers are answered according to our faith or our spiritual blood pressure. (Mosiah 27:14, The Book of Mormon) We repent by faith or an unshaken spiritual blood pressure. The trial of your faith or gaining good spiritual blood pressure is more precious than gold. (1 Peter 1:7) There will be no turning back once one discovers how nice life is with a good nourishing spiritual blood pressure. (Alma 32:42)

Everyone has heard of Essential Hypertension. This is a blood pressure that is hard to treat because the cause is unknown. This blood pressure is hard to reduce, but we cannot ignore it. Wouldn't it be interesting if Essential Hypertension is caused by our many stresses, the fuel sources we have substituted for our Natural Fuel Source, and the lack of faith and meekness in our lives? Essential Hypertension is an indication that the alarms are going off on our faith monitor because our spiritual blood pressure is beyond or below normal limits.

Joseph Smith, the head of this, the last dispensation of time, told us how to build faith. He titled these steps "The Articles of Faith." I believe these steps are our mustard seeds of faith. Our actions must match our beliefs. We cannot claim to have faith in Jesus Christ and His Atonement for us while we are breaking the laws of the land in which we live. Grace will save us. This is drawing near to the Savior with our lips, but our hearts are far from the Savior. (Isaiah 29:13)

The Articles of Faith

1 WE believe in God, the Eternal Father, and in His Son, Jesus Christ, and in the Holy Ghost.
2 We believe that men will be punished for their own sins, and not for Adam's transgression.
3 We believe that through the Atonement of Christ, all mankind may be saved, by obedience to the laws and ordinances of the Gospel.
4 We believe that the first principles and ordinances of the Gospel are: first, Faith in the Lord Jesus Christ; second, Repentance; third, Baptism by immersion for the remission of sins; fourth, Laying on of hands for the gift of the Holy Ghost.
5 We believe that a man must be called of God, by prophecy, and by the laying on of hands by those who are in authority, to preach the Gospel and administer in the ordinances thereof.
6 We believe in the same organization that existed in the Primitive Church, namely, apostles, prophets, pastors, teachers, evangelists, and so forth.
7 We believe in the gift of tongues, prophecy, revelation, visions, healing, interpretation of tongues, and so forth.
8 We believe the Bible to be the word of God as far as it is translated correctly; we also believe the Book of Mormon to be the word of God.
9 We believe all that God has revealed, all that He does now reveal, and we believe that He will yet reveal many great and important things pertaining to the Kingdom of God.
10 We believe in the literal gathering of Israel and in the restoration of the Ten Tribes; that Zion (the New Jerusalem) will be built upon the American continent; that Christ will reign personally upon the earth; and, that the earth will be renewed and receive its

paradisiacal glory.

11 We claim the privilege of worshiping Almighty God according to the dictates of our own conscience, and allow all men the same privilege, let them worship how, where, or what they may.

12 We believe in being subject to kings, presidents, rulers, and magistrates, in obeying, honoring, and sustaining the law.

13 We believe in being honest, true, chaste, benevolent, virtuous, and in doing good to all men; indeed, we may say that we follow the admonition of Paul—We believe all things, we hope all things, we have endured many things, and hope to be able to endure all things. If there is anything virtuous, lovely, or of good report or praiseworthy, we seek after these things.

Joseph Smith, Articles of Faith 1:1 - 13, <u>Pearl of Great Price</u>

How is your physical blood pressure? Do you experience Essential Hypertension? Have a good checkup with your physician if you have high blood pressure. How is your spiritual blood pressure? Is it stable or does it fluctuate between rage and pride or doubt and depression? Have you had a checkup lately with the Great Physician? Repentance works wonders.

Many individuals do not want us to have faith in our selves, our family, step family, God, Jesus Christ, and mankind. They increase the temperature of the furnace in our homes seven times hotter than normal, and we blame God. I suspect these individuals do not want us to know how to manage the stoney places, the fertile ground, the thorny places, the withersoever I will spots, the good spots, the poor spots, and the poorer spots of our life with faith in Jesus Christ. They can make money off us if we have poor spiritual blood pressures.

Do you live in a fiery furnace? Do you want your family and fellow citizens living in a fiery furnace where they will be consumed? If you placed them in a fiery furnace which is seven times hotter than normal, you will be consumed, too.

Are you of little faith? Do you take thought (worry) or give thought (plan)? What devises do you use to ease discouragement? Do your devises give function or take function from you? List the company which you keep when you are lonely. Does the company you keep have faith in Jesus Christ? What or who is your cornerstone?

Are you developing and trading for many mustard seeds of faith, or are you trying to bury your one mustard seed of faith? Does your mustard seeds stay within the parameters of a nourishing spiritual blood pressure? Do you have an alarm going off on your faith monitor? Remember. Your spiritual blood pressure will rise with you when you die, and you do not have a physical body to rely on. I suspect that faith in Jesus Christ is the first principle of intelligence.

18 Whatever principle of intelligence we attain unto in this life, it will rise with us in the resurrection.

<u>Doctrine and Covenants</u> 130:18

Our many mustard seeds of faith in Jesus Christ are going to blend into one as we age. We do not call it grace. We call the aging process of maturity and self-esteem meekness.

Chapter Thirteen

Meekness

One of the most common commands which parents and step parents state to children and step children is: "Settle down!" Parents and step parents may be running faster than they can walk, but they want their children and step children to settle down. Most children realize if they want something now as well as a future inheritance from their parents and step parents, they have to settle down somewhat. This is exactly how our Heavenly Father and Jesus Christ feel.

Blessed are the meek: for they shall inherit the earth.

Matthew 5:5, The Holy Bible

I have asked my children and grandchildren to settle down. I wanted them to be more calm or meek. I suspect other parents and step parents experience this, too. Parents do not want their children and step children to become angry at the slightest inconvenience or request. They do not want to have to humiliate their children or themselves every time parents or step parents want their children to do something or to stop doing things that are wrong. Parents and step parents do not want their children and step children to think they are stupid for the kinds of things parents and step parents ask children and step children to do or learn.

Parents and step parents have heard many times: "If you want your children to change, you must change." Most parents and step parents expect their children and step children to change by setting limits on their children and step children. Their children, step children, and grandchildren become experts in extending those limits causing dissension. Parents and step parents become more limited than children and step children. Parents and step parents change the limits instead of changing themselves.

Parents and step parents try to bail themselves out by bailing their children and step children out of the limits they placed on their children. Parents bail themselves out of the trouble in which children and step children continually are in. Depression occurs when you are bailing your self and children out more than you are teaching your children and step children. Meekness is not a part of your family life. Dissension is. Your children and step children keep your family in dissension to extend their limits and limit the boundaries of parents and step parents.

I suspect the changes that we want in our selves and in our children and step children come through meekness. Meekness will restore the normal limits for parent and child. The peace that passes understanding is meekness. (Philippians 4:7) Meekness will not take all problems from us. It does open a new world for us. Since there will be more challenges where we need to learn to persist with meekness, we need to learn the opposites of meekness and the synonyms of meekness. When we find out what meekness really is and what is not meekness, we will be able to discern between The Left Hand (Adversary) and The Right Hand of Christ's day and our day.

Look around you. Have you noticed any one that is meek? I do not mean someone that is scared of his shadow. I mean really meek. List their qualities. They are usually patient, easy to get along with, easy to manage, and easy to work with, or supervise. Meek people have a clean sense of humor and are fun to be around. They have a special spirit around them. Prophets are good examples of meekness. I have also had some dear friends who followed this pattern.

I have learned in many Sunday School classes that meekness means submissive, humble, and teachable. People who are meek are gentle, patient and mild. They are not inclined to anger or resentment and are trustworthy. Using the synonym of humble, this is how the Lord defines meekness in scripture.

> *23 And now I would that ye should be humble, and be submissive and gentle; easy to be entreated; full of patience and long-suffering; being temperate in all things; being diligent in keeping the commandments of God at all times; asking for whatsoever things ye stand in need, both spiritual and temporal; always returning thanks unto God for whatsoever things ye do receive.*

Alma 7:23, <u>The Book of Mormon</u>

In this verse, we find many synonyms of meekness. Ponder their opposites. I have made a list of the opposites and synonyms of meekness. This is what we are trying to eliminate in our children and step children and ourselves. This is why parents and step parents receive so much opposition and resentment from their children and step children. Of course, we really can only eliminate these things within ourselves. Parents and step parents should be good examples for their children and step children. You will be able to think of more opposites.

Left Hand	*Right Hand*
Humiliation	*Humility*
Resistant	*Submissive*
Argumentative, defensive	*Easy to be entreated (Easy to ask requests)*
Hard-hearted, hard-headed	*Gentle*
Complaining, resentment, whining	*Long-suffering (Enduring)*
Rage, indifference, indulgence	*Temperate (mild)*
Lazy, will do commandments of men	*Diligent in keeping God's Commandments*
Ask parents, governments for things need	*Ask God for things we need*
Ingratitude, ungrateful	*Grateful*

Now, we know why the Lord wants us to be able to discern between our right hand and our left hand. From which sides do depression, our identity, self-esteem, happiness, and meekness come? We are free to choose the aspects of either hand in our personalities. We are not free to choose the consequences of the Left Hand. Our behavior of the Left Hand affects too many people. The burdens of the Left Hand bring heavier burdens and depression which consume us. The behavior of the Right Hand eases burdens for everyone.

The Right Hand

One does not have to be humiliated to be humble and oppressed to be submissive. Parents and step parents can still set limits on their children, step children, others, and yourself and be gentle. We do not have to allow ourselves to be led around by the nose while begging for mercy to be easy to be entreated. Patience is not ignoring hardship and long-suffering, but enduring hardships. Parents and step parents can still become angry and reproof softly their children.

The Savior taught us the methods to become easily entreated and also to endure our hardships. Temperance is the key to meekness. Temperance is the key to being diligent in keeping the commandments of God at all times, asking for only what we need spiritually and temporally and being grateful for what we receive. Individuals who are temperate are pleasantly mild. They are not lukewarm, but they do not indulge to excess in their appetites, tempers, alcoholic liquors, or their actions, and speech. A temperate climate is mild. A temperate climate in your home begins with soft answers. Let's begin with the way the Right Hand taught us how to control our appetites. With the Word of Wisdom, meekness can be an option in our lives.

The Word of Wisdom. Jesus Christ gave us a Word of Wisdom which is found in <u>Doctrine and Covenants</u> 89. The Word of Wisdom is for all things, not just food. This chapter teaches the way to develop moderation (meekness). This will fulfill the words of Christ in each generation.

Our bodies are created by certain principles. Food has been placed on the Earth to maintain these principles in new cells in each generation throughout time. Lack of energy, poor health, and death comes when these principles are altered in any way. Diabetics are well aware of the difficulties when they cannot breakdown sugar and carbohydrates for immediate use or store glycogen for later use. Diabetics have difficulty absorbing food nutrients due to poor circulation.

Oxygen is easily displaced on the hemoglobin molecule for a carbon monoxide molecule. This results in carbon monoxide poisoning. There is too much illness in the world. We are not eating healthy foods. The foods which we do eat have too many preservatives in them, and we are taking other medications with food. We seek ways for energy such as pills and caffeine. It would be interesting if vitamins, minerals, and proteins, the building blocks for the body, are displaced in a similar manner as carbon monoxide poisoning by all the preservatives, caffeine, and medications we are taking. Even large amounts of sugar, protein, fats, and vitamins affect our health.

We cannot be meek and gluttonous at the same time. In other words, meekness is the absence of gluttony. A glutton greedily eats too much. They may have great capacities and great potential for something such as work, but they devour or neglect important things in their life or their family's life. They want more and more and covet more and more in spite of what they have. Their gluttony is never satisfied. Gluttony reduces our capacity and potential to function. Gluttonous people may achieve more by deception, but they also become more angry and depressed. As they devour people, their heart waxes cold. Gluttony occurs in many things.

Be yoked together as a family or step family. In a beautiful scripture, the Savior asks us to take His yoke upon us. He is meek and will give us rest. Labor comes with trials of having and rearing children. "Heavy laden" describes the depression and oppression which comes with our burdens and trials. Christ gives us rest from our labors, not parents and step parents. His yoke lightens our burdens. Parents, step parents, children, step children, and spouses are part of his yoke. His yoke is also the commandments and covenants of our Father in Heaven.

28 ¶ Come unto me, all ye that labor and are heavy laden,
and I will give you rest.
29 Take my yoke upon you, and learn of me; for I am meek
and lowly in heart: and ye shall find rest unto your souls.
30 For my yoke is easy, and my burden is light.

Matthew 11:28 - 30, <u>The Holy Bible</u>

Our stipes–His Stripes. In my summer travels to museums, I have heard an interesting story about yokes. Two oxen are placed in a yoke to pull a plow or wagon. One ox is usually stronger. This ox is known as the "nigh ox." The weaker ox is known as the "off ox." The wagon or plow is pulled in the direction of the "nigh ox," the stronger ox. Someone walks along the side of the "nigh ox" to keep the ox going in the right direction. When the stronger ox tires, the ox is placed in the "off ox" position for a rest. If the "off ox" decides to go in another direction, the "off ox" usually receives a stern call or lash from a whip. If we accept the Savior's yoke, someone walks along beside us to keep us going in the right direction. If we decide to walk away from the one helping us, we do not receive lashes from a whip from the Savior. We receive lashes from behavior of ourselves and others. Depression is not meekness. We are not healed by our stripes to ourselves.

But he was wounded for our transgressions, he was bruised for our iniquities:
the chastisement of our peace was upon him; and with his stripes we are healed.

Isaiah 53:5, <u>The Holy Bible</u>

The Left Hand

Giving in to your Goliath is not meekness. The Story of Uriah, David, and Bath-sheba will illustrate this for us. This story is found in the Old Testament in 2 Samuel 11:1 - 12. It is depressing to read of the greatness in David as a youth, but as an adult he succumbed to both adultery and murder. In his youth, David killed Goliath with stones and a slingshot. The real Goliath in his life was a beautiful woman, named Bath-sheba. She was married to a faithful soldier in David's army. His name was Uriah. At this time, David's army was fighting Syria.

In the evening, David arose from his bed and walked upon the roof of the king's house. He saw a beautiful woman washing herself. David inquired about the woman. He was told that sounds like Bath-sheba, the daughter of Eliam, the wife of Uriah the Hittite. Apparently, others had seen her bathe, too. David sent messengers, and she came to him. They committed adultery, and then she returned to her house. Bath-sheba conceived and told David. To cover his actions, David sent for Uriah, the Hittite.

David demanded of Uriah how his servant, Joab, delivered his message, how the people did, and how the war prospered. He then told Uriah to go home and bathe. David sent meat to his house. However, Uriah slept at the door of the king's house with all of the servants of David. The servants told David that Uriah did not go to his house. David asked Uriah why he did not go home. Uriah told David, "The ark, and Israel, and Judah, abide in tents; and my lord Joab, and the servants of my lord, are encamped in the open fields; shall I then go into mine house, to eat and to drink, and to lie with my wife? *as* thou livest, and *as* thy soul liveth, I will not do this thing." David told Uriah to stay in Jerusalem until tomorrow which he did. David gave Uriah a large meal and made him drunk. Uriah still slept with the servants of David.

In the morning, David wrote a letter to Joab, and sent the letter by the hand of Uriah. The letter stated, "Set ye Uriah in the forefront of the hottest battle, and retire ye from him, that he may be smitten, and die. Joab is the eldest son of David's sister and was Captain of David's army against Syria. Uriah was sent to a place where the hottest battle was taking place. Syria had their most valiant men there. They fought with Joab's army. Some of the servants of David were killed, as well as Uriah the Hittite. Joab informed David of Uriah's death. David pretended to be angry. Bath-sheba mourned for her dead husband. When her mourning was past, Bath-sheba became David's wife and bore him a son who died. What David did displeased the Lord. (2 Samuel 11:1 - 12) After all he had done so valiantly, all of David's wives and concubines and his children were given to others. He lost exaltation. (Doctrine and Covenants 132:39)

I have always been a little suspicious of this story. I have suspected for a long time that some things does not ring true. I do not believe, and this is my belief, that Bath-sheba, Joab, and the men who ignored Uriah's plight are completely innocent. I do not believe in that day that a woman would innocently bathe so a king could see her bathe and risk being raped by soldiers. Women have sexual desires which overtake them. Her husband was at war. He was gone for long periods. From stories, I have heard from soldiers that I have cared for, they always knew when the commander was mad at or jealous of an officer. The officer was put on the front line, or the point as it is now called. The company or battalion was always sent to the fiercest battle.

Step parents have had similar experiences as David. David's kingdom was finally snatched by a Goliath, a beautiful woman. Children and step children try to seduce parents and step parents. This is the quickest way to get a step parent to divorce a parent. If their parent and step parent do not divorce, this is the quickest and complete way to snatch and control their parent's kingdom or household. Children and step children now expect parents and step parents to give into their every whim.

Step children and children try to control the physical space of parents and step parents. Step siblings and biological siblings are forced to go along in this nightmare, or they will be sent to the front line, too. Friends and neighbors can send parents to the front lines also. Parents and step parents, siblings and step siblings, friends and neighbors are all held hostage by a child who prefers to be a Goliath instead of a child or a sibling in his family.

When biological parents or step parents married, they did not expect a Goliath in their children or step children. We know rage and angry outbursts are not meekness. Being silent and withdrawn in this situation is also not meekness. Ignoring this situation is not meekness.

Holding back is not meekness. Holding back usually results in screaming, angry outbursts, and depression to relieve the tension caused by these great trials. Depression is not going to make people more kind and thoughtful to you. They usually avoid you because they cannot do anything to help you, and they cannot take on anymore burdens on themselves, especially burdens that cannot be satisfied. Depression invites victimization, causing more depression.

Children of the Desolate. There are many children of the desolate in this world today.[19] They range in all ages and sizes. Children of the desolate are not just children of unmarried mothers. Children of the desolate are children of depressed parents and step parents, widows and widowers, divorced spouses, drug addicts, and alcoholics. All are experiencing the buffetings of Satan. Children and step children experiment with trouble and blame the consequences that children and step children receive on desolate parents and step parents. Children and step children of the desolate feel they must control their parents and step parents, not themselves.

The behavior of parents and step parents cause heartache in children. Parents and step parents and spouses obtain psychiatric therapy for themselves, their spouse, children, and step children to restore order and proper authority to their homes. Children of the desolate often prefer to live with psychiatric problems than with parents' and step parents' authority.

When individuals do not want to change, they live in a psychiatric limbo instead of a plateau of meekness and humility. In some Christian theologies, a limbo was a region bordering hell. It is a prison and a place or condition of oblivion and neglect. A limbo is a void with no borders. The limbo is also a dance in which dancers bend at the knees as far back as possible to pass beneath a bar that is put lower and lower. Of course, if you cannot bend underneath the bar, you are so far off balance, you fall to the ground. This is how the bar gets lower and lower in psychiatry and psychology and in our families and step families.

The Psychiatric Limbo. In my nursing career, I have noticed the increased incidence of psychiatric disorders. I have done as many suicide watches over married people as I have done over children of divorced parents or unwed mothers. I have even watched over children of fighting parents. The parents could not bury the hatchet even in the hospital. Their family members became worse, and they could not understand why. After all, their family members were receiving psychiatric therapy. *The family members and the patient created the same "non-therapeutic" environment in the psychiatric office that exists at home.* This is how this non therapeutic environment has created more desolation in families and step families.

Psychiatrists and psychologists have seen the things the Savior and apostles warned us about. However, psychiatry and psychology have limits. These limits are set by the organizations which the psychologist, psychiatrist, and social worker belong. These organizations provide their licensing, testing, and continuing education. Psychiatry and psychology does not know everything about the human mind and personality. The limits of psychiatry and psychology also must include the boundaries for malpractice insurance. Psychiatry and psychology are bound by the patient's insurance plan. Psychiatry and psychology are also bound by their patient's free agency. *A patient is always going to be tempted beyond the current level of psychiatric knowledge.*

Patients are as vindictive to their counselor and employers as they are to their family. No one wants to work hard at several degrees for several years only to lose their degrees and their livelihood for someone who is not thinking clearly or who is experiencing uncontrolled anger. Businesses cannot pay high costs for psychiatric care and psychiatric drugs, especially when they do not seem to accomplish anything. Psychiatry and psychology are most limited because psychiatry and psychology do not include God, the one who created the human mind. God created the principles that are designed for the mind and body to work together efficiently.

---

[19]Isaiah 54:1, The Holy Bible, p. 926.

A patient presents himself with a group of symptoms. He cannot accept blame for his decisions, actions, or take any criticism. The patient cannot handle any stress. The patient tells the psychiatrist or psychologist about incidents which have happened in the past to his best recollection. He was angry at the time. He is angry now. The patient is also depressed. His memory is not so good.

The psychiatrist or psychologist hears many incidents where family has wronged the patient. The doctor hears very little about how the patient has wronged the family or about the many ways and times parents and step parents have tried to help their son or daughter. The psychiatrist or psychologist does not know who to believe although he or she has seen and heard the same symptoms over and over. The psychiatrist and psychologist try to maintain a therapeutic relationship with the patient. If the psychiatrist and the psychologist could or would include God in therapy, they would know that by their fruits they would know what is wrong with their patient. *Forbidden fruits have signs and symptoms.*

Their patient is trying to reconcile with someone they are very angry with. It may be their parents. It may be spouse or siblings. Patients are most usually trying to reconcile with their self or with God. The psychiatrist and psychologist want to make a comfortable environment for the patient to change. Psychiatrists or psychologists exclude the ones the patient is angry with. Can you imagine excluding the one they are trying to reconcile with in family, especially if they are trying to reconcile with themselves and God? There would be no results because there would be no one to forgive and to be meek with. The patients become more and more depressed until they are suicidal. The patients are medicated into oblivion.

Parents cannot make a decision because the patient is over eighteen. Parents are not consulted if the patient is under eighteen because of the rights of privacy. Step parents have no rights. The rights of privacy does not include the bill! Who is making decisions for the care of the patient? The sick and depressed patient and a counselor who is too busy to see the patient regularly.

If the patient is angry with spouse, the psychiatrist limits the powers of the spouse. The patient who is angry with the spouse limits the spouse's powers in the home. Spouses are limited or eliminated in the doctor's office. Now, spouse and parent cannot make a decision to help their child and spouse. Spouses can be excluded to the point of divorce. Parents are at their wit's end. Spouses are at their wit's end.

Is anyone in charge of this depressed and suicidal patient? If there is no one making mature decisions for your loved one, if the patient only receives guidance for one hour of the week or month and medications for the rest of the time, and if God is excluded, the Adversary will be in charge of their care, not a counselor. No medication can stop the buffetings of Satan.

The psychologist or psychiatrist makes the decision within the bounds of his knowledge and his malpractice insurance. Since their time together is limited to prevent dependency, the patient is heavily medicated. The patient of age is his or her own person. The patient can have as many types of anti-psychotic medications on hand as they want. Their memory is poor. They get tired of existing and being babysat. They want to be cured in a hurry. Family gets tired of doing a suicidal chase. Patients take or are given more medications than are needed. All were never knowing or able to understand that the patient and his family could have gone to the Mighty Counselor between appointments.

For unto us a child is born, unto us a son is given: and the government shall
be upon his shoulder: and his name shall be called Wonderful, Counsellor,
The mighty God, The everlasting Father, The Prince of Peace.

Isaiah 9:6, The Holy Bible

Medication. We can choose to be meek or try for a medicated-induced meekness with illegal drugs or a large amount of prescription medications. A medicated-induced meekness usually makes you sleep twenty to twenty-four hours a day. This is going backward to the period of infancy, when we slept twenty to twenty-four hours a day. This causes severe depression in your children and step children. They do not understand why their mother or step mother, father or step father is so sad and stoned all the time. Sadly, there are parents who have children and step-children who deliberately create this situation in parents and step parents. It is an easy way to shift blame to parents and step parents for the dissension that children caused.

I suspect that the increase in obesity is caused by the increased use of anti-depressant medications and illegal street drugs. These medications depresses your metabolism. Eating fast foods with excessive sleeping puts on the weight just like it does in babies.

Parents and step parents are indulging in depression. This kind of indulgence is very confusing and depressing for children, especially when the child realizes that he does not get meals, Christmas presents, even a home, etc., like the other kids do because parents have spent their money on useless items, excessive shopping, and pills. They do not have money for their house payment, food, or the energy to cook for the family. Children and step children have a hard time growing in the best of circumstances. They cannot bear your burdens and grow mentally and spiritually. Children will never grow spiritually if parents do not rely on spiritual things to help them. Children will not grow mentally if everything they do never satisfies or delights you. Home is not suppose to be hopeless.

Humans do not like to admit that their depressions come from sin. Now, if the sins of others and a lack of meekness in others can hurt us terribly and cause depression in us, our own sins and lack of meekness will oppress us in the same manner. Making a lack of meekness and our sins legal is not going to cure our depressions and turn scarlet sins into white sins.

18 Come now, and let us reason together, saith the LORD:
though your sins be as scarlet, they shall be as white as snow;
though they be red like crimson, they shall be as wool.
19 If ye be willing and obedient, ye shall eat the good of the land:

Isaiah 1:18 - 19, The Holy Bible

Jacob of Israel had many trials with his twelve sons, his daughters, and his brother, Esau. We are of the House of Israel and experience the same trials with our children and siblings. Jacob had to learn to be meek so he could lead, not follow his children. Following The Left Hand or not being able to discern The Left Hand from The Right Hand sets the stage for children or siblings to be in charge of families and step families.

Catalysts. A catalyst brings about or hastens a result in a scientific experiment. Catalysts are affected by temperature. In His refining process called meekness, the Savior also uses catalysts for His children. The Lord's catalysts hasten or bring about a desired result when we experiment on His words. (Alma 32:27) The Savior uses heat and cold with His catalysts, too.

Children gauge their life by celebrities and idols, the way they dress, their homes, the drugs they ingest to perform, and the movies and sports in which children see them. Individuals from Hollywood and your children's peer group are setting the stage for your family instead of parents and step parents. Celebrities and idols are not the gauge nor the catalysts for our lives. Jesus Christ, the Atonement of Jesus Christ, and our meekness are our catalysts.

The most important catalyst in our life will always be the Atonement of Jesus Christ. Through the Atonement of Jesus Christ, we are redeemed from our sins, not in our sins. The Adversary wants to redeem us in our sins with more sins which oppress us even more, and he wants the glory for doing this to us. The Adversary accomplishes his tasks by hardening of hearts. Jesus Christ accomplishes His tasks through softening of hearts which is meekness. The Savior tames us by softening our hearts. This eases our oppression which eases our depressions. Christ gives the glory to our Heavenly Father.

The Left Hand of Our Day	**The Right Hand Forever**
Idolatry	*Atonement of Jesus Christ*
Self-Medicated	*Word of Wisdom*
Gluttony, Without Natural Affection	*Temperance*
Dissension	*Yoked Together as Family*
Goliath	*Recognize Our Goliath*
Silent, Withdrawn, Lukewarm, Yell	*Soft Answers*
Parents Held Hostage	*Obey Parents and Step Parents*
Shift Blame	*Accountability*
Psychiatric Limbo	*Prayer and Fasting*
Suicidal Chase	*Do Not Run Faster Than You Can Walk*
Sin	*Faith in Christ, Repent, Baptism, Gift of Holy Ghost*
Our Stripes of Depression, Anger, Hate	*His Stripes*
Neither Root Nor Branch	*Root and Branch in an Eternal Family*

Inventions. We live in an age of many inventions. These inventions are improved upon year after year and have become more important than families and step families. Companies have us chasing these new and improved inventions so they have to keep changing.

Among these many inventions, we hear of catalytic converters. "A catalytic converter is part of the exhaust system in cars and trucks which contains a chemical catalyst to reduce pollution. Wood stoves and other machinery have catalytic converters. I have often wished that there was a spiritual catalytic converter for us to convert the superheated gases of this life from hurt feelings to energy without chemicals. I suspect there is. Our spiritual catalyst for us is called meekness. These are the things that meekness can convert to make us happy.

Meekness, Our Spiritual Catalytic Converter

LOINS GIRT WITH TRUTH

1. Without natural affection
2. False accusers
3. Ever learning, but not able to come to the knowledge of the truth
4. Resist truth

BREASTPLATE OF RIGHTEOUSNESS

1. Lovers of their own selves
2. Disobedient to parents
3. Despisers of those that are good
   a. Self
   b. Parents
   c. Siblings
   d. Spouse
   e. Neighbors
   f. Country
   g. World

PREPARATION OF THE GOSPEL OF PEACE

1. Unthankful
2. Unholy
3. Trucebreakers
4. Traitors
5. Lovers of Pleasure

SHIELD OF FAITH QUENCHES THE FIERY DARTS OF THE DEVIL

1. Blasphemers
2. Incontinent
3. Fierce

HELMET OF SALVATION

1. Form of Godliness, but denying the power thereof

SWORD OF THE SPIRT WHICH IS THE WORD OF GOD

1. Heady
2. Highminded
3. Proud
4. Boasters

Are you, your family, and step family members ready to inherit the earth as a joint-heir with Christ? To be a joint heir with Christ, we must be meek. Meekness comes when we are able to discern between The Left Hand and The Right Hand and by preserving the words of The Right Hand in each generation of our families in stead of the words of The Left Hand. You are a generation, too. To be ready to be a joint-heir with Christ, you must decide if you want to be saved in your sins or from your sins. This determines who is your Savior. The Left Hand did not present a way to save us. The Left Hand only wanted glory for himself.

Most of us understand that we need to be more meek. It is that part of being meek while we are being stonewalled, manipulated, cheated, and isolated that gives us grief. We usually have more meekness when we can afford our problems. I suspect this is why we are told to not run faster than we can walk. Today, the stage for families and step families is being set with a standard of living that does not allow us to run and walk according to our ability. Society wants tributes from their countrymen. Our children and step children want tributes from parents and step parents. Let's learn some things about forcing others to make tributes

Chapter Fourteen

Your Tribute

I have worked with many nurses who had families and step families. Many times, they were up all night with a sick child. Some of these nurses were also pregnant. They still showed up for work the next day. Many occupations have mothers or fathers who do the same. Many fathers and step fathers work in the heat or the cold of the day at two and three jobs to provide a roof over their family's head, food in their mouth, and clothes on their bodies. They somehow find time to play with their children. They also want to buy their loved ones something special. Many parents and step parents have had only five to ten dollars left till pay day or for Christmas. They came up with some mighty miracles for their family and step family. I suspect they did it by prayer and fasting and sacrifice. They may have not realized they were praying and fasting. They just said a quick prayer and went without to provide for their children and step children.

In spite of all the things that parents and step parents have provided for their children and step children, their children and step children are angry and are making poor efforts in school. They are most angry with their parents and step parents. Their parents or step parents are not as attractive as the parents which children see on television and in movies. Children accuse parents and step parents of never being there for them. Parents scratch their heads in disbelief. Parents and step parents do not understand that their child has lost respect for the enmity or authority which God placed on the Earth in parents and step parents.

Many parents and step parents do not feel that God's enmity, or Authority, is important to pass on to their children and step children. Their child can choose which religious affiliation he wants when he becomes of age. Of course, the child usually chooses none. His idols, those movie stars and sports stars which parents have been taking their children to, have no religious affiliation. As parents wipe away their tears, they wonder what is going on with their child. In much frustration, they begin searching for their son or daughter, step son or step daughter.

First, parents wonder if they are dealing with a prodigal son or daughter. Parents are not merely dealing with a prodigal son or daughter. Prodigal sons and daughters waste their own living, not the living of all those with whom they come in contact. The brother was angry with his prodigal brother. Parents, grandparents, and siblings did not waste their living waiting for their prodigal relative to come to their senses or to find themselves. Parents, grandparents, and other siblings did not become prodigal parents, grandparents, and siblings to give their prodigal child or brother self-esteem. They had their senses, and they wanted to keep their senses. Most step parents have prodigal sons or daughters who would not return to them anyway.

Second, parents wonder if they are dealing with "lost coins." Parents search and search for their "lost coin," but realize this is a dead end, too. When a parent or step parent searches for their "lost coin," they find it. There is joy. Now, parents find a lot of other "lost coins" with their "lost coins." They keep each other company. These "lost coins" do not feel they are lost. They do not want to be found. There is no joy. What are parents and step parents dealing with?

Parents are dealing with a child who wants parents and step parents and the government to pay them "tribute money" for every inconvenience, boredom, opposition, and sadness in the child's life. The inconvenience of having a step parent is really expensive. The richest of parents will not be able to keep up with their child's demands. Both parent and step parent become a servant unto tribute. (Genesis 49:15) Parents and step parents are encumbered by children and step children to keep the tributes coming or when parents refuse to pay tribute.

Here is another opposite that is wise for us to learn and teach our children and step children. The Savior took the time to teach us all about this opposite in the last week of his life. If you recall, this week was an emotional week for the Savior. He wept several times over the city–just like parents and step parents become depressed and weep over their families and step families when someone asks them to pay tribute.

Tribute–Render. In our day, a tribute is an expression of admiration or congratulation. It is suppose to be a formal gesture of appreciation and admiration for high achievements, not minimal efforts or approval when doing evil things. Eulogies and the gifts we give each other at Christmas time, birthdays, and to employers are tributes between two people or a group.

In the Savior's day, a tribute was a special tax that one nation forced upon a conquered nation. This was to keep a conquered nation from invading the conqueror. Likewise, in our day, a tribute is money paid regularly to a ruler or nation by another nation for protection or to keep them from invading our country after they have already invaded our country.

In our day, a child or step child expects money in spite of his or her minimal efforts. Mother or step mother gives them money to keep them from doing more wrong. The child still does what he promised not to do. Mother or step mother may love her children very much, but this forced payment was not given out of love and gratitude or praise. It was given after many guilt trips and misbehavior. A tribute is bribery, and bribery never works.

> *15 ¶ Then went the Pharisees, and took counsel how they might entangle him in his talk.*
> *16 And they sent out unto him their disciples with the Herodians, saying, Master, we know that thou art true, and teachest the way of God in truth, neither carest thou for any man: for thou regardest not the person of men.*
> *17 Tell us therefore, What thinkest thou? Is it lawful to give tribute unto Cæsar, or not?*
> *18 But Jesus perceived their wickedness, and said, Why tempt ye me, ye hypocrites?*
> *19 Shew me the tribute money. And they brought unto him a penny.*
> *20 And he saith unto them, Whose is this image and superscription?*
> *21 They say unto him, Cæsar's. Then saith he unto them, Render therefore unto Cæsar the things which are Cæsar's; and unto God the things that are God's.*
> *22 When they had heard these words, they marvelled, and left him, and went their way.*
> *Matthew 22:15 - 23, The Holy Bible*

Notice. The ones who asked the Savior if it was lawful to pay tribute to Caesar were probably helping to enforce the payment of tributes to Caesar. Parents and step parents often wonder if it is "lawful" or the right thing to do to pay tributes for their children and step children. Is your tribute given out of love or is it to keep your child out of trouble? Tributes with children are bribery. I know that bribery does not bring about the desired results we want in our children. Instead of increasing their efforts, children continually misbehave to keep the bribes coming.

The Cycle of Paying Tribute. Paying a tribute without contribution to your family tribe creates the painful cycle of paying tribute. This cycle is very depressing, especially to mothers. Parents and step parents must bribe their child or step child until their deaths for every effort, or they must watch their child make mistake after mistake. These mistakes hurt a lot of people. Again, this is trying to learn from same and same: good and better or bad and worse.

Paying a tribute without contribution isolates parents and step parents. This cycle intimidates, stonewalls, and manipulates parents and step parents, not children and step children. Your family does not represent the image of God that we are trying to obtain. This cycle does not increase agency (power to choose) for parents and step parents or children and step children. This cycle decreases or takes the power to choose away from both parent and child. Children have more authority over parents and step parents and the family. They do not need God or deny that God exists. They need the bribes. Children and step children's resources are too limited by themselves or God for parents, step parents and a family to rely on. Let's identify this cycle.

First, all families have a dictator. Dictators create their own little kingdom within their parents' and step parent's home. Dictators do as they please, but are financially dependent on parents. If dictators obtain money from parents, they can save their money for other purchases. Dictators manipulate allowances from their younger siblings. They manipulate parents' time and parents' money. They also manipulate the parents' image in their children's mind. Dictators manipulate the image of children in parents' minds.

Second, as the dictators age, this money is not enough for their needs and desires. Allowances from siblings will not pay car payments, college tuition, rent or house payments, utilities, food, and their children's clothes. If they work, their money pays for eating out frequently, technology, clothes, sports, recreation, travel, movies, drugs, alcohol, gambling, and furniture. To receive this amount of money from parents, dictators create sob stories called broken-wing acts. They are unwilling and unable to work for money because of their broken wing-acts. However, their broken-wing acts do not interfere with their energy for shopping, partying, sports, recreation, and travel. As drugs, alcohol, cigarettes, and excessive stress affects their financial status, their ability to function and work decreases. The Holy Ghost withdraws. Pride and desires cause individuals to compel others.

Third, parents and siblings begin to have difficulty keeping up the pace which the family dictator has set for them. Parents will work, and they add extra jobs. Your children know where the cash flow of the family or step family is going. Parents and step parents complain about the dictator and the pace they set for the family often enough. Siblings see the dictator of the family is not working, but they have every need fulfilled. The siblings of the dictator who are your children and step children become jealous and angry. Other members of the family, siblings and step siblings, want their needs, wants, desires, and obligations fulfilled like the dictator of the family has their needs and desires fulfilled.

Fourth, many children and step children do not believe in God, the one that has helped parents and step parents provide for them. Children and step children do not believe in angels or resurrections either. They believe in a cash flow. Their choices are limited because they do not believe in God, angels, or a resurrection. They must create their own broken wing acts.

Everyone goes from one crisis to another to make sure they receive their tribute money. Have they learned anything from their mistakes? Yes. This is why children keep repeating their mistakes. *They have learned: In order to keep the cash flow coming, they have to keep the mistakes coming to obtain tribute money!*

Their broken wing acts have to be pretty good. If younger siblings take money from Mother and Father, they are taking money from the dictator of the family. Siblings know they have to still keep the dictator happy to have any peace. Younger siblings do not want to pay any more tributes to the dictator of the family than they already have had to pay. They have their families to raise, too.

Fifth, finally Mother and Dad cannot keep up the pace of the dictator, imitators, and agitators of the family. They are too old. They are living on a fixed income. Mother and Dad now have poor health with poor insurance benefits. Mother and Dad may even be angry because parents have needs, wants, desires, and obligations, too. They are tired of working all their lives for one member of the family and his or her creditors.

Sixth, everyone is angry. They are angry with their parents, especially a step mother. They are not angry with the dictator. They fear the dictator. They are aware of the cruel acts and injustices over the years. They are not going to invite more cruelty on themselves. They know if they chasten the dictator, they will always have to pay more tributes and work twice as hard to prevent any further acts of cruelty and injustices to their families.

Seventh, in frustration, everyone avoids each other. Parents avoid children. Children avoid parents. Siblings avoid siblings. The Holy Ghost leaves this family, too. They live in spiritual darkness. Their physical countenance even darkens. Your children have not been rendered to God. They have been rendered to the dictator of the family. Parents have also been rendered to the dictator of the family. All have rendered their families, not to God or Caesar, but to the adversary.

The Savior warned us there would be many who would deceive us. There would be many with devious plans to trap us. Parents just did not expect it to be in their own household.[20] They did not expect their children would betray parents or grandparents over junk and the inconveniences of a child's life. Parents did not expect their children would abandon parents when parents and children were experiencing trials because parents would not or could not pay children and step children tribute money.

AREAS WHERE IT IS COMMON TO PAY TRIBUTE MONEY

First and second marriages. All marriages and families have trials. It does not matter if they are a first marriage or second marriage. Second marriages are an excellent breeding ground for parents to pay tribute money to your children to keep children happy and to buy step

---

[20]Matthew 10:36, The Holy Bible, p. 1204.

children's loyalty. Second marriages have some insatiable appetites that parents and step parents cannot quench. It is difficult to care for a normal appetite when a step parent receives no daily spiritual bread. The difficulty increases when those for whom you care do not want you to have any daily bread for yourself. *The balance of power in this struggle is in parents' and step parents' favor as long as parents and step parents receive daily bread. Do not give up your daily bread in battles over tribute money. Your daily bread comes from God and your spouse.*

Tribute money is a cause of much depression in men as well as women. Most men like to do things with their children, especially their sons. Fathers or step fathers are always going to expect some effort from their children, especially their sons, after the entertainment is over. It is heart-breaking for a father when their adult children will not go to school or work. Children expect biological parents to provide an expensive life-style for them. They expect their step parent to not interfere with this lifestyle arrangement. It does not matter how old or what state of heath their parents are in. It is tribute money if you are trying to keep your children interested in you and trying to keep them from hating you. Neither you nor this child's family will be able to rely on this child as everyone ages.

Mother usually becomes so bogged down with the burdens of the dictator of the family and his or her needs and crisis'. She is not so quick to pick up the behavior and burdens of another dictator. She just knows she does not have the time, the patience, the energy, or the money to care for all of the burdens and behavior which accompanies her children's and step children's broken wing acts.

If parents refuse to pay tribute money, children despise their parents and step parents and look to others for their needs. Fathers cannot understand why children love junk more than fathers. Fathers do not understand why his family wants fathers to work long hours in the cold and the heat of the day for junk. Children claim they want more time with their parents, but children do not want to sacrifice anything for that time. In their hurt and anger, parents withdraw. Soon others are doing more for your children than parents are doing. These individuals wonder what is wrong with parents and step parents.

Tribute money affects the finances of the family. This tribute cycle can drain the assets of a family like the thin cows devoured the fat cows of Egypt.[21] These kinds of thin cows, we have never seen before. Parents, especially mothers, are put in a position where they must pay tribute to their children to keep them happy and loving mother. It does not matter if there is money in their parents' bank account or for parents' retirement. It does not matter if there is little food in the cupboards or food storage.

Parents pay tribute money to children who have attention deficit disorder or attention deficit disorder with hyperactivity so they will not have an attention deficit disorder. Parents do not really understand these disorders. They just hope they will find something to cure these disorders in their children. Money is going to postpone or talk them out of this disorder.

When their child is victimized, parents buy them something to make them feel better. Soon the child goes out of his way to be victimized. When their child is victimizing others, and they do, parents, particularly mothers, pay tribute money to keep their child from victimizing others. Mothers especially know when this behavior is occurring. They know their children.

---

[21]Genesis 41:14-21, The Holy Bible, pp. 62-63.

Parents and step parents know when they are lying. This behavior is hard to accept for mother. They can see the light in their children's eyes diminish. Does paying tribute money work? No. Tribute money makes their behaviors profitable.

Smoking, Alcohol, and Drugs. Smoking, alcohol, and drugs is a very expensive tribute cycle. Parents and step parents pay tribute money to children to keep them from stealing and harming others. Parents cannot give gifts of money or proudly loan their son the car for a date. Their children and step children will buy more drugs, "energy enhancers," cigarettes, and alcohol. Their child may be killed in a car accident, and parents held responsible. Parents and step parents sooth their emotions with alcohol and anti-depressants.

In a tribute cycle, children never learn to do things for themselves. Children only learn to do just enough to get by or to obtain what they want. Self-esteem is not obtained this way. I suspect this is why parents and step parents have not been given the energies, health, and life-span to meet every need, want, desire, and obligation of their children and step children. This is why the Savior told us not to run faster than we can walk in scripture. Our children and step children must learn the many values of work and not running faster than they can walk, too.

Movies, Television, Video Games, etc. Children and step children like to see the most current release of movies, and the most popular television program and video game. Movies, television, violent video games quickly show a child a tribute cycle over and over. These movies, etc. are not only dangerous, but they portray false doctrine on the screen. Children accept this false doctrine. It does not matter how much sex and violence they are portraying. They insist the doctrine that parents and step parents are teaching is false. Children become angry because their parents and step parents do not provide a living for their families like they see on television. This type of living is where the father or mother hand the child money, nothing less than twenty or more dollars, every time the parent wants the child out of the room or the child asks for money.

Children can watch these programs twenty-four hours a day. Parents and step parents bought televisions and cable televison for their children to have in their children's rooms. They have computers with the Internet in children's rooms. They added telephones in children's rooms. They can contact individuals who have ulterior motives in mind. Parents can now watch their programs in peace. However, your children and step children are doing poorly in school, are easily agitated, and are very argumentative. They are tired. They have disobeyed their parents and step parents. Peace will not be coming to this household. We pray for help for them and then turn to an R-rated movie and X-rated video game to ease our tension.

Parental money should be put away for their parents' retirement. The time should be spent together monitoring homework and activities so the child has some grades that will be acceptable for college and attitudes acceptable for raising a family. Your child needs an education, or he or she will become depressed. He will lose his identity in a tribute cycle.

Children who require tribute money of their parents will never be able to provide feasts for their family. Parents, step parents, and siblings have not allowed their child to experience and learn from opposition (God's authority) the things our Heavenly Father wants us to learn. The first thing you and your child must learn is that you will not receive a wedding feast or tribute for every inconvenience in your life. When parents pay tribute to their children and step children, this is the kind of wedding feast which parents and children experience.

134

1 AND Jesus answered and spake unto them again by parables, and said,
2 The kingdom of heaven is like unto a certain king, which made a marriage for his son,
3 And sent forth his servants to call them that were bidden to the wedding: and they would not come.
4 Again, he sent forth other servants, saying, Tell them which are bidden, Behold, I have prepared my dinner: my oxen and my fatlings are killed, and all things are ready: come unto the marriage.
5 But they made light of it, and went their ways, one to his farm, another to his merchandise:
6 And the remnant took his servants, and entreated them spitefully, and slew them.
7 But when the king heard thereof, he was wroth: and he sent forth his armies, and destroyed those murderers, and burned up their city.
8 Then saith he to his servants, The wedding is ready, but they which were bidden were not worthy.
9 Go ye therefore into the highways, and as many as ye shall find, bid to the marriage.
10 So those servants went out into the highways, and gathered together all as many as they found, both bad and good: and the wedding was furnished with guests.
11 ¶ And when the king came in to see the guests, he saw there a man which had not on a wedding garment:
12 And he saith unto him, Friend, how camest thou in hither not having a wedding garment? And he was speechless.
13 Then said the king to the servants, Bind him hand and foot, and take him away, and cast him into outer darkness; there shall be weeping and gnashing of teeth.

Matthew 22:1 - 13, <u>The Holy Bible</u>

If you have been to any Sunday School class, this is one of the parables which is quickly passed over. The teacher tells us that the King is our Heavenly Father, the Son is Jesus Christ, His servants are prophets, and the wedding feast is for the world. It is also known as the Atonement of Jesus Christ.

Keep in mind that while on Earth we are to follow Christ's example. This means we will be doing what the Savior did in His ministry. We will be preparing some feasts for our sons and daughters. We will be preparing some wedding feasts for ourselves. Our Heavenly Father has prepared a wedding feast for us, too.

The Age-Old Family Battle. A man and a woman decide to marry. They bring to their marriage feast what they have prepared for their marriage. It may be meager. It may be a feast. Their feast is according to their ability and what they can afford. They even have a marriage feast in their honor where a large amount of food is served. Individuals help pass out the wedding invitations. If the couple is wealthy and popular, individuals come. If the couple or their parents are not wealthy, most individuals do not come. They have sports and recreation to attend.

Even family members do not come. If family members do come, they are not there mentally with the couple. What the couple has prepared spiritually for their marriage, no one eats. Family members flatly refuse to eat the dinner, or they throw the dinner in the garbage. Children won't even eat what their mother has prepared on limited funds. There are things, other than food, that Mother has prepared for her children which children and even a spouse will not accept or partake. Children and others laugh about this marriage and make bets that the marriage will not last a year. These uncaring individuals then go back to their jobs and their merchandise. They become busy with their lifestyles while the ones they have hurt become ill with depression.

Some of these couples have been killed because they did not serve at their wedding feast what their children wanted. Most couples are killed spiritually. They withdraw. They wonder, if my children and family are laughing at me and my wedding feast, just how many people really are laughing at us? This couple loses their confidence in themselves and in each other at a time when they must work hardest as a unit. Through self-doubt, these couples lose what self-esteem they had. Marriage becomes a drudgery. No one is happy about their wedding feast, the most important day in their life. It would be very awkward at a wedding if the guests at a wedding did not accept what the bride and bridegroom had prepared for their wedding guests. The bride and bridegroom would be extremely hurt.

When this marriage ends in divorce, the same things happen at another wedding feast in their honor. Since they are angry with family, only friends are invited to the wedding this time. For those who come, there is always someone who does not have the respect for this couple and what they are about to build. They do not dress appropriately for the wedding. They may not even dress appropriately for their own wedding.

The King who blesses all wedding feasts becomes angry. Is he angry with the couple? No! He is angry with the children and people who would not eat what their parents prepared or listen to what parents had to teach children. The King knows. If children will not come or partake of the wedding feast their parents and step parents have provided, children are not going to come and partake of the wedding feast which the King has provided for the world. The King knows that parents cannot prepare other feasts for their children until the first feast is partaken.

It does not matter whether you are married only once or are married many times. The King takes your marriage seriously. The King blesses those who bless the wedding feast of the parents and curses those who curse the wedding feast of the parents. He blesses and curses through the Abrahamic Covenant. Unfortunately, the couple is blamed for the curse which was received from the King, our Heavenly Father.

Individuals do not have to become depressed to control others or manipulate them to their wedding feast. Bribery will not get children to partake of the wedding feast of the King or parents. Parents and step parents, remain steadfast and loyal to each other. Though you will be blamed for the darkness in your family, share the wedding feast that you have prepared with your spouse. There will be enough left over for your guests, your children and step children. There is no need to pay tribute money to your guests. Don't let tribute money set the pace for you and your family and the many blessings waiting for you.

136

Render. Render has many definitions. This is another word that should be looked up in the dictionary. Cooks roast meat to drain the meat of fat and impurities. This is called rendering. Soloists or organists render or deliver to the audience a song. We lave legal tender to render payments for various things. Judges render a verdict.

Parents and step parents all have a marvelous work and a wonder to do with their children and step children. They are to teach their children and step children how to render unto God the things that are God's. Children are in His image. Parents are in His image. Parent and child, step parents and step children are to be rendered to God. We all will be tenderized by God and Christ and their message of peace to their children of the World. Hopefully, both parent and child will present themselves to God in a lifelike image of God, not Satan. We will reach this final day of reckoning or rendering with charity, mercy, and forgiveness.

On the Day of reckoning or rendering, parents may be more than willing to give up their claim or possession on children who cared so little about parents. Neither parent or child has the image of God. They have no agency and refuse to be accountable for their actions. They cannot express themselves in any language very well. Parents and step parents still must deliver an indictment or verdict on how their children and step children received what they taught them. Parents and step parents have to admit there was no cooperation in their family or step family. They do not understand why. Parents may have to admit they did not teach their children how to avoid opposition. They taught their children how to create and experience opposition. Parents may have to admit they did not let the Savior be their children's Savior.

Rendering God's children to God will not be done according to one's artistic notions imaginations, and conceptions. There are principles, covenants, and ordinances in which we render the things that our God's to God. These things would be His children and the families and step families in which they dwell. The entire family will learn how to express their fears, needs, wants, desires, and obligations in this language form. It is the language of God. Parents will render or deliver an indictment or verdict on what they tried to accomplish as a family. Parents and step parents will tell how their children and step children performed according to the laws of God which are communicated to us by prophets.

List the contributions of each member of your family or step family to your family or their family? Are children or step children asking parents and step parents to give them tribute money instead of making an effort in their lives? Are you rendering yourself and your family to God or Satan? Is this why you or a member of your family is depressed?

Do children and step children have respect for the enmity or authority of parents and step parents? Do your children and step children refuse to partake of the King's Feast and also parent's and step parent's feasts? They just want tribute money.

Are parents purchasing things which the prophets and the Savior told us to turn away from to pay tribute to their children and step children? Is the Lord going to bless us when we have disobeyed Him, His prophets, and our parents and step parents?

By now you have learned that you cannot establish meekness if you are paying tributes to children. You are learning that you cannot keep up the pace of tributes. There are ways to make a contribution to our families and step families without always paying them a tribute. There are ways to maintain God's enmity on the Earth without tributes. Revelation is how we learn to contribute to ourselves and our families and step families.

Chapter Fifteen

Revelation, Part I

Tribute Versus Contribution. In the previous chapter, we discussed tributes. In this chapter, we are going to learn how to make a contribution instead of a tribute to our selves and our children and step children. Many individuals have forced us to give them tributes. Revelation teaches us how to make a contribution, something to offer or a way to be included in things in your family or community.

Parents and step parents make many contributions and some tributes in order to raise God's children and to maintain the country and state and home in which they live. Parents and step parents have received revelation or personal disclosures of wisdom from God in prayer or from others to accomplish this task. Our school teachers educate us and our children so that their students have the ability to detect fact from fiction. Our school teachers did not know they were talking about revelation.

Many people are frightened of the word "revelation." They think revelation is just a fancy term to control others by claiming they have had a revelation for us. Actually, revelation is a fancy term for answers to prayers. For those who pray and wait for an answer, they learn how to control themselves. This is why revelation is called personal revelation. There are people who will not accept any kind of limits. They may pray or may not pray. Depending on their behavior, the Lord withdraws His answers to prayer. These individuals are controlled by a lack of personal revelation. They must settle for their own strength, others' generosity, or devices.

Several thousand years before His death, Jesus Christ created this Earth for the time and place for God's children to be tested. The Savior was crucified and resurrected to provide a way back to our Heavenly Father. The Savior provided revelation to prophets in scripture about His Birth, Life, Teachings, and Death Experiences. The Savior has also explained in scripture what is our responsibility in this part of the history of the Earth. The Adversary restrains us from these revelations of our Heavenly Father and the Savior with various temptations. The Adversary also restrains us from the revelations given to our Earthly parents and step parents for our behalf.

Without revelation in our lives, we are not able to come to the knowledge of the truth. This is like having to take a test on material without having the book. Without a way to discern truth, we view evil good, and good evil. Sweet things becomes bitter, and bitter things becomes sweet. Darkness becomes light, and light becomes darkness. Without revelation, families and step families are not meek with each other and themselves. They also do not know where and how to set limits with each other and themselves. Families become neither root nor branch.

We had no intentions of betraying the Savior, our families, and our selves in this manner. So how did this happen? We abandoned revelation as a young teenager for the ways of the world. The ways of the world are very tempting and trying.

The Definition of Revelation. As the word implies, revelation is a revealing to man. This revealing may be a confirmation of what a man or woman suspects, knows, or is seeking to know. In religion, revelation is God's manifestation of Himself and His will to prophets. All men can have revelations about God's will and man's will, not just prophets. Overtime, revelation or God's disclosures to man about Himself and His will for His children has become known as darkness, evil, and bitter. Revelation is the exact opposite. Revelation is light for our lives and is good and sweet. It is not bitter. Revelation does depend upon the source.

The Source of Revelation. The source of revelation is our Heavenly Father, Jesus Christ, and the Holy Ghost. Man has come good ideas. Only God, Jesus Christ and the Holy Ghost know the hearts of all generations to the end of time. God knows how these generations will blend together and what entangles these future generations. Jesus Christ was willing to lay down His life in order for us to have revelation, the way to progress in the middle of opposition.

The Forms of Revelation. There are many good people on the Earth who have good ideas to better peoples' lives. Many conspiring men and women and boys and girls twist these ideas to deceive us, to hurt us, and make large amounts of money. The form of revelation will be dictated by the severity of the lies circulating and how many people these lies are hurting. The form will be determined by the emergencies that are about to happen, by our prayers, and by our faith.

There are many things by which we can be injured. The Lord is not going to request an angel reveal himself every time personal revelation is needed or to keep us from the temptations of the world. This would interfere with our agency. This would also cause too much fear and trembling and arguing in His children. Our Heavenly Father placed us in families and step families instead. Children and step children, if willing, can depend on the disclosures of God to parents and step parents for them until they become of age.

As a member of the Godhead, the Holy Ghost will be the source of most of the revelations to parent and child. He works under the direction of our Heavenly Father and the Savior. These directions or revelations come in a dream, a vision, through our conscience, pondering, and inspiration after prayers. A voice comes from a person that is not seen, but is felt. Impressions come to our conscience.

Many revelations or inspiration comes from our prayers. Prayer is a disclosure to God of our needs, desires, and wants. This is probably why the Lord asks us not to use vain repetitions in our prayers. We pray for specific guidance, not just generally for the day. God's answers to our prayers are God's disclosures to us. His disclosure may be a simple "no," "not now," or "yes." We will be led to where we can obtain more information. As well as impressing ourselves, our Savior will impress others to warn or help us. The Lord has revelations for our emotional emergencies. Most revelations will be handled by a still small voice which has a certain sound or a certain feeling which instructs, directs, and calms us at the same time.

Everyone is entitled to receive revelation or come under the influence of the Holy Ghost. We do this through our conscience. All have been given different abilities. Most of us have been given the chance to develop a conscience. We may want a clear conscience. It is important that our conscience is able to tell good from evil. It is important that our conscience does not become seared. (1 Timothy 1:1-4) Humans often call evil good so their conscience seems clear, but their conscience really matches their desires, ideas, and wants. They cannot discern their Right Hand from their Left Hand because the Holy Ghost is not with them. The Holy Ghost is the spiritual being who helps us discern our Right Hand from our Left Hand. The Holy Ghost can work with us with this knowledge. We do not work against the Holy Ghost.

The Gift of the Holy Ghost. Baptized members of The Church of Jesus Christ receive the Gift of the Holy Ghost. There is a difference between being influenced by the Holy Ghost to make a judgement occasionally, or help someone occasionally, or all the time. When we have the Gift of the Holy Ghost, the Holy Ghost remains with us at all times as a protector and comforter. Gifts of the spirit, or self-esteem, are developed. With the Gift of the Holy Ghost, we learn to minister and be an administrator in The Church of Jesus Christ, sometimes at the same time. Many administrators have been ministered through visiting teaching and home teaching.

Patriarchal Blessing. The Church of Jesus Christ has an office called a Patriarch. Worthy, baptized members who are about sixteen years old receive a patriarchal blessing. This blessing comes to the Patriarch from God through revelation. A member who has received his or her patriarchal blessing receives a copy of the blessing. If we could keep track of the many times that we needed and received personal revelation, we will find that our personal revelations will follow this patriarchal blessing.

Parents and step parents do not have to depend on a change in body mannerisms, especially the involuntary movements that we all have. They can pray about their child and receive revelation. The Lord knew that our spouses, children, and step children who look so beautiful would stare parents and step parents straight in the eyes to control their involuntary movements, and lie. The public can do this, too. No one knows who to believe. Thus, the Lord gave us revelation. It is a skill we need to develop. The skill of revelation will help us understand why some things do not happen they way we dreamed they would. We do not have to inflict unworthy dreams or our anger on a large amount of the population.

The Process of Receiving Revelation. There is a process in receiving revelation. It depends if the situation is an emergency, an educational experience, a desire to change, or a request for help. In an emergency situation, one often hears or feels a voice. The voice pierces you like a trumpet. "Move the car!" "Leave!" "Check on your spouse or children!" "Do not proceed." Many lives have been saved because individuals heeded this voice. They did not know where the impression or the voice came from. Most likely, it was a ministering angel from family members who have passed on.

For all other situations needing revelation, there is a process. *First, no murmuring.* Lay aside your anger so you can feel the Holy Ghost instead of hate and anger. Many will try to stir you to anger so you cannot think of a rational way to solve a problem. *Second,* study and ponder *the information available, especially the scriptures.* Scriptures are going to carry more weight than the Internet, a friend's opinion, a television talk show, or a parent's fear. *Third,* we ask our Heavenly Father in prayer how to respond. When our prayer is answered, we can ask again in prayer to see if we understood His inspiration to us. *Fourth,* we wait in prayer long *enough for the Lord to give us a burning in our bosom to let us know we are right or a stupor of thought to let us know that we are wrong.* Parents and step parents sometimes are given a stupor of thought to know how to guide their children. *Fifth,* we can be right, but the timing is wrong. Individuals, like myself, have acted hastily with a stupor of thought, or we waited two years with a burning in our bosom to respond to a disclosure given to us by the Lord in prayer.

Learn the difference between this burning in your bosom and a stupor of thought. I have learned just as much from both. I have been able to save patients' lives with both. With the stupor of thought, you usually forget the wrong course of action–if you lay aside your anger.

Without faith, we can do nothing. Ask in faith with an honest heart. This process is the spirit of revelation. The Lord works this way to speak peace to your soul. We can learn to speak peace to others, too, through revelation. We can speak peace to our own soul by revelation.

Revelation Follows God's Rules. Revelation from God will follow God's rules, and revelation from man or the Adversary will follow man's or Satan's rules. Satan's revelations are usually no-rules. Man's rules are usually secret combinations which change often to benefit a few. Jesus Christ did not give us a Word of Wisdom, commandments, covenants, principles, and ordinances and then give us permission to go against them. The Holy Ghost who is the Comforter, is not going to disclose to us a way to bring discomfort and harm to others. Everyone, including biological parents, step parents, siblings, and step siblings are entitled to be comforted from the Holy Ghost. The Holy Ghost will not inspire you to eat, sleep, drink, work, play, etc. in a manner that is contrary to the commandments of Jesus Christ to comfort you. It will not even happen once. The Holy Ghost is not going to inspire you to cut your self, to kill your self, to kill others, to rob a bank, to destroy another's reputation, etc., to solve your problems or protect yourself and family from the consequences of your behavior. *In other words, our Heavenly Father did not give people agency and then instruct the Holy Ghost to give other individuals permission to take this agency away from others and from Christ and Himself.*

Stewardship. There is a key to understanding and using revelation. Revelation works by stewardship. A steward is someone who is in charge of the affairs of a household or organization. This is not a new concept for us in this day. There are union stewards on a job site and stewards and stewardesses on planes and trains. Some individuals have received special schooling to care for, teach, be elected to, and employ people. They have added responsibilities to themselves. Doctors, nurses, and other medical staff are stewards for patients for several hours, several times a week. A lifeguard is a steward over us while we are swimming. Parents, and this includes step parents, are stewards of their children and step children until their children and step children become of age.

We only receive revelation or disclosures about the things or people that we have in our stewardship. In other words, I am not going to receive revelation for another's spouse, children, my grandchildren, my son-in-law, employer, my church, my community, and my nation. They are not in my stewardship. I can be honest, kind, charitable, and assist where I can when I can as I meet various individuals in different settings. The Lord has given us the stewardship to help others bear their burdens. We can be wise stewards who help others more than harm them if we just obey the laws of the land and the laws of God.

Repentance. When we make mistakes in our stewardship, revelation stops. Repentance is available so that we can continue to remain under the influence of the Holy Ghost to receive revelation for our stewardship. A stewardship functions more smoothly if one is repentant and humble (tame). Stewardships are difficult if one is unrepentant, stubborn, stiff-necked, hard-hearted, etc.

The Benefits of Revelation. Since revelation or disclosures by God to man are given for the benefit man, there are benefits to revelation given to us. Revelation was the way Moses brought the children of Israel on dry ground through the Red Sea. If Moses can accomplish this through revelation, the Lord can assist us with the mysteries of getting along with a spouse and raising children and step children.

141

First, revelation from the Lord will deliver us from the hand of our enemies, those who would slay us and who would bring our souls to destruction. (Doctrine and Covenants 7:3 - 9) Sometimes, we can be our own worst enemy. *Second,* revelation from the Lord will comfort us in our grief when we discover members of our family and step family are our enemies, and they want to humiliate and destroy us. With revelation and a lot of faith, a step family can be friends again. Daily revelations from the Holy Ghost can put an end to the strife in our families. (Helaman 11:23 - 24) *Third*, we learn knowledge by revelation. Our revelations will not fail us and those we have in our stewardship. (Doctrine and Covenants 9:1 - 14) The most important revelation that we can learn and know is that Jesus is the Christ, the Son of God, and He died for all of us. This revelation will never fail us and our families and step families. *Fourth*, through revelation, we learn how and where to stand in this life. This gives us organization.

Organization. As a nurse, I assisted physicians and other nurses in the change of dressings, insertion of various kinds of tubes, suturing wounds, and cleaning of wounds. Before we started, I gathered bandages of all types, scissors, hemostats, treatment trays, tape, ointments, disinfectant, q-tips, a stand for the clean equipment, and a garbage for dirty dressings and a pan for dirty instruments. The treatment cardex told us what size gloves and gowns the doctors wore. Not all doctors are the same size. Nurses quickly learned to have extra pairs of gloves and gowns at the bedside. We also learned to give the patient a pain medication about twenty minutes before the doctor began. We prepared every needful thing to make a painful experience a little more pleasant for the patient. Some nurses had a few jokes to lighten a tense situation.

One time, when I was helping a doctor who was noted to be stern, he moved the stand as I was opening the outer package of a sterile vial containing some very expensive medication. The vial fell to the floor and shattered. My eyes were as big as silver dollars. I can still remember waiting for him to yell at me. He didn't. I breathed a sigh of relief when he laughed. I laughed a little, too. We then both realized that we had to order more medication. I would have to open a new treatment tray, and we both had to re-gown and re-glove. My patient was lying there with an open incision so I could not leave him to do other work. This doctor and I got to visit while the patient dozed from the pain medication. I found out that the doctor was not as stern as portrayed by other nurses. Many times after this experience, the doctor always spoke to me when he came on to a hospital floor where I was working. *However, I quickly learned to guard that clean stand every time I assisted another doctor or nurse. I even guarded that stand when I was caring for a patient myself. I also realized I needed a stand for the clean things in my life and a receptacle for the garbage that would appear in my life.*

In latter-day revelation, the Lord has asked us to organize ourselves, prepare every needful thing, and establish a house of prayer, a house of fasting, a house of faith, a house of learning, a house of glory, a house of order, a house of God. We are to organize, prepare, and establish our house so that things coming into our house and leaving our house and our salutations to everyone are in the name of the Lord. (Doctrine and Covenants 88:119-120) This is beautiful scripture. Every mother, father, step mother, and step father wish they could do this.

It is difficult to organize a household in a hurried world which has high prices caused by conspiring individuals. This creates extra work for parents and step parents. No one wants to cooperate. Organize yourself with a stand for clean equipment and a receptacle for dirty garbage. *Your stand for your family organization and its supplies is revelation. Your receptacle for garbage is repentance.* The Holy Ghost tells you what supplies to gather, what supplies to discard, what has a more pressing claim, and what can wait. The absence of the Holy Ghost, and you can feel this, will tell you when you need to repent. We cannot organize ourselves by placing clean equipment in the garbage and dirty equipment on our clean stand for use. Parents, especially fathers or a step mother, are not dirty receptacles for the garbage you are carrying.

Two or Three Witnesses. In The Church of Jesus Christ, every word is established to us by two or three witnesses. This includes inspiration as well as accusations. This began in Moses' time. (Deuteronomy 17:6) There are even two nations who testify of Christ for all nations. (2 Nephi 29: 7-9).

Christ continued this law when brothers had faults with each other. (Matthew 18:15 - 16) The law of two or three witnesses continues this day. (Doctrine and Covenants 6:28) I suspect this is why there are three distinct individuals in the Godhead, God, the Father, His Son, Jesus Christ, and the Holy Ghost. These witnesses are one with each other which means they agree. (1 John 5:7 - 8) Can you imagine what the state of the world would be if these three witnesses of Christ and His principles did not agree? How would we believe in Christ? Even the courts of our land (USA) have two witnesses or "it is a my word, against your word situation." Disagreeing witnesses in the courts of our land create havoc in our court system.

When we receive revelation for our stewardship from the Holy Ghost, it usually is confirmed to us a second time several days later that we did the right thing. This may be through a scripture, a hymn, a friend telling you of a similar experience, or the same inspiration is sent after you have calmed. Sometimes, people came to me and told me to try things that I had already tried. In my youth, I misunderstood this as interference. As I matured, I learned this was my second or third witness. I learned to not take offense and now thank them politely.

Creating dissension and stacking witnesses against people we disagree with or do not like is not the law of two or three witnesses. The law of two or three witnesses confirms. This law does not condemn or oppress. I suspect the law of two or three witnesses is the reason God and The Savior hates lies so much. Lies destroy the ones to which God has sent two or three witnesses. False prophets and false prophecies come from stacking false witnesses and condemnation of others with false information. When we work against the law of two or three witnesses, revelation will not be sent by the Holy Ghost.

The Gift of Tongues. The Church of Jesus Christ of Latter-day Saints is also a church that believes in the Gift of Tongues. This is not a new concept. My gift of tongue is English. It is a great gift to be able to speak and interpret in a tongue simultaneously to oneself and to others. It is a greater gift to speak peace to others in times of conflict. Most people do not speak in a foreign language if there is no one in the room with them that cannot understand that language. The Holy Ghost will not speak in a manner that you cannot understand his message. This explains some of the impressions that we have been impressed to give others. Someone in the room or the world will understand your message if this message is given through revelation.

Prophesy. Naturally, prophesy follows revelation. There are many kinds of voices in the world, and none of them is without significance to the Lord. (1 Corinthians 14:1 - 10) Parents and step parents are going to warn their children of many things. It does not take rocket science theory to know in advance that our children will not do well in school or graduate from high school if they do not do any homework , or they attend school sporadically. Usually, we prophesy in anger when we are suppose to prophesy with charity. Our prophecies do not edify, exhort, and comfort. Prophecies which bring peace are going to do the most edifying and be the most comfort. Prophecies that are visions of vanity and anger will not edify us.

We may not realize it. We prophesy through song. Brigham Young did this by asking a young man, William Clayton, to write a song to inspire the saints moving westward. This song is known as "Come, Come Ye Saints." False prophecies can be given through song also. A cute, catchy song can lead many to do wrong in the future. If there is no one around that can understand your gift of tongues or be comforted and exhorted by your prophecies or music, there is a good chance your information or impression came from the Adversary to make you look stupid or lead others from Christ–not to Christ.

Application of Revelation to Families and Step Families. Revelation is the major cause of the problems in step families. Let's review briefly revelation. Revelation is a disclosure about God and man. There is a source from whence true knowledge of God and man comes. It is called revelation. There are different ways we receive revelation. There is a process of receiving revelation which involves no murmuring, studying, pondering, asking in faith, and prayer. We usually feel a burning in our bosom or a stupor of thought. Our revelations will follow God's rules of conduct and His commandments. We must be repentant. Above all, we must have stewardship over the ones for whom we are seeking revelations. Revelation is not a curse. There are benefits to revelation. Two or three witnesses confirm the words of Christ to us.

Since time began, fathers or step fathers of the family are the revelators of the family. Joseph of Bethlehem is a great example. Fathers and step fathers will have more revelations or disclosures on where to live and how to run their family unit than a wife, ex-spouse, children, extended family, employers, and grandparents. If a wife or step mother is doing all the work of the family or step family and working outside of the home, she will have more revelations than the revelator of the family. A revelator who has to work several jobs and is gone from his family for long periods of time may delegate to his wife. The wife and mother will do for the family what she feels impressed to do in certain situations. This is a large burden for a mother or step mother. Your children and step children make many demands of your wife and step mother while father or step father is gone. Her revelations may become mother's intuition or the quickest thing to solve the problem for the moment. Her revelations may not be from the Holy Ghost. She may be reacting to the many burdens placed on her and only be comforted by a talk-show host.

Disclosures to the revelator of the family or step family, the father and step father, will organize you and your family. Without organization by revelation, we often find that we have no family organization because we have not learned to choose priorities. Family members come and go as they please and do what they please. Family members go from one crisis or emotional emergency to another. Children and step children are rescued by parents and step parents constantly. This does not develop faith in Heavenly Father, Jesus Christ, parents and step parents, or even ourselves. Faith is a benefit of revelation.

Children Receiving Revelation for the Family. In a step family, children and step children seem to receive more revelations about their family or step family than parents and step parents. Some parents allow children to decide if a step family can be created. Children and step children who do not know their right hand from their left hand, insist they are the ones that have

144

the best interests at heart for the family and will now make the decisions for the possessions, assets, and siblings of the new step family. They do not call it revelation. Children and step children call it "their rights" to govern their parent, step parent, family, and step family. Natural parents gave up their rights when they married again. Step parents do not have any rights. Children become very angry if parents and step parents do not give-in to their children and step children.

Naturally, none of the children and step children in a family agree. They are not going to allow any power to dominate them. Therefore, they will not and do not intend to follow any revelations of their parents and step parents regarding their own children and assets. Any revelations to parents and step parents are for parents and step parents only. However, children feel parents and step parents do not need revelations. Children are making the major and minor decisions for parents and step parents.

Children and psychiatry feel that step fathers and step mothers could not possibly have the best interest at heart of the entire family. Children do. Children and step children have to be protected from the step parent. It is better to err for the sake of the child. Psychiatry has father presiding over his family and mother presiding over her family to prevent child abuse. Naturally, a house divided cannot stand. If a father and mother tries to work things out with the assistance of the Lord through revelation, step children receive more and better revelations or feelings for their parents, step parents, siblings, and step siblings. Children and step children's revelations always seem to counter the revelations that a biological and step parent receive.

The Source of Revelation. Children and step children determine how assets are dispersed and how their siblings, step siblings, parents, and step parents are disciplined and treated. Children and step children feel they also get to determine how this step family and step parent are recognized in the world. Hence, the many sob stories to neighbors and psychologists. Many of these revelations and prophecies were determined by a step child's fears, anger, and grudges with parents and step parents. These revelations were not sought out of love, gratitude, understanding, forgiveness, mercy, and what was best for the entire step family. They wanted to control their parents and step parents. Their source of revelation was from the Adversary.

The Form of Revelation. The goal of revelation between God and man is to strengthen, guide, and comfort man. The "revelations" that many children and step children receive are to weaken and dishearten parents and step parents. They want to humiliate their parent and step parents for correcting them. They also want their parent and step parent to divorce. Step children's revelations or disclosures drift between their siblings, peers, the neighborhood, and heavy metal music, R-Rated movies, not between parents, step parents, God, and themselves. Their revelations has become gossip.

False Prophecies. Children and step children begin to experience the consequences of this behavior which the Lord calls a cup of iniquity. They experience both the wrath of God and the wrath of parents and step parents. The step parent is quickly blamed for the behavior of step children. As children and step children blame their step parent or parent, many fears are related and embellished to others. Parts of secrets or false prophecies are told to parents, step parents, and others to find out more information, to cause a step parent to look stupid and disorganized, and to lead parents and step parents from the truth. Parents, step parents, siblings, and step siblings usually respond how the child or step child wants parents and step parents to respond to the revelations about them in the neighborhood and family. When parents and step parents become angry, the child or step child has more disclosures and false prophecies for the neighbors.

The Benefits of Revelation. In my nursing career, one doctor would order a heating pad while another doctor ordered an ice pack for the same condition. This became confusing even to the most experienced nurse. When it was my turn to experience the heating pad therapy from one doctor and the ice bag treatment from another, I finally realized why it was done this way. It was not a matter of agency or blood thinners, etc. It was a matter of circulation. The doctor knew when he wanted to increase blood circulation or decrease circulation to an affected area. The physician in charge of our care, the Savior, does the same thing with hot and cold or good and opposition. The Savior increases, but controls the amount of our circulation by the Holy Ghost through revelation. This assures us that with all the many opinions and philosophies in the world, Jesus Christ is not changing, we are. We develop tender shoots, instead of tinder shoots.

Children and step children like to keep parents and step parents out of circulation. When parents and step parents seek revelation about something that is false, there are no benefits to their revelations. There are also no revelations. Parental actions easily become the wrong course of action, resulting in frustration, anger, and feelings of failure. With no revelation, the family is tossed to and fro with everyone's opinions, anger, conspiracies, hurt feelings, and mental fatigue. Disgust and outbursts become their kind of revelation. The assets of families or step families benefit only one member of the family with this kind of revelation. All should receive comfort, inspiration, knowledge, peace, and organization by revelations of parents and step parents.

The Process of Revelation. Children and step children swear they are telling the whole truth and nothing, but the truth. Their revelations or disclosures about their family or step family are so full of truth. Their church leaders, family, psychologist, and neighborhood do not have to pray about their disclosures, the process of revelation. The law of two or more witnesses do not confirm to children and step children and the neighborhood. Children and step children confirm to the two or three or ten witnesses against parents and step parents in many different ways. The step family speaks the same tongue, but their revelations or disclosures cannot be understood with any degree of rational reasoning by parents, step parents, siblings, and step siblings.

Repentance. Children and step children who are not keeping God's commandments and rules of behavior claim they receive more revelation than parents and step parents who do keep God's commandments, pay tithing, have an education, etc. The child or step child's revelations are not for the benefit of the family. Their revelations are about the family or step family. I do not believe the Holy Ghost will give revelations to individuals who are unrepentant about the hurt and dissension which they have created in a step family. These individuals may also be breaking other commandments of the Lord. These individuals are going to be compelled to be humble. (Alma 32:12-16) When they do decide to pray, their revelations are going to be about their own repentance, restitution, and mercy, not about your repentance, behavior, your stewardship, and justice for you.

Stewardship. In all of these situations about revelation for your step family, there is one big problem! *Children and step children do not have stewardship over their family or step family!* This is true if children decide to split the family and become head of a portion of the family which will listen to their revelations to keep some peace in a portion of their family. Even if children and step children's intentions were just and honorable, children and step children will never have more stewardship of the family or step family than fathers or step fathers. This is why we are asked to honor our parents and step parents by the Savior.

A temporary stewardship over minor children may be given to adult siblings by the courts of our land if both parents are deceased. If parents and step parents are married for eternity, their stewardship never ends. The family and step family forms again on the other side of the veil. Even in a civil marriage, the Lord is not going to give us a commandment to honor our fathers and mothers and then allow the Holy Ghost to teach us to dishonor a parent and step parent who are the legal stewards of children and step children. The Holy Ghost is not going to dishonor a father or step father who may have now or will in the future hold the priesthood of God. Remember. God, Jesus Christ, and the Holy Ghost work together.

The Holy Ghost is aware that without revelation and stewardship the words of Christ cannot be preserved in this generation of the family or step family. A generation is about forty years, but includes both parent and child. Most of us will have the experience of a generation as a child and as a parent and grandparent. This was not meant to give us experience in offense and defense, but in receiving and accepting revelation. Without revelation and stewardship, children and step children often manipulate their siblings and step siblings into dishonoring their biological parent as well as their step parent. The Holy Ghost is not going to be manipulated into this kind of mess. For wrong courses of action, the stupor of thought is for us to change, not for the Holy Ghost to change.

Recognizing the stewardship in a family or step family. I have noticed that children and step children recognize a boy-friend or girl-friend of their parent until their parent marries. The dating couple will be recognized or tolerated even if they have committed adultery or fornication with each other or other crimes. Immediately after the marriage, children and step children will not recognize the stewardship of their parents and step parents over children and step children. After a parent and step parent marry, the children are concerned about their behavior and these crimes. Many couples do not marry because they receive more privileges and respect from their children and step children if they do not marry. They are being controlled by children. Eventually, children and step children lose respect for those who they control.

Psychiatry and others may feel that children have more stewardship in a second marriage instead of the parent and step parent. Psychiatrists and psychologists are always telling the step parent to not discipline or make waves with a step child. Lawyers convince parents to put family assets into a child's name. This is false doctrine. The best psychiatrist or psychologist is not going to be able to convince a child to recognize the stewardship of his parent and step parent. The best lawyer cannot protect your assets after a child of age has signed a contract with your assets as collateral. Who has your assets decides who controls your other children as well as you. A biological parent and step parent often wonder if they will ever get to have any stewardship over anything in their second marriage again. You will. Prepare for the day when it comes. (Isaiah 40:31)

Stewardship in Divorce. An ex-spouse often wonders why their ex-spouse is so harsh with their ex-spouse and their children. Divorce has removed the stewardship over an ex-spouse and the family. A feeling of loss appears when this happens even though they wanted the divorce. The parent who retains custody of children receives the stewardship of the family. The family courts in our land have tried to make things fair for fathers and mothers who have divorced, but they cannot restore the stewardship that was once there. In other words, a stewardship of a family cannot be split into pieces. Christ called this asunder. (Matthew 19:6) If children and step children are asked to serve a split stewardship, they will hate the one and despise the other. (Matthew 6:24)

When a spouse remarries, the stewardship which belonged to an ex-spouse is given to another. This increases their sense of loss. Ex-spouses are obligated to pay child support for their children. This is determined in a court of law. Ex-spouses want to support their children. They do not want to support the new spouse of an ex-spouse and their children, especially if their marriage and stewardship was lost by adultery of the one who retained stewardship over the family. Paying child support is not stewardship fees. It is an obligation when one has children.

Expenses in a stewardship of several individuals will be tied together. It does not matter whether you like them or not. With revelation, a former spouse can learn if child support money is spent wisely in this new stewardship. Ex-spouses do not have to ride shotgun on a stewardship in which they are no longer a part. It is normal for an ex-spouse to become jealous of the privileges and time that a new spouse has with his or her children. Ex-spouses are entitled to be comforted from the Comforter, The Holy Ghost, too.

It is not normal or wise to continue to control and cause distress in a previous spouse, their new spouse, and your children with repeated trips to court. This hardens and devours your children. It hardens and devours yourself. An ex-spouse may claim they are looking out for their children, but they really are fighting over a territory which is no longer theirs. Their children become pawns, the ones that are sacrificed to keep the game going. Your ex-spouse may be deliberately spending child support money extravagantly and irresponsibly to anger you. You take your ex-spouse back to court over and over. This controls your children's view of what you really are and is very expensive for the household which you do have stewardship over. There are times when custody needs to be changed. Rely on revelation, not just an attorney's view or your child's anger at not receiving all his whims.

Grandparents. Most grandparents love their grandchildren and are hurt by a divorce in a family. They wonder what rights they have with their own grandchildren. Grandparents can take over the battles between their child and his or her ex-spouse. Grandparents also claim to have concerns about this step family and revelations on how parents and step parents should act or change things. There is just one problem. They also do not have stewardship over this family. Their name is not on the marriage license, and they are not or should not be making the sacrifices for this step family. Children will let grandparents make more of an effort for their grandchildren than children make for their own children. In their love for their children, grandparents forget this new step family has a period of adjustment and will experience the storms of life caused by the Adversary. By experiencing the storms of life, grandparents are wiser, but it is more important this step family learn the wisdom which grandparents have learned. Grandparents, your children and grandchildren learn more by doing–not watching you do.

Adultery. A stewardship works on trust as well as revelation. Adultery affects the stewardship of marriage. Adultery devours everyone, including the stewardship in a marriage. Children cannot learn trust, integrity, and honesty while watching a parent betray his or her spouse. Children get to watch their betrayed parent and grandparents grieve over adultery instead of developing trust. I suspect this is why the Savior told us that adultery is the only reason that we can divorce. A marriage and self esteem are very hard to maintain when the stewardship is lost with continual acts of adultery.

When someone is experiencing adultery in a marriage, personal revelations are very hard to hear and trust. If adultery is continuing, I do not feel any revelations will be coming. This is breaking one of God's commandments. Everyone is angry when this happens. What are children receiving revelations and inspirations about at their age? School, God, friends, and sports. One does not have to receive revelation to play sports. Its part of the natural man and reflexive. It takes revelation, trust, and inspiration to learn what to do about God, school, and friends.

If one sins greatly, such as adultery and murder, stewardships are lost. I have cared for women who knew when their husband committed adultery or crimes. They could feel it. I suspect, they were feeling this loss of stewardship of a husband over a wife and children. It is devastating to be married to a spouse who has no stewardship over the family because of sin.

Death. Death cannot take away the stewardship of their family and step family if a couple is married in The House of the Lord, a temple of The Church of Jesus Christ of Latter-day Saints. If a couple is married for time only, the stewardship is for this life. However, after their deaths a couple may be sealed by proxy to restore this stewardship by family members. They also can join The Church of Jesus Christ and do this work for themselves.

It is interesting to note. Christ has given stewardship to parents and step parents just as His Heavenly Father gave His stewardship of His children to Jesus Christ and stewardship of His Only Begotten Son to Joseph of Bethlehem, a step parent. Christ's death did not end His stewardship over us. It enhanced His stewardship.

Siblings. Parents and step parents often wonder why their children and step children are so harsh with each other. Siblings and step siblings do not have the stewardship to discipline their siblings. They also do not have the patience. Children do have a lot of murmuring between themselves. This bounces us back to the first step in receiving revelation. We will not receive the burning in our bosom or a stupor of thought with murmuring.

Discipline of siblings by siblings is usually loud and harsh, and their discipline carries that uncertain sound of a pipe, harp, or trumpet which the Apostle Paul talked about in the New Testament. When siblings are disciplined and led by siblings, they know they are not obligated to obey their siblings. Siblings just have to redirect the wrath of a sibling from them to someone else. The most likely and convenient ones are the surviving biological parent and step parent. This is how younger siblings control older siblings and their biological parent and step parent.

The child has learned to live by control and dominion. He has not learned what it like to live with authority and revelation from parents and step parents, the leaders of their family or step family. When the good in parents and step parents is unrecognizable, the good of any leader in a church, the community, the state, and the world is unrecognizable. Without revelation, children and step children do not know their left hand from their right hand. It does not help the situation if everyone follows someone who does not know their right hand from their left hand.

Children. If parents and step parents have no confidence in their decisions and become inconsistent, children and step children will detect an uncertain sound in your voice. They will disobey you and laugh at you instead. Children and step children are going to laugh at parents and step parents anyway. Parents and step parents might as well have revelation in their lives.

A child may try to honor his or her two biological parents, a step parent, and the leader of their siblings. However, what usually happens is the ex-spouse, biological parent, step parent, grand parents, and sibling leader never agree on how the child should be cared for, visited, provided for, and disciplined. Children and step children learn to control and limit the stewardship of parents and step parents in self-defense. Children do not learn to manage, control, and enlarge their own stewardship.

Managing a Stewardship. The Lord asks that we be worthy of hire spiritually and temporally (worldly matters) in our stewardships. (Doctrine and Covenants 70:12) This is accomplished by following the Lord's instructions for managing a stewardship. His instructions for stewardships are found in Doctrine and Covenants Section 70 and throughout scripture. These instructions are for everyone. None are exempt from these requirements. This includes biological fathers and step fathers and single women who are head of household because of death, divorce, or marital status. There are things that women are stewards over.

Parents and step parents are to manage their household, its concerns, and benefits. This stewardship is not to be given unto the church or the world. In other words, parents and step parents are the chain of command which receives revelations or inspirations for the family and step family, not children, step children, neighbors, or extended family.

Parents and step parents are stewards over the revelations and commandments given to them. An account of their stewardship will be required in the day of judgment. (Doctrine and Covenants 70:1 - 18) I suspect there will also be an accounting for the stewardships in which we purposely caused mismanagement. Children's siblings and friends will have to account for the times they lead a parent's child astray, diminishing the effectiveness of a parent's stewardship.

Many stewardships receive more than is needful for the necessities of life and our wants, needs, and desires. These things come by the manifestations of the spirit. We are to give the excess to the Lord's storehouse. The benefits shall be consecrated unto the inhabitants of Zion and their generations as they become heirs according to the laws of the kingdom. (Doctrine and Covenants 70:1 - 18) Notice. Our benefits are not to consecrate our boredoms. Your temporal things are to be equal without grudges. Equal in this sense probably does not mean exact, but balanced. Otherwise, the abundance of the manifestations of the spirit shall be withheld. What is a manifestation? A revelation or a disclosure.

The Lord wants us fulfill our stewardships in His way. Why? There are more benefits coming from more manifestations of the spirit due to our diligence and for our security. There are more problems coming that we cannot foresee, but the Lord can. We need to know how to organize the Lord's blessings and ourselves. Manifestations will be given for our food, clothing, inheritances, houses, and our lands. Many disclosures will be given for the many circumstances we are placed in. If we are faithful over many things, have done well, and have not sinned, the Lord is merciful and will bless us. (Doctrine and Covenants 70:1 - 18) The Lord will also teach us how to manage many blessings.

We do not mature by limiting or eliminating someone's stewardship. We do not mature by cutting off someone's access to the Holy Ghost. This enlarges wounds. We extend our borders, or mature, by fulfilling our own stewardships and allowing others the chance to mature by fulfilling their stewardships. First, we must let others, including parents and step parents, have a stewardship. The Lord knows when we are ready to extend our borders and will give us a stewardship that we can handle. This maturity and these changes happen by revelation and a lot of work and faith.

Mocking of Revelation. Near the time of His Crucifixion, our dear Savior was mocked and blindfolded. He was hit and then asked to prophesy who hit him. (Luke 22:63 - 64) Parents, step parents, teachers, and even nations have been treated the same way. The perpetrators use spit wads, stones, or bullets. Their victims, their parents and step parents get to guess who mistreated them. This are many ways by which revelation is mocked in the world.

The Lord can give victims revelation about their food, clothing, houses, inheritances, and their lands. He gives inspiration for deliverance from our enemies and for improving family relationships. Yet, there are many who deny the revelations of the Lord. They say the Lord no longer works by revelation, by prophecy, by gifts of tongues, by healing, by miracles, or by the power of the Holy Ghost! If the Lord no longer works this way, why is the Holy Ghost then a part of the trinity in most Christian religions? Is the Holy Ghost, The Comforter and The One who teaches how to discern things, going to be dormant for over 2000 years? I don't think so.

We who do not know our right hand from our left are trying to turn the right hand of God unto the left. (3 Nephi 29:6 - 9, <u>The Book of Mormon</u>) There are revelations, prophecies, gifts, healings, speaking with tongues, and interpretation of tongues which manage the stewardship of Jesus Christ. These same principles will help us manage our stewardships. They are recorded in scripture. This is how God is the same yesterday, today, and forever, and in him there is no variableness neither shadow of changing? (Mormon 9:7 - 10, <u>The Book of Mormon</u>) We do not have to create a god who varies to cover our sins, pride, opinions, and failures. There is repentance. We cannot heal our land, ourselves, and our families with false prophecies, a twisted gift of tongues, a twisted interpretation of tongues, without knowledge, and without revelation. We cannot heal our land by mocking the many stewardships which were created in the Lord's chain of command, namely parents and step parents.

The Lord did not give us the burden of a stewardship which includes fighting against powers, principalities, rulers of the darkness of this world, against spiritual wickedness in high places and tell us to tough it out *and support them all. It may not seem like it, but even the Apostle Paul reminded us that we wrestle not against flesh and blood.* (Ephesians 6:12) The Apostle Paul reminds us: "For I am persuaded, that neither death, nor life, nor angels, nor principalities, nor powers, nor things present, nor things to come, nor height, nor depth, nor any other creature, shall be able to separate us from the love of God, which is in Christ Jesus our Lord. (Romans 8:38 - 39) The Lord remains connected with us through revelation.

Teaching About Revelation. Most of our revelations or inspirations will come through prayer and a still small voice that answers these prayers. Teaching children about prayer and repentance teaches them about personal revelation. This is why we are to teach our children and step children to pray and to repent. This is why so many people do not want us to pray and have succeeded in passing laws against prayer. It makes you wonder: What are these individuals who are opposed to prayer a part of that they do not want us to know the truth? Why do they not want us to learn how to make decisions for our selves, or receive help in the various situations in the world. Prayer and personal revelation do help us overcome the evils of this world.

Remember. The Holy Ghost cannot answer vain repetitions. There is nothing to answer or confirm. Teach your children and step children the difference between sincere prayer and vain repetition. If a child always needs to pray about his own behavior and repentance, he does not receive inspiration about other things in his life. Prayer is a vain repetition if it does not come from the heart. Your child will stop seeking revelation without answers to his vain repetitions.

Ministering Angels. Revelation can come directly to a few individuals from angels. However, the Lord has many children who need help managing their stewardship. Most of us will receive help for our stewardship from ministering angels and the Holy Ghost. The amount of their help is determined by our faith and humility. Prophets have seen these ministering angels in vision. (1 Nephi 11:30) The Priesthood of Aaron contain the keys of the ministering of angels. (Doctrine and Covenants 13:1) Since there are so many people in the world now, I suspect our ministering angels are a beloved brother, father, or grandfather who has passed away and who holds the priesthood of Aaron. This is why we feel at times family members who have passed away around us. This is one of the reasons why members of The Church of Jesus Christ seal families in temples, and fathers are given the Melchizedek Priesthood after they have passed away. If worthy and the individual accepts this work done on his behalf, your family members are allowed to make a contribution to the work of the Lord and their families again.

Sadducees and Pharisees argued with each other whether their were visions, angels, and resurrections. Prophets have testified there were visions, angels, and resurrections. In Acts 2:14 - 16, the Apostle Peter reminded us that the prophet Joel told us in the last days the Lord would pour out his spirit upon all flesh. Your sons and your daughters shall prophesy, your old men shall dream dreams, your young men shall see visions: Upon the servants and upon the handmaids in those days will I pour out my spirit. "Whosoever shall call on the name of the Lord shall be delivered." (Joel 2:28 - 32) The Lord will tell us how to handle the problems of the last days by revelation in dreams, inspiration, and visions to men and women, sons and daughters. Many ideas and inventions have come from these dreams, prophecies, and from calling upon the Lord. Lives are improved or saved by revelation and prophecy. Whether the Lord sends an angel to Earth depends on your stewardship and the angel's stewardship.

Church leaders such as bishops feel the absence of their stewardship and ministering angels when they are released from their calling. For awhile, the congregation feels the absence of a released stewardship, but they soon feel the stewardship and ministering angels of their new bishop. I suspect the grief that children experience in a divorce is the absence of the stewardship of their father and mother. Children feel the absence of this stewardship even though they see their divorced parent often. I suspect children also feel a change in their ministering angels, too.

A family ministering angel can be a step parent, too. New ministering angels would be assigned to children and step children as they join a step family. This keeps a step family within the new stewardship of a parent and step parent. (Exodus 23:20) If inspiration is not wanted, these angels will be assigned to minister to others who will allow them to comfort them.

Children and step children are angry after a death or divorce has occurred in their family. Children do not want the revelations, administrations, and ministrations of their parents and step parents, especially after their parent and step parent has committed adultery or other crimes. They do not care if they have repented. At best, children view revelations, authority, and service by parents and step parents as interference or control. To control their parent or step parent, children and step children will not recognize or allow others to acknowledge the stewardship of their parent and step parent. When this happens, children do not recognize their own stewardship. Power struggles replace stewardship for parents and step parents, children and step children.

Children and step children usually do not want the ministrations and revelations that come to parents and step parents by ministering angels. It is no wonder our children and step children are tossed to and fro with the philosophies and conspiracies of men and women, boys and girls, and the propaganda that peer groups try to sell to each other. Some of these men and women, boys and girls are siblings. It is interesting to note. Children and step children do not view the wicked ways of their siblings and peers as interference. It would not be interference if all siblings and your child's peers were part of the conspiracy to destroy or reduce the effectiveness of their parent's and step parent's stewardship

Parents and step parents often do not seek their own revelations regarding their personal stewardship. They are too angry, or they are too busy reacting to outside interference and the revelations of others for their stewardship. With their anger and doubt, parents and step parents could not determine the difference between a burning in their bosom, a stupor of thought, or that voice that moves you like a sudden, sure sound of a trumpet. No one would listen anyway.

A family ministering angel is there to comfort you and may be a deceased brother, parent, or grandparent. They will not impress you to cut yourself or humiliate yourself or others. The individuals who you want to hurt or control may be in the same stewardship of your family administering angel. Fathers and grandfathers did not like to witness fighting and backbiting among their loved ones on Earth. They do not want to hear it when they have passed on. I can think of nothing more distressing than to not be able to abide the presence of God as well as our ministering angels, a beloved grandfather, father, or brother. (Doctrine and Covenants 67:13)

Angels. The Lord is able to do his own work, but He has shared the work of the world with angels. These angels are mentioned in The Book of Revelation. Even Satan admits there are angels in Heaven who have charge concerning the Savior. (Matthew 4:6) Since angels seem to accompany many of our revelations, and there are now individuals in this world who claim angels told them to commit crimes, let's learn to distinguish a real angel from the Adversary or an hallucination.

Many years ago, a fourteen year old boy, Joseph Smith, discovered much about revelation when God, the Eternal Father, and His Son, Jesus Christ, paid a personal visit to him. After reading James 1:5, Joseph Smith prayed to know which church was true. He received a Heavenly Visit from our Heavenly Father and His Son, Jesus Christ. Our Heavenly Father introduced His Beloved Son, Jesus Christ, and allowed Him to speak. The Adversary tried to prevent this visitation. Joseph now knew that God and Jesus Christ did exist, and they communicated with man. Joseph knew the feeling of the presence of His Heavenly Father, and His Son, Jesus Christ. Joseph also discovered the feeling of the presence of the Adversary. This knowledge led to many other questions and revelations. These feelings are what we learn by ministering angels and the Holy Ghost. Our parents and step parents can tell us of their experiences, but we must learn for ourselves the difference between the Left and Right Hands.

After his experience with the adversary, I often wondered how Joseph was so completely trusting of the Angel Moroni. How did Joseph Smith know the Angel Moroni was from God? Joseph recognized the same peaceful spirit. I suspect at the time of the First Vision, Jesus Christ told Joseph that an angel would come to teach him the gospel. Christ taught Joseph Smith how to recognize an angel sent from God. This is one of the things which Joseph Smith has shared with the world.

1 THERE are two kinds of beings in heaven, namely: Angels, who are resurrected personages, having bodies of flesh and bones—
2 For instance, Jesus said: Handle me and see, for a spirit hath not flesh and bones, as ye see me have.
3 Secondly: the spirits of just men made perfect, they who are not resurrected, but inherit the same glory.
4 When a messenger comes saying he has a message from God, offer him your hand and request him to shake hands with you.
5 If he be an angel he will do so, and you will feel his hand.
6 If he be the spirit of a just man made perfect he will come in his glory; for that is the only way he can appear—
7 Ask him to shake hands with you, but he will not move, because it is contrary to the order of heaven for a just man to deceive; but he will still deliver his message.
8 If it be the devil as an angel of light, when you ask him to shake hands he will offer you his hand, and you will not feel anything; you may therefore detect him.
9 These are three grand keys whereby you may know whether any administration is from God.

Doctrine and Covenants 129:4 - 9

It is interesting to note. The Angel Gabriel and the Heavenly Hosts who announced the birth of the Savior and sang praises to God followed this pattern. Jesus Christ was the first Resurrected Being. The Angel Gabriel and the Heavenly Hosts were just men made perfect. They gave their message and left. (Matthew Chapter 1 and Luke Chapter 2) *Their message was a message to help, comfort, or praise, not a message to harm, to discourage, or to cause murmuring. In this temporal world, you do not have to be dead to receive a handshake from which you feel nothing. Just ask a step parent or a divorced spouse.*

In this life, we learn the principles of healthy bodies and healthy spirits. Our spirits will become whole with the things we learned in our lifetime. Our physical bodies will become perfected at our resurrection. It does not do us any good to have a whole body with a sick spirit at the time of our resurrection. If we did not learn much, we will not become whole. If this happens, we most likely will be in the Second Resurrection. We accomplish the task of healthy bodies and healthy spirits by revelation.

Are you aware that as a joint-heir with Christ you are entitled to revelation about your life, ministry, problems, etc.? If you have received personal revelation, you will experience trembling moments–aha moments. Does the word "revelation" scare you so much that you or family members call revelation evil and bitter? Are children replacing parental revelations for family with their false prophecies? Are children receiving "revelations" for your stewardship of your family or step family? Do they have stewardship of the family? Learn the difference between burning in your bosom and stupor of thought. Your family will learn from both.

Chapter Sixteen

Revelation, Part II

Revelation to the Women of The Church of Jesus Christ and the World. In this chapter, I would like to tell you about the revelation given to Emma Hale Smith, wife of Joseph Smith. I feel this is a revelation that can bring comfort to the mothers and step mothers of the world. This is why I call it a revelation for the women of the world. This revelation certainly has inspired me in some difficult times. Step parents can relate very easily with Emma Hale Smith.

Emma Hale Smith fell in love and married a young man who was directed to gold plates which became The Book of Mormon. Emma married Joseph Smith against her parents' wishes and walked into a very difficult life. After their marriage, Joseph's name was always had for good and evil, mostly evil. Employment for Joseph Smith was hard to find because of Joseph's reputation. Many members in society felt they had to teach Joseph some very difficult lessons violently. No woman wants her husband, herself, and her family to be treated or viewed this way. Even Emma wondered about The Church of Jesus Christ which Joseph was trying to reestablish on the Earth. This was no small task for Joseph Smith and his family. It was not a task that he sought out. He was only fourteen years of age.

In all the commotions surrounding her husband, Emma never got to be head of her own kitchen. She usually lived in another's home because Joseph could not find work, for Joseph to work on church business, or for safety reasons. Joseph did not inform Emma of many church matters. He was gone for long periods of time, and Emma did not know where he was. Joseph was even in prison. Several of Emma's children died of exposure in violence against the Smiths. The Lord gave this revelation to Joseph Smith to give to Emma to comfort her.

In this revelation, the Lord tells Emma to be faithful and virtuous. As a reward, the Lord would preserve her life, and she would have an inheritance in Zion. Emma's sins were forgiven. The Lord called her an elect lady. The Lord asked Emma to not murmur because she was not informed of the things that were going on at the time and for not being shown the Golden Plates. (Doctrine and Covenants 25:1-4)

Emma was told to be a comfort to her husband in his afflictions and to console him with meekness. Emma was Joseph Smith's first scribe when he was translating the plates that became The Book of Mormon. She acted as a scribe for Joseph when Oliver Cowdery, Joseph's scribe, was traveling on church business. I imagine it was exciting. However, her excitement lasted a short time. Emma needed to fix meals for Joseph, change diapers, and bathe their children, too. Emma could explain the scriptures to others under Joseph's guidance, and she could exhort the church as prompted by the Spirit. Emma was given the Gift of the Holy Ghost by her husband, but she was told to receive this gift. Receive means to accept or acquire something or someone such as visitors. A host or hostess receives visitors or patrons.

In all this, Emma was told not to fear. Her husband would support her in the church. Through her husband, Joseph Smith, all things would be revealed, according to the Lord's will and everyone's faith. Emma was asked to lay aside the things of this world and seek for the things of a better world. (Doctrine and Covenants 25:-10)

Emma was asked to make a selection of sacred hymns for church services. The Lord told her, "For my soul delighteth in the song of the heart; yea, the song of the righteous is a prayer unto me, and it shall be answered with a blessing upon their heads." (Doctrine and Covenants 25:11-12) Emma did make that selection of hymns for The Church of Jesus Christ of Latter-day Saints. These hymns were and continue to be a blessing to many in their trying circumstances. These hymns have soothed many broken hearts and frazzled nerves.

Emma was told to cheer up, rejoice, and cleave unto the covenants which she had made. Emma was to continue to be meek and to beware of pride. The Lord told her to delight in her husband and the glory he would be receiving. She was told to keep the Lord's commandments continually, and she would receive a crown of righteousness. The Lord warned: "And except thou do this, where I am you cannot come." (Doctrine and Covenants 25:2 - 15)

Notice. Emma was told to delight in her husband, and his glory which shall come upon him–not her children or herself. (Doctrine and Covenants 25:14) Emma heard many unkind things, lies, and gossip about her husband. It must have broken her heart and wore her down. I have often wondered if Emma wondered who to believe. After Joseph was killed, Emma's life was preserved. Emma remarried. Her remarriage formed a step family.

The step family experience is similar to Emma's experiences. Step parents marry with the same unrealistic expectations that all couples have. They often marry against the objections of their parents and children. Step parents hear many things about their spouse. The parent and step parent try to make a life centered around their children and soon discover this is not possible. Step parents have many fears and concerns for their own safety and the safety of their children and step children. Step parents hear many stories about their step children and spouse. Step parents do not know who to believe. The neighborhood hears many stories about step families. The husband in the step family receives no glory. Employment maybe hard to come by, or the father or step father works three or more jobs. He receives no thanks.

The only glory that a father or step father will receive is the organization that his wife brings to their household. The same is true for a step mother. The only glory that she will receive comes from the organization that a husband brings to the home. The Lord gave Emma many ways to ease her anxieties and be a part of Joseph's life. We can ease our depressions and anxieties with the same methods which Emma was given to relieve her depressions and anxieties.

Since Emma was told she could expound on the scriptures under Joseph's direction, I suspect she included Doctrine and Covenants 88:119. Others may deliver more plagues and sunshine to you than is necessary for you to learn by God and opposition, but they cannot take your prayers, fasts, faith, learning, glory, order, and house of God from you. They cannot take your song in your heart from you. Only you can give it up or refuse to develop these things by ignoring or mocking revelation from God and by murmuring.

A Revelation to the Men of The Church of Jesus Christ and the Men of the World. Your marriage is a stewardship of two, a man and a woman. Both of you are to organize yourselves and prepare every needful thing so you can establish a house of prayer, faith, learning, glory, and order. (Doctrine and Covenants 88:119) Naturally, there are revelations to gather the men of The Church of Jesus Christ and the men of the world as well as the women of The Church of

Jesus Christ and the world. The men of The Church of Jesus Christ will always be gathered physically and mentally under the priesthood, either Aaronic or Melchizedek. There are revelations for the priesthood which are found in the <u>Doctrine and Covenants</u> Sections 42 and 102. They are worth reading.

There is a revelation for all men of the world to comfort them, too. It is found in this verse. This verse is preceded by the verse telling us about a commandment to love one another as I have loved you. (John 15:12) There are compensatory blessings for you.

Greater love hath no man than this, that a man lay down his life for his friends.

John 15:12 - 13, <u>The Holy Bible</u>

Men, if you do not lay down your life for your family, you will be ambushed. I am not talking about your mortal life, although some men have been ambushed. I am talking about those teenage dreams of yours. You know the ones. You are going to be a millionaire by thirty. You will always be the hero of the team. You will make the last second touchdown or hoop to win the game. You are going to have the body of Adonis. The girls will fall all over you. You are going to marry a rich wife or a younger wife who will work so you can retire by the pool side. If you succeed at these kinds of dreams, you will be ambushed, and your family will be ambushed also. You may feel the attacks on you and your family come suddenly and without warning. You have been warned by many prophets. You may feel that nothing will hurt you, or you are tired and need a break. There are many things that will hurt you. I have cared for many mothers and fathers who have been ambushed by the things they thought would not hurt them.

At this time, I am going to add a few things to the birds and the bee talk that your parents probably tried to give you many years ago. This is not from a preacher's point of view. It is from a nurse's point of view. I tell you these things because you would expect me to act professionally as a nurse. If you were hemorrhaging from a leg wound, you would expect me to put pressure on that wound, not strong-arm you, play games with your mind, or isolate you.

Men may not know how to express it, but men feel and know when they are neither root nor branch, too. Men are affected deeply by the things going on in their home and place of employment. Men would like to know what is going on. Parents, wives, children, siblings, friends, employers, and governments are skillful in communicating this disconnected feeling to sons, husbands, fathers, brothers, friends, employees, and fellow citizens. You may feel they do this because they are angry or jealous with you. They want to make money off of your efforts.

I have been head of household for a while. I cannot think of anything more frustrating after having worked ten to twenty hours a day at two jobs to come home and to find a wife or child who is pouting over something you said two weeks ago. Dinner is not fixed. The house is not clean. The lawn is not mowed. Homework is not done. Your children are lazy and truant at school. Your wife has been watching soap operas and videos all day. Your wife or child may be back to sleeping twenty-two hours a day like an infant because they are depressed and angry. Wives may have been out shopping again. Your children are probably using alcohol and drugs.

To add insult to injury, your employer brings in out of state workers to fix the machines that you have been working on for years or may have built for the employer. These out of state workers receive the expensive overtime, benefits, and retirement which your family needs. Your employer cannot or will not pay benefits for both in state and out of state workers. Your employer can afford the cost of private suites for the many sports teams which are in your area.

As head of household, you know that you cannot afford the furniture, figurines, junk, clothes, and court costs for wife and children who insist on buying something every time they are angry, bored, or have an emotional emergency. You feel like you should work three or more jobs, and often you do. This feeling waxes old quickly. Intimacy and romance is not the same under these circumstances. Men suffer from high blood pressure and become depressed.

Your family doctor will give you a medication for high blood pressure and may give you anti-depressants. Both husband and wife may be receiving anti-depressants. Both may self-medicate with street drugs or alcohol. Several drug addicts or their wives have told me that street drugs destroyed their sperm counts. All anti-depressants and mood elevators have side effects. The most common side effects are weight gain, muscle and joint pain, impotence, and pancreatitis. Women gain weight in their hips and thighs and have no desire for sex. Men gain weight in the abdomen. The diploma nurses who trained me told me the worst place for a man to gain weight is around the layer of fat called The Great Omentum in the abdomen. This weight puts more strain on the heart. It affects your breathing. This weight in this layer of fat is near a large blood supply where cholesterol, as well as other chemicals, can be readily absorbed or stored. In all of our medical discoveries, we still do not know the complete role that cholesterol plays in our bodies and how all of the chemicals which we insist on ingesting affect our bodies.

As your weight increases, the same dosage of anti-depressant does not work. Your depression increases, and your self-esteem decreases. Dosage strengths are increased and different types of medications are added. You are working and experiencing these things for a wife, biological children, and step children who seem to have no concern for you. As your anger increases, you first began to think that for this I went to twelve years of schooling and four years of college or trade school. Men begin dreaming about what they thought they would be experiencing in marriage, the sexual experiences which they are missing or which are not as great as Hollywood portrays.

Women read soft-porn romance novels with steaming chapters of sex. Males resort to pornography in magazines, videos, and the internet. Both are using these things as a replacement for the normal intimacy of their marriage. The couple's intimacy does not improve because they have substituted something very bitter for a special part of marriage. If you think your children do not know that you are using pornography as a way of escape or entertainment, you are wrong. They are too knowledgeable with the computer. All of your family become entrapped and repeatedly ambushed by your way of escape–pornography.

Spiritual Anorexia. Both husband and wife are using anorexia and bullimia as a way to solve their marital problems. Their example causes or forces their children to be anorexic and bullimic, too. Individuals may want you to be anorexic so they can be bullimic. Children and step children can force parents and step parents to be anorexic and bullimic. Girls begin with appetites. Boys begin with no desire to learn and a desire for an increase in muscle mass and sports. Of course, they need an income, too. We have become a nation who is bullimic over sports to avoid an education, spiritually, emotionally, and intellectually. Bullimia, an excess appetite and then disgorging to counter the effects of gorging, has the same effect on your personality as it does your body. In other words, there is a physical and spiritual side to bullimia and anorexia. Your personality becomes irregular just like your heart becomes irregular.

There are people with money and businesses who sit in board rooms discussing new products for the world to buy through their expensive, private cliques. We use to think they were thinking of our benefit. After conversations that I have overheard on cell phones, I realized these businesses are keeping track of what you want, what you buy, where you travel, how you travel, what sports teams are nearby, if these teams are losing at the time of your traveling, and most of all what you are missing because of your depressions and the drugs and alcohol that you are using. Oil companies have the market on gas prices where you travel, how much you can heat your home, and the cities where large conventions are held. We will never know what their profits are funding. Other businesses have the market on the things you are missing because you are on anti-depressants, alcohol, or street drugs. These businesses are tracking your age, too.

There are companies that know you are missing sex because of impotence, dysfunction in your marriage, or you are working two or three jobs. The products of other companies which they own may have caused the dysfunction and impotence of your family. These companies take advantage of your fatigue, your generosity, your age, and your dysfunctions. They have clever substitutes for your pain. Their products are suppose to compensate for a lack of education, a lack of communication skills, a lack of sex, and boredom in one's life. Companies even have multiple ways of dealing with pornography, alcoholism, and drug addiction. They add more pornography, alcoholism, and drug addictions.

Our Testing. When you were in school, your teachers usually assigned you a project or term paper due at the end of the school year. Your grade depended on how many things from the class course that you included in your project or term paper. Many do not believe it, but this life is a test for us. Marriage is the class and the project that includes everything our Heavenly Father gave to us to succeed at marriage, not fail at marriage. He gave us scriptures and prophets and His Only Begotten Son. He wants us to pass the test, not invent or buy more products which harm and humiliate us.

If you are familiar with Christ and The Holy Bible, you know there is a New Testament in The Holy Bible. Marriage is a part of this New Testament. In your New Testament, wives do not control their husbands with pouting like they did their parents. Wives cannot decrease their stress by spending sprees. There is no room for an eye for an eye justice in the New Testament or your marriage. Men have physical structures to work long hours at heavy duty, not women. A woman's structure is for bearing children. Men will never be happy if they retire, and their wife works for the benefits of the family. The New Testament of marriage is not a relationship like you had with your mother. You do not need another mother. You already have one.

Someone has to toil for the family money. Many people fight over your family money. They scare men by telling you that you must save a million or more dollars for retirement. Many men are trying to do this. Every catastrophe in the world is used as an excuse to take a larger portion of your savings and increase your property values which increases your property taxes. Interest rates climb. We do not know who and what the profits of your labors are financing. Husband and wife are trying to control the shape of their family by being anorexic or bullimic in all aspects of their marriage. Anorexia and bullimia does not work in dieting or marriage. Saving money for others to steal from you, and it is stealing, is not the principle of saving.

Marriage works best if you learn as many skills as you can before your marriage. These skills can be combined in many different ways for your marriage as well as your employment. Your Heavenly Father knows you. *He will support and give to you your noble and worthy dreams and desires of your heart. It usually comes after the children have left home. Work smart. Dream smart. Subdue your dreams so you can have noble dreams.* Your dreams as well as your prayers should not be vain repetitions so the Lord can bless you.

If your wife and children are struggling, give your family direction in family home evening. Tell your family of the dreams that you have laid down for something that had a more pressing claim–them. Give your family things to accomplish daily, weekly, monthly, and yearly as well as praise and sports. This is why fathers are in charge of family home evenings. You are the provider, the protector, and the revelator for the self esteem and the physical needs of the family. Wives, let your husbands develop their agency by accepting direction. If mother cannot follow directions from her husband, then your children and step children will not follow the directions given to them from their father or step father.

Many problems occur in your home because your wife and children do not know how to cook satisfying food. Their appetites control them and you. They should be controlling their appetites, not controlling others with anorexia or bullimia. This sets the stage that all aspects of personality, conflict, and marriage, and family will be controlled by insatiable appetites. Husbands and wives, do not be controlled or ambushed by sex and pornography. *Do not substitute revelation in your family with pornography, anorexia, and bullimia.* If you do, you will always dream of what might have been with what cannot ever be. There will be no peace for you. You will regret it. *Remember. Personal revelation is not the same as personal agency nor personal glory.*

Do you seek revelation or assistance from God for your problems within your self, family, or step family? Are you familiar with the source of revelation, the forms of revelation, and the process of revelation? How are you persuaded to abandon assistance from the Lord which comes through revelation? Does your personal revelations benefit you and your stewardships?

Again I ask: Do you have stewardship for those whom you seek revelation? Can you recognize the stewardship of others? Do you recognize your own stewardship? Has your stewardship been stolen from you? Have you stolen the stewardship of others with your high school dreams? Have you given your stewardship to the church or the world, such as children, step children, and neighbors, and creditors?

Are you worthy of hire? Are your dreams noble? Do your dreams create anorexia and bullimia in your spirit? Do you control others, especially your parents and step parents, with anorexic and bullimic attitudes?

Does your song in your heart match your beliefs? Do you have an idea how to make a contribution to society when so many are working against you and the family unit you are trying to build and care for?

Chapter Seventeen

Revelation, Part III

John, The Revelator. We cannot discuss the gift of revelation without discussing The Book of Revelation, written by John, The Revelator. The book of Revelation is found at the end of The Holy Bible, King James Version. It was written by the Apostle John by commandment to bear witness of Jesus Christ.

The Apostle John asked Christ if he could tarry on Earth and have power over death to bring many souls unto Christ until Christ came again. Christ gave John the righteous desires of his heart. John would prophesy before nations, kindred, tongues, and people. (Doctrine and Covenants 7: 1 - 8) Since John would prophesy till the end of time, it is logical that John would write the history of the world. Other prophets have seen what John saw. They were told that an apostle named John would write the history of the world. (1 Nephi 14:17 - 30) Since John asked to remain alive till Christ tarried, I suspect that John was given a tour of the events that he would be seeing or experiencing for many years. John would know which seal was opened at all times.

We do not know the year, but John is exiled to the Isle of Patmos for preaching the word of God. John is in the spirit one day and hears behind him a great voice, like the sound of a trumpet. This sound of a trumpet was not necessarily loud, but it was piercing, such as truth. John's vision is one large vision or revelation about Jesus Christ and things which must shortly come to pass. The angel bears testimony of the word of God, of Jesus Christ, and of the things John saw. John was told to write a book and send it to the seven churches which are in Asia. Descendants from members of these seven churches live all over the world.

John turned to the sound of the voice. He saw seven golden candlesticks. The seven golden candlesticks represent the seven churches. In the midst of these seven churches, was the Son of God. Ths Son of God had in his right hand seven stars. Out of his mouth went a sharp two edged sword. I suspect the seven stars are the prophets over the seven dispensations of time. It is possible The Stick of Judah (The Holy Bible) and the Stick of Joseph (The Book of Mormon) are the edges of the sword. (Revelation 1:11-20; Ephesians 6:17; Hebrews 4:12) Mercy and justice would come from these two edges of the sword carried by Jesus Christ.

I have often wondered if the Menorah represents these seven golden candlesticks or seven churches mentioned in the first part of Revelation. The tallest part of the Menorah would represent Jesus Christ. I know there are stories that the Menorah is in commemoration for a time a priest had an amount of oil for the temple for only one day. Through a miracle, the oil lasted seven days. If you think about it, the Menorah does represent oil for seven days, but in God's time. His days are a thousand years, and John tells about the oil that Christ has over these seven periods of time, called seals. The oil comes from plagues as well as the blessings and revelations in our life.

John's book contains his vision concerning a door in heaven opening, seven seals that only Jesus Christ is worthy to open, four horses, earthquakes, wars, seven stars, seven vials of plagues, eating a book, the pre-existence, the events both good and bad from beginning of time to the end of time, beasts, harlots, Satan bound, the final judgement, and the celestial glory that can be attained if we repent.

The Book of Revelation is not written chronologically with the other books of The Holy Bible. I suspect the Book of Revelation was placed at the end of The Holy Bible so one could compare all the events which happened prior to John's vision as well as after John's writing of his vision. John ends his book by saying: "Blessed *are* they that do his commandments, that they may have right to the tree of life, and may enter in through the gates into the city." (Revelation 22:14) "For I testify unto every man that heareth the words of the prophecy of this book. If any man shall add unto these things, God shall add unto him the plagues that are written in this book: And if any man shall take away from the words of the book of this prophecy, God shall take away his part out of the book of life, and out of the holy city, and from the things which are written in this book." (Revelation 22: 18 - 19)

There has been much debate and fear over these two verses. We are thinking take from or add to John's manuscript. I suspect these verses mean to take from or add to people. Families and step families like to add plagues, too much rain, hate, justice, and injustice to each other, when sun, love, and mercy are due. Parents and step parents like to take away plagues with excessive efforts and money for and to children. Parents and step parents add so much sun. The children are not receiving sun. They are receiving too much heat. Too much water will not compensate for too much heat. In these conditions, children and step children do not produce fruit like a plant would normally do. When a plant receives too much water, it produces too much vine and little fruit. Children do, too.

The ridiculous behavior, isolation, intimidation, manipulation, and secrets by step children and biological children add plagues to biological parents and step parents. Removing these plagues bring more plagues to both parent and child. These plagues come at the time when parents and step parents are scheduled to have authority in the world by becoming parents to maintain the chain of authority of God to man till the end of time. There is that chain of command again. A mother may be pregnant, nursing a child, sick, or elderly when her children and grandchildren trifle with sacred things and give their mother and grandmother more plagues.

There is a point which every generation reaches. The Lord does not let parents and step parents go pass this point. Parents and step parents begin to notice that all the blessings and efforts of parents and step parents do not help their children. The efforts of the best psychiatrists and best lawyers will not help. This is the time for children to make an effort with revelation in their life. Learn to recognize this time in your child and step child's life and your own life. Do not become depressed by this period of time. This is the period of time when your child is preparing himself to establish the words of Christ in the next generation–when your child becomes a parent. Notice. The words of Christ are to be established not the ideas of parents and step parents, scientists, teachers, employers, coaches, movie stars, politicians, etc. in each generation.

If I want to be blessed, I have to keep the words of John the Revelator. If you want to be blessed by Christ, you have to keep the words of John the Revelator. To begin with, we have to keep the commandments of Christ for these blessings. It is better if we choose to keep Christ's commandments than if we are compelled to keep His commandments.

None of us can escape the influence of the four horses, the seven seals, the seven vials of plagues, and the angels sent to guide us back to God and Christ in John's vision. The preaching and acceptance of Christ's gospel, His commandments, covenants, ordinances with the plagues from the seven angels provide a balance of mercy and justice for us. Neither you nor I can change John's vision. When we change John's vision, there are many other prophets who have had similar visions that we would be changing or trying to nullify in our life and other people's lives. This is a major cause of depression in its self.

The Opened Door. John, the Revelator, was invited through an opened door in heaven. He was shown things which must be hereafter. He saw someone sitting on a throne. Around about the throne were twenty-four elders. Out of the throne proceeded lightning and thundering and voices. I suspect what they were discussing was as powerful as thunder and lightning. (Revelation 4:1 - 5) This also is not mysterious or a new concept for us. Many preachers, including parents and step parents, have given fire and brimstone talks, especially when someone in their congregation or family needed repentance.

It would be interesting if the same door which was opened for John is mentioned in Revelation 3:20. "Behold, I stand at the door, and knock: if any man hear my voice, and open the door, I will come in to him, and will sup with him, and he with me." This is the door with only one door knob which was made famous in a painting. If we open the door, the Savior will sup with us. He will give us comfort and revelation.

We are not to add to our discomforts or take away comforts like we embellish gossip. The Lord knows our works. He has set before us an open door which no man can shut, including step parents and step children. (Revelation 3:8) In many of the problems in the history of our families and nations, we insist on shutting the door for people. All of these years, we thought this famous painting represented an open door for us. Many of us have tried opening this door and discovered it has been very difficult to keep open. A door without a doorknob and latch will not stay shut unless there is a latch inside. I suspect this painting also represents a door that cannot be shut. What is the door that cannot be shut to you–revelation?

The Twenty-Four Angels. Twenty-four elders sit with the Savior. (Revelation 4:10) Four beasts gave seven of the angels vials of the wrath of God. (Revelation 15:7) It would be interesting if these seven angels were the ones who had authority to manage the opposition to the enmity or authority placed on the Earth by God after Adam and Eve ate the forbidden fruit. The other angels visit mankind to guide us while on Earth. This is how a balance between sun and rain, sweet and bitter, good and bad, light and dark, mercy and justice are maintained on the Earth. We are able to discern between good and bad or the right hand from the left hand.

A little vial accomplishes a lot on Earth. When we think of a vial, we are thinking of a small glass jar for medicine. Vial probably comes from the word "phial" which is a shallow drinking vessel. Many medicines are packed in small glass bottles with rubber plugs or which can be easily broken to draw out the medication by syringe. There are scriptures about drinking from the cup of wrath from God and a cup of iniquity from man. There is a difference. (James 1:20) There is also a difference between the wrath of parents and step parents and the wrath and iniquity of children and step children who want to trap siblings and parents and step parents.

If we fulfill the words of John in our life, the words of Christ will be fulfilled in our life. This will be done by revelation. Revelation is for all who ask of Christ. We do not need to

163

doubt and argue whether there are angels, visions, and resurrections. We just need to connect the angels in the Book of Revelation with the angels who have appeared on the Earth throughout time or the angels that Christ talks about. For example, Christ told us that no man knows the day and the hour that Christ shall come again, not even the angels of heaven. (Matthew 24:36) I suspect these angels are the twenty-four angels sitting with Christ. These angels may not know the hour of His Second Coming, but they do know how to prepare us for this great event in the history of the world and our families and step families. I suspect these twenty-four angels are the twelve apostles in Jerusalem and the twelve apostles appointed when Christ visited ancient America. (Matthew 10:1-4; 3 Nephi 19:4)

Take Heart. Parents, step parents, and spouses will receive many revelations for their stewardship, their family pr step family. The Lord has given us a thorn in the flesh so pride will not overtake us in the abundance of received revelations. We usually ask that these thorns be removed from us. We are left with pride, not peace. His grace is sufficient for us. His strength is made perfect in weakness. We would be nothing without these thorns and infirmities. (2 Corinthians 12:7 - 16) If we want the graces the Savior had, we develop the graces the Savior had–precept by precept. These precepts will come to us as we study the scriptures and by revelation about the thorns in our life as well as His principles, covenants, and ordinances.

Have you tried to shut the door of Christ to others, especially family and step family members? Are you trying to shut the opened door for yourself with anger, depression, drugs, alcohol, and thoughts of suicide?

What kinds of thorns do you have in your life? Do these thorns want you to choke physically, emotionally, psychologically, financially, intellectually, morally, and spiritually? Do they want you to choke at work, over your attempts at service, and in obedience? Are they trying to prevent you from making sacrifices for family and God and shorten your ability to endure and persist? You and your thorns will choke in the same manner that you choke the efforts of others.

Are you trying to change the Revelation given to John, the Revelator? This is the history of the world. Other prophets have seen parts of John's revelation. Lehi and Nephi in The Book of Mormon saw the river, the Tree of Life, and the fruits upon the Tree of Life. (I Nephi Chapters 8 and 11) Are you changed by revelation? Are you trying to pollute the water that flows from the Throne of God? Are you trying to change Christ's stewardship and your stewardship by ignoring revelation or mocking revelation? If so, you will be depressed.

Revelation brings many changes. With change, there is always a transition.

1 AND he shewed me a pure river of water of life, clear as crystal, proceeding out of the throne of God and of the Lamb.
2 In the midst of the street of it, and on either side of the river, was there the tree of life, which bare twelve manner of fruits, and yielded her fruit every month: and the leaves of the tree were for the healing of the nations.
3 And there shall be no more curse: but the throne of God and of the Lamb shall be in it; and his servants shall serve him:

Revelation 22:1 - 3, The Holy Bible

Chapter Eighteen

Transition

We all have many transitions in our lifetime which take us from an embryonic stage to a senior citizen. We can see many of these changes in our physical body. Our minds and spirits experience transitions also. With transition, our mental age matches our chronological age. If our minds do not experience these changes, we will have many setbacks in our life. We will suffer from depression or cause others to suffer from depression. These transitions in life may be abrupt, brief, or gradual. However, transitions are meant to have a lasting effect on us.

A transition is when we change from one form or stage to another. Stories and songs are formed by the transitions in sentences, paragraphs, chapters, and musical notes and keys. There are transitions in education, personality, and birth. Transitions smoothly connect one part of life to another part. Learning takes place when we connect precepts upon other precepts. These precepts become our transitions. Transition is not to be confused with transitory. Transitory is temporary while transitions have lasting effects.

It seems like our family or step family members feel changes in life come by attention, broken wings acts, power struggles, secrets, manipulation, oppression, and isolation. These methods do not bring about change. These methods stonewall the transitions needed to make a connection with our identity, Heavenly Father, Jesus Christ, and Earthly parents and step parents.

Christ experienced many transitions which changed his life from carpenter to the Savior of Mankind. He did this by overcoming the three kinds of temptations which come from Satan. If you recall after fasting forty days and forty nights, the tempter or Satan came to Jesus when Christ was hungry and said: "If thou be the Son of God, command that these stones be made bread." Jesus answered: "It is written, Man shall not live by bread alone, but by every word that proceedeth out of the mouth of God." The devil took him into the holy city, and sat him on a pinnacle of the temple. Satan said: "If thou be the Son of God, cast thyself down: for it is written, He shall give his angels charge concerning thee: and in their hands they shall bear thee up, lest at any time thou dash thy foot against a stone." Jesus replied: "It is written again, Thou shalt not tempt the Lord thy God." The devil then took Jesus to an exceedingly high mountain, and showed him all the kingdoms of the world, and the glory of them." The Devil said unto him: "All these things will I give thee, if thou wilt fall down and worship me." Jesus said unto the devil, "Get thee hence, Satan: for it is written, Thou shalt worship the Lord thy God, and him only shalt thou serve. The devil left Christ, and angels came and ministered to Christ. They did not minister to the devil. (Matthew 4:1- 11)

Temptation–Transition. Satan may have left the Savior. However, Satan now tempts us in the same manner that he tempted Christ because Satan knows we are always hungered. We have never made those transitions that individuals make when they refuse to cast stones into bread and also refuse to allow bullies to force us into casting our bread into stone with our anger. Satan knows that it is popular to control others with pinnacles of power. Our love of money will keep us in our temptations. We take outrageous chances. Instead of enjoying a beautiful view, we are endangering rescuers and forcing family to live with grief over our indulgences the rest of their lives. Satan tells us that idolatry will give us what we need. We are tempting the Lord and have been for over two thousand years. It is interesting, to note. Satan is trying to wear the Lord down through us–just like a child or step child tries to wear his or her parents and step parents down by controlling his or her siblings, parents, step parents, and grandparents.

The Prevailing Theory of Our Day. The prevailing theory of our day is that Hollywood, excessive recreation, and excessive sports, most of which is idolatry, are going to make these transitions for us. We do not need an education, God, parents or step parents. It does not matter if we use drugs and alcohol. We are going to learn history, English, leadership skills, money, etc. via Hollywood or our favorite sports team. This is false doctrine. We do not learn by being a spectator. We learn be doing and by adding precept upon precept.

Casting Our Nets. After His Death and Resurrection, Jesus showed himself a third time to some of His disciples. Simon Peter, Thomas called Didymus, Nathanael of Cana in Galilee, and the *sons* of Zebedee, and two other of His disciples were at the sea of Tijeras together. Simon Peter decided to go fishing, and the others decided to go with him. By that night, they had caught nothing. When the morning came, Jesus stood on the shore, but the disciples did not know it was Jesus until Jesus spoke to them. Jesus said: "Children, have ye any meat?" They answered him, "No." And he said unto them, Cast the net on the right side of the ship, and ye shall find fish. They cast therefore, and now they were not able to draw it for the multitude of fishes." The disciples came in a little ship; dragging the net with fishes. As soon as they reached land, they saw a fire of coals with fish laid upon the coals and bread. Jesus told them to bring the fish which they had caught. Simon Peter drew the net to land full of one-hundred-fifty-three great fishes, but the net was not broken. (John 21:1-12)

After they had dined, Jesus asked: "Simon Peter, lovest thou me more than these?" Simon Peter said to him, "Yes, Lord; thou knowest that I love thee." Jesus said unto him, "Feed my lambs." He asked Peter a second time, and Peter replied: "Yes." The Savior replied: "Feed my sheep." For the third time, Christ asked Peter if he loved Christ. Peter said yes for the third time. Jesus again said, "Feed my sheep." (John 21:15 - 18) We also have lambs and sheep to feed. In order to have food to feed them, we cast our nets where the Savior told us to cast our nets–on the right side of the ship. It is on the right side of the Lord's ship, the Right Hand of God, where your full nets will not tear with the great burdens of the weight of your great fish.

We will become neither root nor branch if we do not make those transitions that enable us to provide for the sheep and the lambs in our life. This includes children and step children, parents and step parents, siblings and step siblings. Parents and step parents will not be happy if they do not feed their lambs or the sheep which will come and go in their lives. Children and step children will not be happy if they do not feed their sheep and their lambs in their life. This is why the Lord told us to honor and obey our parents in scripture. Let's begin with the lambs to see where our nets are being torn, and the fish for our lambs and sheep are slipping away.

Birth. I first heard of the word transition in nursing school. It was in my obstetrical nursing class. My instructor was teaching us that babies about to be born experience several stages of rotation to deliver safely the head and shoulders. Otherwise, internal damage occurs to mother, and brain damage occurs to children.

New mothers experience transitions, too. There is nothing more exciting than to see a new life come into this world. It was interesting to watch the changes that an expectant mother experiences in pregnancy, labor, and birth. We student nurses were taught to watch for these changes to make sure mother was bonding with her child, her little lamb.

Most mothers are extremely modest. I first noticed mothers were beginning their transition period by a gauge in their modesty. As labor intensified, she lost her modesty and just wanted to get the whole thing over with. She did not care how many people checked her nor how much her nervous husband was eating in front of her. With some experience, I learned that mother was really entering her transitory phase when she was more concerned about her infant than herself. She could have several catheters in her body, an abdominal wound from a Caesarian section, high blood pressure, or a fever, but she wanted to know how her baby was doing. She asked her husband to check on their baby frequently for her. This was in the days before the concern of kidnaping of newborns at hospitals. It did not matter how experienced the nursery personnel were. She and her husband were the most qualified to care for their baby.

New mothers, I want to caution you. Your husband has to go through transitions, too. Birth is his time to bond with his child. Usually, he has been working very hard these past nine months, possibly at two or more jobs. He may have been remodeling a nursery for you while you have been irritable and uncomfortable. Father has to go back to work soon after the baby is born. I can only imagine how it feels to take a newborn baby in your arms and realize that you have to work for mother and baby the rest of your life. Fathers and step fathers have to go to work in the cold or the heat of the day, inside and often outside. They have to work for their family when this child loves peer groups and rock stars more than his parents and when they are not getting along with their wife. Fathers feel overwhelmed and worry if they can meet the demands of fatherhood and marriage at the same time, too.

Most fathers realize baby will be more attached to his or her mother. Babies feel their mother is the only one that provides their needs. They are too young to realize that father provides the money for the things the baby receives. Mother, you are going through many hormonal changes. You may be going through sadness over a sick baby. I have seen mothers be too abrupt and harsh with fathers. They blame their behavior on their hormones or the fact their husband left his shoes in the living room one too many times. Their husband cannot do anything right. Father's feelings get hurt. He withdraws from the family. He may withdraw from you and those changes that come with marriage and fatherhood. Everyone is awkward with new babies. It is part of the shock of having nine months of anticipation finally come to pass. Mother, it will be your privilege to give opportunities for your husband to bond with his new daughter or son. Read the information that you receive in the hospital together. Bath and diaper the infant together so father can see how to bath and care for his child.

While working in the recovery room for labor and delivery on a quiet shift, I remember wishing that adults could go through transitory phases as easy and as quickly as a new mother and her newborn. After all, the demands of society and pressures of family or a step family kept our minds rotating in several different directions. Naturally, adults would experience after pains or depression, too, like a newly-delivered mother.

Music and Heat. Adults do experience many transitions in our life. A good example of a transition is our favorite song or popular song. As we pull into the driveway, we have to finish the song. The organization in our spirits wants to carry the tune to the end. Musical tunes are connected to many memories. We want to finish the memory. Another example is my burnt offerings which I occasionally cook for my husband. I become busy and do not want to wait for the normal transition period in cooking food. I turn the heat up. I burn our dinner. My husband always ate my burnt offerings and told me what a wonderful dinner to ease my realization, a transition, that I had to do things differently. Likewise, there are transitions from hate to love, anger to forgiveness, justice to mercy, war to peace, denial to repentance, etc. We have to learn to stop turning the heat up on ourselves and others and learn to live life at a more gentle pace. The Lord changes us with heat, but He knows our hearts. His heat is justice and mercy.

We are not going to make the important transitions in our lives with idolatry. For one thing, these industries believe in predestination for everyone, especially our wallets. There are other ways for you to make the important transitions in your life. You do not have to continually respond to the opposition in your life the way the movies want you to respond.

I suspect that the Hollywood and sports industries are adding things to or taking away things from John's Revelation. This is why we do not see positive results. I do not need anymore plagues than I am already dealing with. I do not think you do either. I would rather have those transitions that bring maturity. You usually copy what you line up for. Be careful of what you line up for. Hollywood is not saving you, maturing you, or even entertaining you.

Agency. The Lord gave us agency. We cannot make transitions if we are not allowed to choose to change. Experience, good and bad, comes from our choices. If life becomes so hectic and demanding, we will not recognize that certain choices define important transitions for us. As we begin to notice the transitions in our life, many of the things of this world will beckoned to us also. You begin to chase your agency instead of using your agency. Conspiring men and women, boys and girls, are interested in taking your agency from you–and those transitions which the Savior had planned for us within this agency. Learn to notice what others want you to chase for them. Many times, I discovered I was conned into chasing my own agency in which others thought they had control. Nonetheless, I was still accountable for my use of my agency.

Physical. Our bodies experience many transitions as we go from birth to toddler, to preschooler, and then the school age, pre-teen, teenage, young adult, adult, middle age adult, and finally senior citizen years. Death is even a transition for us. We have vitamins, hormones, and enzymes which stimulate growth when activated in our biological clock and probably by the food we eat. Time is a great transition for us if we use our time wisely. Our joints and our emotions could not take sudden activity after sudden growth spirits without connective tissue. This is what a transition does for us. A transition is our connective tissue spiritually. We have connective passages in all aspects of our personality. We have to slow down and look for them, not avoid them with a fast-paced life. We are not suddenly modulated into a wife and mother, husband and father. It takes time and many changes to learn how to make sacrifices for multiple people.

Intellectual. Education is not only an important transition for a child to accept, but it is an important transition for mother to experience. She has something to teach her children. Mother learns to live calmly without her child around her twenty-four hours a day. Education is a two-fold transition. It is easier to learn subjects at age level instead of postponing our learning till adulthood. This way, life comes in spurts, not floods of adult-level learning. Parents and step parents have to be willing to allow children and step children the time and space to be educated.

Not every mother is going to have straight A students. Don't expect this. Be glad if you do have an A student. I preferred working with B and C student nurses. They had to work for what level of education they achieved. They seemed to develop more common sense than a photographic memory. Your student must realize that others' transitions are as important as his transitions and opportunities.

If I had it to do all over again, these are the changes I would make in my children's education. They might have had a better transition from school class to the working class. We had seven children who attended school. We could not afford to send them to college. Teachers would not help them before or after school because teachers had to sell donuts for fund-raisers for the wrestling teams and football teams. I would take out a loan to send them to a private school in those junior and high school years. Parents take out loans to help pay for new cars for their children and themselves and the drug and alcohol rehabilitation programs needed for their family. They might as well assist their child before they make the biggest mistakes of their lives.

Before I moved into an area, I would check out the schools more. Find out if your school district is sending the truant juveniles to the schools your children will be attending because that school has detention and truancy programs. Parents, homework is an important transition in your children, especially if you help them on a regular basis. The spirit at your home is more conducive to learning. Children will focus more at home. We might as well face it. School is not what it used to be. Parents have to fill in the gaps. You may want to home school. If not, use the material which home-schooled children use.

Psychological. All children experienced isolation and teasing at school. I am grateful that my schools did not resemble a reformatory for boys and girls. This was an easier transition for my mother and myself. It is very frustrating for parents when you do not know if your child is safe at school. This gave school more credibility to my parents. Your child must make the adjustment to school to build his data base for life. Hopefully, your child will be able to make the decision that he or she is not going to be a victim or a victimizer in their lifetime. They learn more this way. The best way to accomplish this task is to learn what the teachers have prepared for you each school year. The first person which your child learns not to victimize is their self. It is very difficult to not act like a victim when you have bullied yourself.

Spiritual. There are emotional, psychological, financial, and moral transitions that we need to make before we can make acceptable offerings of service, sacrifice, obedience, work, and persistence to both lamb and sheep. Education is a great transition for work. It is a transition that is over twelve years long. We must be willing to persist with the long-haul of an education which includes homework and criticism from teachers instead of persisting with the quick methods of sports and praise of the world. I found that the spiritual transitions that I made in my life accomplished all the tasks needed to get me through my entire life–from lamb to sheep. I had to learn how to sort priorities.

Our Heavenly Father and Jesus Christ are seers. They can see what lies in the future for each of their children in their infant, toddler, pre-school, school age, teenage, young adult, adult, and senior years, and finally death. This is why Christ has provided principles and ordinances of His gospel in The Church of Jesus Christ to take us successfully through these stages of life. The ordinances that we participate in accompany these periods of transition for parent and child. Those ordinances are: blessings of babies for the infant stage; nursery for the toddler stage;

primary and baptism at the age of accountability or eight years, the school age; Aaronic Priesthood for the teenage boys and Young Women for the teenage girls; Relief Society for women over age eighteen; and Melchizedek Priesthood for the men over nineteen years of age. There are priesthood blessings for illness at any age.

There are additional transitions which create growth spurts for these ages: patriarchal blessings for the teenage years and the rest of your life, your endowment in the temple for worthy members over nineteen years, and temple marriage for young adults and adults. Missions are growth spurts for boys at age nineteen and women over twenty-one years of age. Senior couples can also go on missions. Mothers have to let their children grow up and experience the hard work and separation in these transitions for these growth spurts. The men have to be worthy to obtain the priesthood and want to go on missions. Teenagers have to be worthy to receive their patriarchal blessing formally. Otherwise, these blessings lie dormant in your life.

Financial. The Lord knows it takes money to feed His lambs and His sheep. This is why He has provided tithing for us. I suspect, the Savior pays tithing on what He receives from us. This is why we are blessed through tithes and offerings. When one is willing to pay a full tithe to the Lord and budget their remaining money, they achieve great growth spurts and blessings.

One must first learn about credit. Your first experiences with credit were in school when your teacher gave you extra credit for work beyond what was called for. Some teachers gave credit when you did not do work she had assigned. You were willing to do this extra-credit to achieve a passing grade, even if it was a D. As an adult, you or your parents will live under a different kind of credit. The definition of credit which you are now living under is not the same definition of credit which you learned in school. The cost of living is so high. It feels like you cannot have anything without credit. Banks take over the role of teachers who were willing to give you extra credit instead of insisting you do the assignments. This credit costs money. Banks do not care if you learn financial stability. This means more money for them. Financial institutions are not making it easier for you to buy things. They are selling credit with interest. They are more interested in the interest than the credit. Your possessions become a curse instead of a blessing with high interest rates. Tithing and budgeting are worthwhile transitions for you.

Repentance. We have repentance to clean up the rough spots in these stages of life. There are things which happen to us. Repentance does not clean up the rough spots entirely. We have to endure the rough spots. Remember. The Lord has given us the Comforter for these rough spots. Here are some rough spots that we must endure along with raising wayward lambs and being married to a wayward sheep. Often, we care for people who cannot make transitions in life while we are trying to make transitions in our progression.

Postpartum Depression. Let's begin with postpartum depression, the depression which occurs after delivery of a newborn. There are many hormonal changes that occur in a woman's body which allow a woman to become pregnant, maintain her pregnancy, stimulate labor, and stimulate the production of milk after delivery. Hormones stimulate a new mother's uterus to contract after delivery to keep her from hemorrhaging at the site of placental attachment. These hormones affect the new mother's emotions and cause depression after delivery.

Women always worry about the safety of their newborn. The first thing which they ask is: "Is my baby alright?" Women may have been worried about the medications they ingested, the cigarettes which they were smoking, and the alcoholic drinks which they drank at the time of conception. Once they find out their baby is okay, and the excitement settles down. The depression usually subsides. Mother also has some wounds that need healing. Breast feeding makes additional demands on a new mother's time and body.

Mothers do worry about their added responsibilities. Babies are not like playing dolls. Babies have demands twenty-four hours a day, seven days a week, three-hundred-sixty-five days a year for the rest of your life. Mothers worry if they can meet the demands of their children. They quickly grow tired of being tired and sleepy all the time. They become frustrated as household chores begin adding up Mothers tend to lose their identity in children. Mothers grieve at having to go back to work soon after their baby is born. It is a terrible worry to place your infant in another's arms and wonder again if your baby is alright and if the baby will forgive you for leaving them with a stranger. Sometimes, it is easier for women to become depressed so they have an excuse to stay home with their children.

Some women experience postpartum depression. Some have killed their children in these depressions. These women were probably suffering from a psychosis, a neuroses, or a personality disorder before they became pregnant. Added responsibilities causes confusion which worsens a psychosis, a neurosis, or a personality disorder. Some women have noticed they have more energy when they are pregnant due to the pregnancy hormones. Women have also discovered they have an excuse to be pampered and demanding if they are pregnant all the time. Some women feel their identity is only to have children. They forget raising children comes along with having children. They forget there is an identity and responsibility in being a wife as well as raising children. Sadly, women have discovered having more children increases the amount of money received on a welfare check or a recovery services check. It does not matter if they want to or can raise their children. Their nets become torn and all their fish wander away.

These women have not made the transition from being cared for to care-giver. A depression will occur and hang on when you are not willing to make this transition. Adults are to care for the child they conceived, not siblings. Siblings are not mature enough to raise children. They may babysit nicely for you for a few hours, but they will never make plans for your child's future. This is not their stewardship. Their stewardship is to obtain their own education and help mother or father at home. Children are not usually multi-tasked enough to obtain an education, clean your home, cook your meals, do your wash, and care for your children, etc. It is frustrating for a child to have to choose between his education and his time off and a new sibling and a mother who has the time to watch television and movies, but not cook for her family. The Lord is not going to bless a mother in this recovery period if this is happening in your home.

Fathers, as the revelator of the family, it is your responsibility to evaluate your wife to know if another child can come into your home, or the child-bearing period of your marriage has ended. If mother cannot handle her newborn and the other children and some household chores without losing patience, screaming, or hitting, the child-bearing period is probably over. You are entering the child-rearing period. Of course, this is something that should be discussed with the Lord in prayer, your religious leader, your wife, and your doctor. Birth Control pills can cause a hormonal imbalance similar to postpartum depression.

Home is not like a hospital nursery. Mother still needs to wash clothes, fix dinner, keep the house clean, pay bills, and pay attention to others in the family. She gradually adds these things as she feels better. Some mothers are doing these things in a week. Six weeks is about the average time for the household to settle into a routine. Mother's routine has to be flexible at all times. She has to be ready for change in her children as well as her self, her spouse, family circumstance, the neighborhood, and the world. With children, someone is always sick.

If you suspect that your wife is experiencing postpartum depression, contact her obstetrical physician. Wives may not be cooperative at this time. Your physician will give you some pointers. Hopefully, she just needs to catch up with her changing hormones. She also may just need eight hours of uninterrupted sleep. Fathers and doctors need to decide if her depression is from her circumstances, her attitudes to life, fatigue, or her pregnancy.

Intellectually-Challenged Child. As a nurse, I cared for mothers who had babies which suffered brain damage. The brain damage came from prolonged labors, anoxia (lack of oxygen), toxemia, prolapsed umbilical cords, autism, or Down's Syndrome. For some babies, the doctors just did not know why the baby suffered brain damage at birth. Most mothers sense when this has happened. It is a transition period which the Lord gives mothers so the shock is not so great.

I know mother and father had many dreams for their infant. Parents become disappointed and depressed. They begin living their child's entire life in one day, everyday. They are wondering if their child will smile, think, sit-up, crawl, walk, or go to school. They are saddened as they realize their child will never marry and have children in this life. They imagine how their child is going to be teased or excluded over the years. Their world is a world of specialists, not friends, teachers, coaches, boyfriends or girlfriends, etc.

I have often wondered: If I was on rounds with the Great Physician, what would He say to parents who have just given birth to an intellectually-challenged baby? I never was able to tell this to a new mother of a handicapped child. I did not know if I should   I suspect the Savior would hold your baby in one arm and you, the parents, in His other arm. His response would be something like this. "There are two kinds of children in the world. The first kind are children who will be able to develop a conscience, who will be able to go to school, and who will eventually marry and have children, but their conscience will be seared by the temptations of the world. (1 Timothy 4:2) The second kind of children will be children whose conscience will never be seared. They will remain pure. I will be able to use these children for my purposes. When you hear jokes about your child's elevator (brain) not going to the top floor, remember the individuals who have a seared conscience usually have an elevator that went through their top floor. This is why I warned you to not run faster than you could walk. Your child's elevator will be fixed. The individuals with a seared conscience have to have a broken heart and a contrite spirit before the Repairmen will come and fix their elevator. Please love my child as best as you can. I have given you scriptures so you will know how to take care of both kinds of children and yourself. Love him or her so that your offering will be accepted before our Heavenly Father. I can make the hurt go away. I will send you the Comforter."

Your handicapped child will never have a seared conscience. Teach him all you can. Read to him or her even if he cannot learn to read. Teach him all you remember of your school subjects. This will be recorded in his brain. Teach him to pray and about God. At a time later, unknown to you, your child will be able to use this information. You will have been his teacher.

Group Homes. In the past, when parents were not able to keep up with medical bills and their retarded child's behavior, parents have put their retarded children in Developmental Hospitals. Parents have had to sign their rights over to the state in order to do this. Otherwise,

172

parents would be bankrupt with the cost of ongoing custodial care. Siblings are unable to take over the medical expenses and physical care of a handicapped sibling, although some do try. Siblings are usually working for their families. Many siblings are unwilling to care for their handicapped brother or sister.

The trend now is to place retarded children in group homes when they become unmanageable, over eighteen years of age, or parents cannot care for them because of illness or advanced age. Whatever your choice is, remain guardian of your child. At eighteen, you will have to appear with a lawyer before a court of law in order to do this. Their social security disability checks will follow them. This allows parents to have more rights in their child's care than the retarded, autistic child has. Many times, group homes place your intellectually-handicapped child in situations that are hazardous to their health and welfare. Your child is placed in and billed for programs for which they could not possibly benefit. Your child may attend many sporting events in the community and will be taken on vacations. Your child pays for the ones taking them to these events. The group homes call this your child's choice because they are over eighteen. This is the group homes way of teaching them social or group skills.

Be aware. Your mentally-challenged child may make choices. However, accountability comes along with choice. They are not usually accountable. So in reality, no one is accountable for your child's behavior and care. The owner of the Group Homes makes their corporation a LLC Corporation, a limited liability corporation. They magnanimously give part ownership to their client. In a limited liability cooperation, if an accident happens, and the owner of the home owns ten homes, only one home can be taken. However, by giving your child ownership, this home is residential. Now, no one can make claim against the owner of a group home. An unsuspecting motorist or parent is left to pay the bills for property damage or an accident.

Group homes expect to be paid for every minute of time they spend with your child. Medical care is limited in these group homes. They may have a registered nurse on staff, but your child is only allowed so many hours of medical care. Hence, your child may not receive medications for cold relief or diarrhea. Naturally, your child may be billed if the staff has to change their linen. You may not have much recourse over a group home. Work with social security disability on behalf of your child. You may save your child's life. Check on your child frequently to make sure the group home is doing what they claim they would do for your child.

Your child will have a caseworker in a group home. The caseworker should be more concerned about your child's welfare than covering the group home. If all else fails, each state usually has an adult protective service. Call adult protective services and the police.

Handicapped Child. Parents expect to nurse skinned knees, occasionally some stitches, ear aches, colds, stomach aches, or a broken arm or leg in their children. With some medical assistance and prayers, their child recovers, and the family routine is resumed. New parents may give birth to handicapped children. Handicaps may appear later in your child's life from disease or trauma. Their child's mind is okay, but their little bodies have many physical challenges.

Parents did not expect: brain injury, blindness, cancer, deafness, addictions, genetic disease, or paralyzation in a child. Depression occurs because there is no way of escape from the remorse which one feels for their child and the escalating bills. As parents, especially mother, become aware of the enormity of their child's condition, mother and even father become depressed. Their life becomes a life with specialists and surgeries, chemotherapy, etc. I strongly recommend that you view and treat your child as a child with a first name and a personality not as a handicap. My patients could sense when I viewed them as Mrs. Smith versus a paralyzed patient in room 6W14. Train yourself to take care of the task at hand. You will have long-range goals, but you can only worry about the task at hand. Find out as much as you can through doctors, prayers, books, support groups, and the internet about your child's handicap. Pray about the things you are asked to try for your child.

Do not be upset when you have to prove year after year that your child is still blind, crippled, deaf, etc. This the agency's way of proving that the parents are still alive, and the child is still living with his parents, to establish residency in a state, or to prevent scams. For some handicaps, there has been new technology to improve health.

Handicapped children do a lot of sitting. Many times, they do not build skills because it is faster for us if we do it for them. Let your handicapped child experience the role as care-giver as much as they can. Handicapped children can learn to observe what Mom can do to help a sibling or a neighbor. Mom has to include them in the care of their siblings. You will develop a routine with handicapped children. Keep a record of their ups and downs. They have patterns.

Handicapped children may be mainstreamed in school. It is frightening. Yet, they need to learn some independence of mother and father to develop their identity. They need to learn how to deal with other's questions about their handicap. Mother will have to keep up on their school work. Once they become behind, it is more difficult for them to catch up. Be aware of what company your handicapped child keeps. This includes the television.

Handicapped children and handicapped adults have the feeling they have to pay for every ride or favor done for them. I have had patients who bought microwaves or televisions for one ride to the store for groceries. Often, handicapped children have no concept of money. They receive a disability check so they are use to receiving free money to pay for many of the things they need or want. Do not give them all the money. Let them earn it with some chores, too. Let them learn to save money and count change. They need to learn that it takes work to earn money.

Your handicapped children receive a lot of attention and care. Yet, others may be experiencing problems in your home, too. I have noticed in homes with handicapped children that healthy children develop broken wing acts to compete with the real broken wings of handicapped children. Healthy children become lazy and function at the level of the handicapped child. After all, they would like to lie around all day and be pampered, too. This gives the impression that there is a genetic disorder in the family. They do not understand that the handicapped sibling is forced to sit around when they would really like to be playing with others.

Some Words for Your Handicapped Child. First, I am sorry that you must face life with a handicap. Life with a healthy body is hard enough. I know you have challenges that many others do not have. I advise you not to add to your handicaps. Age will add to them soon enough. I am speaking from experience. So I am not saying this with a hard heart.

You may be receiving free money for your handicap. It is called a disability check. This money is not free. Your countrymen have to work for this money. We do not mind helping you out. We do not want our efforts to take from you what your handicap is going to give you if you overcome it to the best of your ability. You need to understand that we have handicaps and handicapped children, too. We have empathized with you. Please empathize with us. We cannot pay for someone who has become depressed and become an alcoholic or drug addict in their loneliness. You are asking us to give you extra credit without doing your assignments. If you think financial interest is high, the interest on this account carries over into the next life.

You may be deaf, blind, crippled, have cancer, or some other disorder. You still must do some assignments on Earth. My handicap forced me to focus on my assignments. I did not have the time or energy to obtain an attention deficit disorder to match my handicap. Your parents may be so protective that you cannot do your assignments. They have to work or sleep. Help them out. Do simple chores. Learn to cook. There are many gadgets that allow you to do things. Make realistic goals and increase them. Discover the ways that you are compensated for your handicap. The person who is handicapped is not compensated through loneliness. If blind, his hearing is better. If deaf, his sight may be better. Develop a sense of humor.

You will have times of loneliness and mocking. If someone does not have a handicap to mock, people, especially children, will invent one. We all have to learn how to deal with loneliness and mocking. You will find these methods in the scriptures. There are ways for the blind to hear the scriptures or feel the scriptures through brail. There are ways for the deaf to learn scriptures in sign language. I told you there was nothing like a newborn. There is also nothing like a smile from someone who is handicapped and who reaches to help others.

Illness in Spouse or Parent. Parents working several jobs do not sleep for more than four or five hours a night. Health problems begin to appear in parents. The stress from lack of sleep and the stress of bearing and raising children bring out a particular illness. Families and step families often find their strengths through enduring illness or injury. Some individuals find their strengths in caring for the sick and injured. Care may be given with much love, but this care is time-consuming and heartbreaking. No one likes to see their loved ones suffer.

This suffering or illness may be acute (sudden) or chronic (ongoing). Illnesses may also be subacute or between acute and chronic, depending on how long we ignore our symptoms. If you have a particular gene for a chronic illness, the stress of an illness or accident may bring out a chronic illness in your self or family members. Type II Diabetes, cancer, and auto-immune disorders are common with the stress in families and step families.

Many fears and depression come when the breadwinner of the family, the father or mother, has an illness or injury. As the bills pileup and the service to the family by others dwindles, a real fear sets in. Families have lost jobs, insurances, their homes, and cars which affect the entire family, some of whom may be chronically ill. Chronically ill patients need transportation to medical facilities often. Someone who is chronically ill may have to go to work. Jobs are lost when insurances have to pay large amounts of money for your illness or injury. Your insurance payments of an illness or injury affect the cost of the group insurance of your employer. With the high cost of medical care, your illness, paralytic injury, premature baby, car accident, or climbing accident can reach a million dollars in one year. At your next job, your illness is now considered a pre-existing illness by your new insurance. States and churches have welfare programs, but they cannot pay house payments of $1500 or more for many members of their state or congregation. Transitions that bring maturity and strength comes when you understand this. Homes have to be sold. Families have to move, sometimes in with other family members.

Drug addiction is common in caring for the sick in your home. This occurs in both patient and care-giver. Some of the illnesses which individuals must suffer are very debilitating. Their body may not resemble a human body anymore. What is left of their body seems to deteriorate before your eyes. The sick family member usually is medicated for pain. It is very tempting for care givers to medicate themselves with the pain medications of the sick to ease the heartache in care givers. Children and visitors can steal these medications. Keep these medications locked up. Do not give children access to the key. You have enough personality changes to deal with in sickness. If you invite drug and alcohol into your homes, you will experience very painful transitions which take you step by step to regression not progression. Drugs and alcohol sear your conscience. Chronic illnesses are increased by stress. It is stressful for families and step families to have someone you love in jail because of drugs.

Most illnesses and injuries have a personality change. Illness or injury affects every system in your physical body and every aspect of your personality. The sick and the caretakers go through these personality changes. I have wondered if this is why so many families fall apart after an illness. Children who are not sick do not like the personal growth in their parent. Power structure is changed by this personal growth. Instead of weeping with a parent or supporting a parent, children try to return the power structure back into their hands with broken wing acts. They are not venting. They are whining. Many times, children are successful in returning the power structure of the home back to children's whims, desires, and, commands.

Our identity is built around the shape of our physical body, what we can do with it, and what we want to do with our body when we want to do it. (Physical) When sick or injured, individuals cannot earn money like they use to earn. Caretakers may have to stay home from work because they are sick or dependent on others. Financial institutions do not care if you have an illness or an injury affecting your job. As the bills pileup, so do the fears of both caretaker and the sick or injured. It is very difficult to budget with severe illness. (Financial)

Patients have many fears, some realistic and some unrealistic. They feel others view them differently when in reality they view themselves differently. Individuals do not like to be dependent on someone when it is not their idea. This inconveniences themselves as well as others. Individuals who are really sick cannot party like they use to because they do not have the energy and money like they use to. Group skills cannot be improved if you no longer have association with your peer group. (Social) They worry if their family will love them like they did though they cannot perform like they use to. Friendships are lost. (Psychological) You can only sit around and read so many books, watch so much television and movies, and do so many puzzles. There is not any money coming in to start a new hobby. Some illness and injuries, such as stroke and head injuries, cause brain damage affecting movement, thinking, and speech. Heavy doses of pain medication and other strong medications affect an individual's ability to think clearly, work, care for themselves, and make decisions. (Intellectual)

Patients do not have the endurance to serve themselves or others when sick. This is very hard on someone who has been a caretaker most of their life. (Persistence and Service) Most mothers let sick children and spouses get away with things the others in the family cannot do. (Obedience) Patients and family sacrifice many things for this illness and injury. (Sacrifice) Now is not the time to be overcome morally with drug and alcohol addictions, pornography, and theft to fill all the empty time you have. (Moral) Most patients watch many R-Rated movies in their empty time. This creates more loneliness, anger, and isolation. Your new image of yourself is like a sponge, and you become what you watch. Many patients return to smoking when ill. I have often wondered if they are craving what they have been watching over and over.

You may be sick, but you and your family cannot easily tolerate all of the personality changes within you. I suspect this is why divorce is prevalent after illness and injuries. I have seen this happen in patients who have only had a broken leg or a gall bladder operation. In two months, they were going to be back to work. With physical therapy, they would regain most of the use of their leg, but they lost the use of their personality and identity while they were sick. They become drug addicts and alcoholics to take away loneliness, not to take away the pain of an illness or injury. This is the difference between psychological addiction and physical addiction

Illnesses or injuries occurs in step parents or in step children. Depression comes when you do not want to care for or be cared for by a family member, especially a step parent or step child. Depression comes when you are not allowed to care for your step child. This unresolved anger usually prolongs your recovery period. Naturally, an aging step parent wonders what they are going to do if they become incapacitated by an illness or injury. I suspect: If a child or step child forces their parent or step parent into a custodial state, our Heavenly Father, Jesus Christ, and the Holy Ghost will withdraw from that child or step child. Your child or step child gets to experience a custodial state of mind. People may not be so quick to serve them.

Medicine has changed since I was in nursing school. Medicine has switched from preventative medicine and an alleviating type of medicine to a type of medicine where it is okay if you injure your body with excessive sports or abuse your body with performance-enhancing drugs. The doctors will fix your body later–if you have insurance. This is called sports medicine. Chronically ill patients are suppose to be grateful for this type of medicine. Many advances have been made through sports medicine and healing of these injuries so these individuals can return to sports quickly, not to work quickly. Doctors forget severe chronically ill patients cannot work. Thus, they cannot afford the fancy equipment, academia, and expensive medicine–unless their spouse works so the family can have insurance. Who is taking care of the many wounds in a sick family member? Hollywood.

Death. Family members with severe injuries die. Chronically ill patients die. Even the most hardened doctor hates to lose a patient. It is very difficult to lose a loved one to death suddenly or to watch them age quickly and painfully before your eyes. Caretakers experience many burdens while caring for the sick and injured. Everyone experiences the stages or transitions of death. Usually, we are in shock while others are in a state of denial, anger, or bargaining. Very few families reach acceptance at the same time. Do not expect this.

Caretakers, often feel guilty after a death because they are finally experiencing some relief. Be aware. This is the time that family and lawyers seek compensation for care that they think you should have given. They also want you to make an accounting of the income of the person you cared for. This could be thousands of dollars. Keep your receipts!! Do not pay cash for any care.

Death is a part of the Plan of Salvation. Many times on Earth, we do not want to cast our nets where our Savior told us to cast our nets. As death approaches, we reach for that extra credit again when we have nothing to take to our Heavenly Home because we did not do our Earthly assignments that we were sent here to do. We are not saved from physical or spiritual death by grace alone. This is that Second Chance Theory. We will have much work to do after a death in the family. We will have to make efforts and restitution when on the other side of the veil. We have been told this is harder for us to do. For one thing, we may have to wait for those needing our restitution to die. This includes our Earthly Judges, a bishop, or a judge that had jurisdiction over us when our offenses were committed. This could be many years after our death. If the wife has to work after her husband dies, children often get into trouble. Everyone is always tempted with something after a death because they are very vulnerable at this time. If possible leave your children with grandparents or friends even if they are teenagers. Hopefully, you will not have to experience the many transitions of wayward children as well as the transitions which come after a death in the family.

Most of us think about our own deaths. We have visions how we would like it to be. We do not think of death as a way to progress. We think of the separations from family and friends and the many other things we planned to do together. Naturally, we become depressed when we realize that our loved one may be out of pain, but we will not recover from our pain of missing them in six weeks, six months, or six years. We will miss our loved one for the rest of our life. Strive to make it a happy meeting when you are with loved ones again. Take care of the things on Earth which would cause you shame when you see each other again.

You may be aware that you have a terminal illness. Your death is a part of your stewardship. Pray to learn how to handle this part of your stewardship. Do not run scared from doctor to doctor for expensive treatments that may prolong your sickness, not necessarily your life. I have noticed patients hanging onto life when it was better for them and their children to let go. Young children were suffering terribly while watching their loved one suffer with various treatments which prolonged their sickness. It is okay to die when it is your appointed time. Death usually happens when you are ready to let go. The Lord knows this time. Your family will have some trials in your absence. They will have trials in your presence, but you cannot help them. Your family will adjust. Your spouse may remarry. They will not forget you nor will you forget them. I have not met anyone who has forgotten their loved ones. You may be needed to care for loved ones and others on the other side of the veil. You will never be helpless again.

Divorce. Many times, the psychological changes in a disorder or injury cause divorce. A parent feels they have to protect younger children from the terrible mood swings or addictions which their spouse now has. Divorce happens for many reasons in a family. A marriage may have been on shaky ground when an illness or injury happens. A spouse may be looking for an excuse to divorce. Usually, if a spouse cannot control their spouse in marriage, they try to control their spouse by a divorce. An ex-spouse can control their spouse's dating and re-marriage, a child's view of their parent, everyone's view of their ex-spouse, finances, emotions, home, cars, visitation, physical space, priesthood, friends, etc. for many years.

Hire an attorney if this happens to you. You would take out a loan for a new furnace if your furnace stopped functioning. You may have to take out a loan for an attorney. You will not be able to save money by being your own attorney and trying to be fair. Usually, someone without an attorney who wants to be fair is victimized by their spouse and their lawyer. You are not aware of current divorce laws which change year to year. Your spouse's lawyer is not going to inform you of divorce laws. Before you sign a divorce decree, look for the hidden ways of losing assets.

In your divorce decree, your assets are divided. You are expecting this, and you are expecting some losses. Ex-spouses do not just control you with child support, medical care, possession of the house, and alimony anymore. Ex spouses control by delaying the divorce with frequent change of lawyers and requesting child-care studies. This delays a marriage in the ex spouse. Time-off from work for court appearances can affect your job.

Child support ends at age eighteen. Alimony ends if your spouse remarries. Controlling ex-spouses will not stop controlling you just because your children are eighteen years of age, or the ex-spouse has remarried. Ex-spouses have ways to control you after your youngest child reaches the age of eighteen. The most common ways are mission expenses and college expenses for all of your children and your retirement. The ex-wife requests that a father pay all of the college expenses for their children. The wife and children get to pick the college. Your children may not even want to go to college. They may have poor grades in high school. Your children may party and do poorly at college. Your children may not want to go on a mission for The Church of Jesus Christ. Fathers still have to pay for this agency of their ex-wife, not the agency of their children. If you want to help your children with college and mission expenses, do so. It does not have to be a part of your divorce decree.

A husband who is about to be divorced forgets he is going to probably have another wife and family. This college and mission requirement will paralyze yourself and your future family. College and missions are not cheap. This college requirement in a divorce decree is a clandestine way to continue to control the husband years after a couple have divorced and their children have passed eighteen years of age. I personally feel that children should be responsible for their own college and mission expenses. They make a better effort when they have made this sacrifice. There are college loans. Your child may have to work to save for his mission. This is okay. Lawyers benefit nicely when you are taken back to court for payment of these expenses.

It is common for children to encourage a divorce in step families. If they succeed, children get to experience the grief of a divorce. They get to experience their future assets and parent's assets and retirement divided in half and a broken-hearted parent. They may lose the home they are living in. Children may not admit it, but they know when they have done wrong in a relationship. They may try to justify their actions in many ways which causes depression.

I have had patients who were in the intensive care unit working several jobs to pay for college educations, child support, and alimony. Their children did not have a kind word for their father who had a heart attack while trying to pay his own living expenses and pay for their college education. Is there going to be depression for this kind of behavior? Yes, there will be. The child may also get the experience of paying for a college education after a divorce. Both husband and wife should map out their divorce decree and see at which age each item in the divorce decree will affect them and for how long.

Those intending to divorce may obtain their divorce and settle property and custody rights (in that order) afterward. I do not recommend this. After the divorce is over, arguing parties will never agree on property settlements and custody rights. They most certainly will stall until the youngest child is eighteen. Children and step children are devoured in these battles.

Soldier. Our Father in Heaven has many children serving their countrymen and dying in battle. There are support groups for soldiers serving in the Armed Services and for Gold Star Mothers, mothers who have lost a child in battle. I encourage you to contact them. They will probably contact you. The Lord will help you. You must first ask. Remember the ministering angels. A soldier who has died in battle is more qualified to minister to his fellow soldiers. We may not like it, but some soldiers have volunteered to do this to keep our country going.

Many mothers have children who do not qualify to defend their country because their children are addicted to drugs, did poorly in school, or are in prison for various crimes. There are

179

some things worse than experiencing death in order to defend your country and your countrymen. Many mothers discipline their sons by telling them at a young age they are good for nothing and the parent will force them to join the army. These children are afraid to die in battle just as we are. If you do this, why should your son make any attempt to achieve in school. Your son and country are worth more than this. You may be left dealing with a very angry drug addict.

Your son or daughter is not a criminal because they are defending their country. Do not allow Hollywood or anyone else to abuse you with this false doctrine. We do not like this war in the Middle East. Neither do the soldiers. We do not like being without our soldiers. Our soldiers want to be home, too. This is what differentiates us from other countries. This war is a terrible woe for us. I suspect this war is one of the woes mentioned in Revelation Chapters 8 & 9. John warned us not to add to or take away from his Revelation. Many protests against this war are adding to our woes. Protestors are trying to stop a part of our history of our world. No one has been able to stop the history of the world. Even the Savior has promised not to stop the history of the world again as he did in the time of Noah. We can stand with our soldiers as they take us through a painful part of our history and pray for their safety in battle and safe return home.

Politics. Politics in this day have become a strange bedfellow. We call ourselves the United States, but our modus operandi is one of divide, smear, and conquer to repress others. Children do this with parents and step parents. It does not matter that this ties the family and neighborhood in knots. Children believe this method has no bounds. The President of the United States and other elected officials are fair-game, and it is open season on them. Naturally, this ties our country in knots. I have never seen so many ways that people use to divide this country. I have never heard anything good about the president of my country since I became aware of politics in the sixth grade. The public does not know who to believe anymore. They do not trust the Legislature, the Judicial, or the Executive Branches of our government. They trust Hollywood and sports teams. They would not lead them astray.

The public is suppose to trust the protestor in the home or on the street. This is not going to happen. What is happening is that we are becoming polarized instead of the country making a smooth transition. Our two-party system has become polarized. One party believes in God and Jesus Christ. The other party does not believe in God and Jesus Christ, and they do all they can do to control those believing in Christ.

We cannot talk of religion and politics for fear we will offend someone or become more angry ourselves. Yet, we are guaranteed freedom of speech in our Bill of Rights. I have an opinion on many things. I have enlarged my opinion through the thoughts and feelings of others. I try to make sure that my opinion stays in line with our Savior's opinion. After all, He died for us. Do not ever give up your opinion for depression and dissension. Just learn how to express yourself gracefully. The Savior learned His graces by grace to grace. This is just a synonym for precept upon precept. Learn history. Take a political science class in high school and college. Take these classes seriously. This is our country that may benefit from your wisdom. This is our country that each generation will need to keep defending. We cannot do this by discarding our sacred honor every time a protestor wants to create dissension to stonewall our leaders.

I would like to caution the youth. Many politicians scream at you in protests and tell you how terrible your government is. Why would they scream at you? You cannot do anything about their protests. You are inexperienced. The only thing you can do is vote for them or contribute to their campaign. Some of you are too young to vote. This is like asking a child to vote for a parent after the parent has screamed at a child over something which the child had no control. This is also like hollering "fire" in a crowded theater. If this does not work in families, society, and friendships, this behavior is not going to work in politics.

It is your family, your parents and step parents who are in the generation that will keep this country going. It is your duty to become educated so that you can take over where your parents leave off. Young people, you will never know what parents and step parents sacrificed for you to have a home, food, an education, some fun activities, and some normalcy in your home structure. You will never understand what parents and step parents had to endure from the decisions by their mayors, city councils, state legislatures, and governors. You will not understand until it is your turn to try to explain to your children why you cannot heat your house, turn your lights on, afford healthy food to eat, have medical insurance, and even have some of the popular gadgets that appear every year.

Years later, you will find that the protest that you attended was just a smoke screen to cover the actions of a politician or a protestor. I suspect this is why our grandmothers use to say to us when we were lying when young: "Me thinks you protest too much." I advise you to not allow music and movies to abuse you. I advise you to not let politics abuse you either. The music and Hollywood industry are controlling the politics of our country too much. They are also controlling our thinking and how we view our country and each other. They are separating us from our leader. They can have a leader, but we cannot. I don't think so.

I know it is difficult when politics affects your finances so much. Young people, it is your parents and step parents, not Hollywood, who will undergo transitions to keep this country going. Be willing to undergo transitions with parents and step parents. Make sure that your parents and step parents, and spouse have as much rights as the protestor in the home or on the street has. If you have a step parent, interact with them so they also can under go the transitions which will keep your family and your country going.

Work. Individuals usually begin working at age sixteen to save for college, a car, clothes, parties, etc. Individuals usually are as committed to their jobs as they were their chores at home. Working for others regularly is not the same as helping parents sporadically. Although your parents did not pay you much, your parents do not stop loving you nor do did they fire you when you failed. So do not view work as a chore. It is not the same. It is a blessing to be able to provide for yourself and those you love. It is a blessing for those you love to have this security in their life. It is a blessing for those you serve while you work. If you do not think so, tell that to someone who is paralyzed or who has cancer and cannot work for his family. They lost their home and cars. They cannot buy a two dollar item for themselves or their children. Their identity now comes in enduring pain. They cannot buy anything with this pain, but sympathy and compassion. Your identity comes in enduring work. You can buy much with your paycheck. Lay down your lives and dreams for time to work. Besides a paycheck, you learn much from work Look for the things you have learned.

It is not always easy to find some kind of work in which you will be happy at all the time. Don't expect to do this. Work is work. You will experience deadlines, frustration, failures, popularity contests, squabbling, layoffs, etc. Try not to be apart of the popularity contests and the many squabbles. Many mind games are played at work. It is an old trick for someone to tell you how horrible their boss is. You think of the times you disagreed with your boss. You tell them how you feel about your boss. They of course run to the boss and tell them what you said. They gave you the bait, you took it, and they switched. You are left with a mess. This usually occurs because of jealousy. Someone is afraid the boss will notice and appreciate your efforts more than their efforts. Many supervisory positions have been attained this way. You cannot afford to quit a job every time there is a squabble at work. You need to be building a retirement and your social security fund.

There will be a time for you to retire. It will occur according to the laws of retirement in your country and your health. You may not be able to do the things that you once dreamed of doing while a teenager. Count the things you were able to do because you were a part of the working force and the Lord's Health Care Plan. They should match your patriarchal blessing.

Be aware. If you are able to work and you retire prematurely from the workforce, you have just retired your patriarchal blessing. There is a depression which comes with this kind of retirement. You seek many things to ease this depression such as smoking, alcoholism, drug addiction, immoral behavior, and pornography. Your money has to come from somewhere. Your wife, parents, and children cannot support you until you or they die. They will become depressed and sick Your children will not be able to provide for their family. Your health will be affected with these ways of escaping depression caused by premature retirement.

The hard part of work is a test for you. We hear all the time that life is a test for us. Many of us wonder what this test really is. I will tell you what your test is. You will learn of things going on at work. These things will not match your belief system. What do you do? Do you quit, become depressed, tell the boss, or stick it out? Here is the test I had to take. I do not know my grade yet, but I still have that part of me that is me.

My parents cleaned doctors' offices to supplement our family income. I read their medical textbooks instead of the comics. I came to love the healing art of medicine. I graduated from nursing school as a green student nurse out to cure the world. I was taught the most current knowledge for nursing by a very good nursing school. I was also taught the wisdom of the diploma nurses. It did not take long for me to find out that the world did not want to be cured with the most basic nursing skills. Doctors and patients prolonged illnesses. Doctors wanted their patients to come back for doctor's visits more than they wanted to cure the patient. Patients wanted more medication. I did not enter nursing school and go through four years of extreme sacrifice to assist doctors while they killed babies by abortion, harmed patients with questionable doses and types of medicine, and obtained expensive academic knowledge. The nursing staff was instructed to call the nursing supervisor if there were problems. We nurses tried to overlook this behavior and make the best of it. It was very difficult to watch sick patients charged outrageous prices for treatment. Nurses began removing evidence from charts of infectious patients, especially ones with AIDS. Finally, we nurses were asked to ignore the fact that our patients had AIDS and Herpes. We could not tell their pregnant wives of their diagnosis. Gene therapy was going to cure our patients. I could not remain the nurse I had planned to be. I was trying to teach my child values, but was asked to lay aside my values at work.

I remembered the story of David and Uriah. Uriah, a faithful soldier in King David's Army was killed by King David. Uriah was placed on the front line where he surely would be killed. The soldiers taking him to the front line knew of the plan. This was not the type of nurse that I planned to be. I prayed and fasted. I am very grateful that I met my husband. However, I had to leave nursing to protect myself and my family. This is not new to nursing or the world. I suspect this is why there is and always will be a shortage of nurses. There are lawyers, politicians, plumbers, carpenters, insurance salesman, car repairmen, secretaries, clerks, butchers, retailers, bankers, stock investors, gas companies, etc. who are taking this same test in their job. Our country has many problems because they failed or refuse to take the test. They do not care for the ones in their stewardship. They care for someone who might benefit their wallets.

We have to decide if we are worthy of hire. We all have to decide if we are worthy of hire in a kingdom that is to come and which will last for an eternity. This is a painful transition that you have to make. If you do not make this transition, your behavior will be like King David with Uriah. Our country may have many inventions, but our behavior has not developed since the time of King David. (II Samuel Chapter 11)

Plan for your job. Plan to have an honest job. Plan for this test that you will one day have to take. There is a depression that comes when flunking this test. I suspect this is the reason why many businesses have increased employee absenteeism. Employees need a break from the dishonesty in the workplace and from deciding so many people are expendable.

You do not have to be retarded to be mentally-challenged. Families, especially step families, are mentally-challenged all the time. This is why step parenting is so difficult. What trials are you experiencing as you work, marry, have babies, care for a mentally challenged or handicapped child, a sick spouse, or experience a death or divorce in the family? Do you recognize the transitions that accompanies these events? Are you chasing your agency instead of using your agency in these trials? Have you retired your patriarchal blessing prematurely?

We learn precept by precept. List the temptations that plague each family member of your family or step family. Are their temptations opposing the precepts you are trying to learn or teach? The temptations in your family consist of insatiable appetites, pinnacles of power, or idolatry. Do you and family members feel that idolatry will meet your needs and give you more opportunities than honest work? List the transitions each member has made and needs to make. Are their temptations leading them from these transitions? Are your temptations preventing you from casting your nets on the right side of the ship? Are you casting your nets at all? Are you depressed because you are taking that major test of life over and over? Are you being tested at home as well as at work? If you have failed this major test, there is repentance.

List the personality changes that are occurring in yourself, family, and step family members. Are more positive or more negative changes occurring in these personality changes in family? Pinpoint where your fears and griefs lie.

If you have the faith to pray and fast, but only feel depressed afterward, there is a log jam in your prayers and fasting. If you pray and then listen to heavy metal music which brags about killing cops and destroying others' reputations in words that I cannot print, your prayers will be on hold like a log jam. Your prayers and fasts will become idle words for which you have to account. If you fast and then break laws or curse others, the log jam gets higher and tighter. If you fast and put in a R-Rated movie to think of something else, your prayers are nullified. If you create miserable circumstances for those who are naked, hungry, thirsty, sick, deaf, blind, or lame because your heart is set upon the riches of this world, your log jam will burst when you least expect it. This log jam has a name. It is called the Abrahamic Covenant.

Chapter Nineteen

The Abrahamic Covenant

People of the world, no matter what nationality, live under the Abrahamic Covenant. It does not matter what religion, what race, what creed, what nationality, bond or free, rich or poor, male or female, we cannot circumvent the covenants made between God and our forefather, Abraham. Wars, laws, attitudes, latitudes, and behavior will never change or end this covenant. We are not going to think of a better way to manage the many families of the Earth than the Abrahamic Covenant. The Abrahamic Covenant will always remain in existence. Step families are not exempt from the blessings or the curses of the Abrahamic Covenant.

The Covenant made between God and Abraham is not just the mission of a group of people. The Abrahamic Covenant is an important principle of health and wealth which we need to learn ourselves and to teach to our children and step children when they are young. In other words, the way we react to this Abrahamic Covenant affects our health and wealth and our very welfare for good or bad. Since we will be judged how we continued the Abrahamic Covenant in our time and kept the Abrahamic Covenant in our generation, let us find out what the Abrahamic Covenant is. Hopefully, we will find out how The Abrahamic Covenant helps us.

> *1 NOW the LORD had said unto Abram, Get thee out of thy country,*
> *and from thy kindred, and from thy father's house, unto a land that I*
> *will shew thee:*
> *2 And I will make of thee a great nation, and I will bless thee, and make*
> *thy name great; and thou shalt be a blessing:*
> *3 And I will bless them that bless thee, and curse him that curseth thee:*
> *and in thee shall all families of the earth be blessed.*

> *Genesis 12:1 - 3, The Holy Bible*

We usually focus on one part of this covenant: God will bless them that bless thee, or God will curse him that curseth thee. The Abrahamic Covenant is now called the mother's curse. This part of the Abrahamic Covenant is an important part of the Abrahamic Covenant, but there are some other important parts to this covenant. They all blend together to bless us and make us whole. *The absence of any part of this covenant creates a great void which curses us.*

Withersoever I will spot. Abraham was told to leave his father's house and kindred and to go to a land which God would show him. Our forefather, Abraham was scattered and grafted like the tame and wild olive trees into the withersoever I will spots, the nethermost spots, some poor spots, the poorest spots, and a good spot of the Master's vineyard. Abraham had to learn how to manage and subdue the wayside, the stony places, the thorny places, and the fertile ground in his life, too.

A Great Nation. God told Abraham that he would make of Abraham a great nation. God would bless Abraham and make his name great. God did make a great nation out of Abraham's seed. Many nations have broken off from the seed of Abraham and have become the countries we now know of today. Abraham's name has become great among these countries. However, the greater Father Abraham's name becomes among his descendants, the greater his descendants want Father Abraham to decide, often by war, who is best among his descendants. Is the mother country best, or are the tribes to which we now belong best? It would be very painful for Father Abraham to have to choose between his numerous great-great-grandchildren. I doubt that Father Abraham sees his seed as foreigners and citizens of various countries. This would be a curse. He sees us all, good and bad, as his great-great grandchildren, many times removed.

Thou shalt be a blessing. Father Abraham is a blessing to us. We will never know all the blessings that has come to us from Abraham's obedience and faithfulness to God. Father Abraham was willing to sacrifice his son to be obedient to our Heavenly Father. The lineage of Abraham continues through Abraham's son, Isaac, and Isaac's son, Jacob. Jacob had twelve sons–each had something to accomplish in this life, not just Joseph. Esau, twin brother of Jacob, also had many sons and daughters. Jesus Christ, the Savior of mankind is of the stem of Jesse. Jesse was the father of King David who was born in the tribe of Judah, son of Jacob.

God will bless them that bless thee, or will curse him that curseth thee. The Holy Bible is full of the stories of how God blessed Abraham and his seed. The Holy Bible also has stories of how God cursed those who cursed the seed of Abraham. God has used heat, water, famines, and pestilence as ways of cursing His children. Those who cursed the seed of Abraham fall into the same pits they dig for others. They receive the oppression which they wanted others to have.

In thee all families of the Earth shall be blessed. The Atonement of Jesus Christ is the greatest blessing for mankind. We have this blessing because Abraham was willing to leave his family and go to the withersoever I will spot which the Lord chose for Abraham and Christ to live. Though Abraham experienced many sorrows and probably some infirmities along the way, he continued to be obedient to his Heavenly Father. Life in his day was not easy. A major worry for Abraham was that he did not have any children to bless the families of the Earth and create this great nation. In their old age, Abraham and his wife, Sarah, had a son, named Isaac.

Abraham and Isaac. God instructed Abraham in a dream to sacrifice his son, Isaac. Abraham took his beloved son, Isaac, on an ass to be sacrificed. Isaac carried the wood on his back that would be used to start the fire on which he would be offered as sacrifice. Abraham journeyed three days to the place to sacrifice his son. Isaac asked, "Where is the lamb for a burnt offering? Abraham told him, "My son, God will provide himself a lamb for a burnt offering." (Genesis 22:8) Abraham built an altar, laid the wood in order, and bound Isaac, his son, and laid him on the altar upon the wood. Isaac did not resist. Abraham stretched forth his hand to slay his son, but an angel of the Lord called to Abraham and told him not to slay Isaac. A ram was provided in the thicket. Abraham unloosed Isaac and killed the ram in the thicket instead of Isaac.[22] The Book of Jasher, one of the lost books of The Holy Bible gives a little more insight into this part of Abraham and Isaac's life.

---

[22]Genesis 22:1-13, The Holy Bible, p. 31.

If the story of Isaac is compared to the story of the last week of Christ's life, there are remarkable similarities. I do not understand what Abraham and Isaac went through and why this incident occurred in their lives. I do know: When children or parents, step children or step parents feel bound by each other's actions, the Lord has provided *Himself* a Lamb to unbind them all.

Abraham learned a little of the suffering that our Heavenly Father would suffer when His Only Begotten Son was sacrificed to save mankind from another child of Heavenly Father. Isaac learned what it was like to be almost sacrificed. As a result, the Abrahamic Covenant was renewed through Isaac, Jacob, and Joseph because of their obedience. The Abrahamic Covenant is important. The Atonement of Christ had not happened yet, but the families of the Earth still could be blessed through the obedience of Abraham, Isaac, Jacob, Joseph, and their own obedience to God's commandments.

The Abrahamic Covenant Today. Is the Abrahamic Covenant in effect in our day and time? After all, each country in which the seed of Abraham now lives has a Constitution or some system of government for their citizens to have order. Yes, the Abrahamic Covenant is in effect today. We obey the Abrahamic Covenant. We also obey the laws of our land in which we live.

Abraham's Account. The account of the Abrahamic Covenant found in Genesis was written by Moses and then translated many times over hundreds of years. Our forefather, Abraham, wrote an account of the covenant between God and himself which is known as the Abrahamic Covenant.

Abraham's record was found in Egyptian catacombs by Antonio Lebolo who willed the papyrus to Michael Chandler. Friends of Joseph Smith bought the papyrus from Michael Chandler and gave the papyrus to Joseph Smith in 1835. Joseph Smith translated the papyrus and found The Book of Abraham and The Book of Moses on the papyrus. These accounts by Abraham and Moses are not watered down by time, opinions, or space on a written page.

Several years before Joseph Smith was given this papyrus, on May 15, 1829, John the Baptist conferred the Aaronic Priesthood on Joseph. A short time later in the same year, the Melchizedek Priesthood was conferred by Peter, James, and John on Joseph. Yes, this is mind-boggling, and we accept this by faith in Jesus Christ, the God of Abraham. If you think about the miracles of the restoration of the Priesthoods to the Earth, there was still something missing–The Abrahamic Covenant–the way that Jehovah promised He would bless the families of the Earth. The prophet Nephi in The Book of Mormon invited us to come unto the God of Abraham. (1 Nephi 6:4) As great as Melchizedek, John the Baptist, Peter, James and John, and Joseph Smith are, the blessings which come to the families of the Earth still come through Father Abraham. (Doctrine and Covenants 132:32-33)

The priests of Elkanah were going to sacrifice Abraham as they did others. Our Heavenly Father and Jesus Christ gave Abraham their Priesthoods. When Joseph Smith was persecuted, he He was given the priesthood. This account written by Abraham and given to Joseph Smith also became another witness for the priesthoods which Joseph Smith and Oliver Cowdery received.

This is the account by Father Abraham which is found in The Book of Abraham in The Pearl of Great Price. At the time of the Abrahamic Covenant, Abraham's father and kindred worshiped idols instead of Jehovah. They believed in human sacrifice. Wicked priests were going to sacrifice Abraham on an altar that he describes like a bedstead because Abraham did not believe in the priests and the gods that his father believed in. Abraham and Lot, son of Abraham's brother, Haran, prayed to the Lord. The Lord appeared to Abraham and told him to leave and take Lot with him. Though there was a famine in the land, Abraham and Lot left. (Abraham Chapter 1 - Chapter 2, Verse 7)

> *8 My name is Jehovah, and I know the end from the beginning; therefore my hand shall be over thee.*
> *9 And I will make of thee a great nation, and I will bless thee above measure, and make thy name great among all nations, and thou shalt be a blessing unto thy seed after thee, that in their hands they shall bear this ministry and Priesthood unto all nations;*
> *10 And I will bless them through thy name; for as many as receive this Gospel shall be called after thy name, and shall be accounted thy seed, and shall rise up and bless thee, as their father;*
> *11 And I will bless them that bless thee, and curse them that curse thee; and in thee (that is, in thy Priesthood) and in thy seed (that is, thy Priesthood), for I give unto thee a promise that this right shall continue in thee, and in thy seed after thee (that is to say, the literal seed, or the seed of the body) shall all the families of the earth be blessed, even with the blessings of the Gospel, which are the blessings of salvation, even of life eternal.*
> *Abraham 2:8 - 11. Pearl of Great Price*

Like in Genesis, the Lord will bless Abraham above measure and make Abraham's name great among all nations. Again, there is mention of one great nation, but it sounds like it comes from those accepting the Gospel and the priesthood which was given to Father Abraham. Abraham's account of this covenant with the Lord tells us this: "Thou shalt be a blessing unto thy seed after thee, that in their hands they shall bear this ministry and Priesthood unto all nations. I [Jehovah] will bless them through thy [Abraham's] name; for as many as receive this Gospel shall be called after thy [Abraham] name, and shall be accounted thy seed, and shall rise up and bless thee, as their father." "I [Jehovah] will bless them that bless thee, and curse them that curse thee. "In thee (that is, in thy Priesthood) and in thy seed (that is, thy Priesthood), for I give unto thee a promise that this right shall continue in thee, and in thy seed after thee (that is to say, the literal seed, or the seed of the body) shall all the families of the earth be blessed, even with the blessings of the Gospel, which are the blessings of salvation, even of life eternal."

The blessing for the families of the Earth is the Priesthood of the Son of Man or Jesus Christ. This priesthood is called the Melchizedek and Aaronic Priesthood to avoid continuous repetitions of the Savior's name. (Doctrine and Covenant 107:4) I suspect that the Savior named these two priesthoods after two very righteous men so man could distinguish the difference between the lesser and higher priesthood. There are important covenants that men make within this priesthood. Worthy young boys cannot administer the covenants and function in the offices of the Melchizedek Priesthood until age nineteen or more. They can gain experience in the lesser priesthood, the Aaronic Priesthood. The chain of authority of God is maintained on the Earth till the end of time by the seed of Abraham who keeps the same covenants as Abraham and teaches the same gospel of Jesus Christ as Abraham and Melchizedek. Apostles were the administrator to oversee the enmity God restored to the Earth.

Father Abraham began the gathering of a great nation. As the virtual seeds of Abraham are scattered and then baptized into The Church of Jesus Christ, they become the seeds of Abraham. Gentiles are adopted into the lineage of Abraham. The seed of Abraham must do the works of Abraham. (John 8:39) This includes trusting in the God of Abraham, not our lineage. (Mosiah 7:19) Thus, all worthy males are allowed to have and officiate in the same priesthood which Abraham received. Now, there is a way to maintain the line of authority from God to man. There is an orderly way to bless the families of the Earth which gives all families and step families structure and function. There is a line of authority from God which determines what is a blessing and what is a cursing for the families and step families of the Earth.

Abraham's Bosom. There is a parable from Jesus Christ about Abraham's bosom. In this comparison, a rich man dressed in purple and fine linen and fared sumptuously (lavishly) every day. A beggar laid at his gate full of sores, desiring to be fed with the crumbs that fell from the rich man's table. Dogs licked his sores. The beggar died and was carried by the angels into Abraham's bosom. The rich man also died and was buried. In hell, the rich man was tormented and saw Abraham afar off and Lazarus in his bosom. The rich man cried to Father Abraham to have mercy on him and asked Father Abraham to send Lazarus to dip the tip of his finger in water and cool the tongue of the rich man for he was tormented in this flame. Father Abraham said,: "Son, remember that thou in thy lifetime receivedst thy good things, and likewise Lazarus evil things: but now he is comforted, and thou art tormented. And beside all this, between us and you there is a great gulf fixed." They which would pass from here to you cannot; neither can they pass to us, that would come from where you are. The rich man asked have someone testify to his five brethren so they would not come to this place of torment. Abraham told him, "They have Moses and the prophets; let them hear them." The rich man told him if one went unto them from the dead they would repent. Abraham told the rich man: If his brothers would not listen to Moses or the prophets, they would not be persuaded by one from the dead to repent. (Luke 16:22 - 31) They most likely did not believe in angels, visions, and resurrections.

The Abrahamic Covenant in Our Lives. We have to grow, mature, and leave the home of our father and mother and kindred. Like Abraham, we have to chose between the false gods and the true God of this world. Our decision, one way or another, will isolate us from our families and step families. The seed of Abraham in this day needs to go to that withersoever I will spot which the Lord wants us to bloom in. I suspect that great nation that all nations will hear of is that one nation under God where there will be one fold and one shepherd. We manage the growing nations that we belong to with the Gospel of Jesus Christ and His priesthood until the Great Shepherd comes again. Our name will be great, and we shall be a blessing to others in the manner that we bless others. The manner we curse others determines the size of the gulf between Father Abraham and us and Christ and us. This is how we become root and branch. The size of the gulf determines if we are neither root nor branch.

I will bless those that bless thee and curse those that curse thee. The most logical way for us to begin the subject of blessing versus cursing the children of the Earth is profanity. *Profanity is not a stress reducer. Profanity creates more stress because you have hurt others as well as yourself. Profanity adds fuel to the fire in families and step families and relationships.*

Profanity–Stupor of Thought Profanity is non other than swearing. I am not going to mention the many words which we use to swear at someone or our self in this day an age. This is what the Savior taught us about profanity or swearing. If you commit perjury, retract on an oath or promise, lie, you are forswearing. Profanity is an oath which we quickly disavow.

33 ¶ Again, ye have heard that it hath been said by them of old time, Thou shalt not forswear thyself, but shalt perform unto the Lord thine oaths:
34 But I say unto you, Swear not at all; neither by heaven; for it is God's throne:
35 Nor by the earth; for it is his footstool: neither by Jerusalem; for it is the city of the great King.
36 Neither shalt thou swear by thy head, because thou canst not make one hair white or black.
37 But let your communication be, Yea, yea; Nay, nay: for whatsoever is more than these cometh of evil.

Matthew 5:33 -37, <u>The Holy Bible</u>

We cannot change the fact we smashed our thumb with a hammer and our thumb hurts terribly. The little old lady will not drive faster by swearing at her. Broken dishes and spilled food are still going to be thrown out. We offend others with our swear words. Our swear words reflect our state of mind and condition instead of others' behavior. Why does it matter if we release tension with a tiny four-letter word? Remember. The Lord gives us revelation by giving us a stupor of thought which prevents us from carrying out stupid actions. You can diffuse an inflammatory situation with just a yes or no answer. You can give others a stupor of thought and let them and you maintain the dignity that you both have and deserve. This way of discipline by parents and step parents is a great blessing for the families and step families of the Earth.

Eye for an Eye Justice. A great curse for the families of the Earth is eye for an eye justice. Step families are a good example of this. Families and step families avenge hurt feelings, real or imagined, with isolation, intimidation, stonewalling behavior, and manipulation. More and more step family members are also killing each other, burning down the homes of those they hate, and killing their own children so a natural parent cannot raise them and love them. Parents and step parents cannot take their children to church without interference from siblings and extended family. A step family member may say they want to avenge their dead father or mother's "blood." However, they did not listen to their father or mother anymore than they listened to a step parent or a step child. In other words, they drew near to their parents with their lips, but their hearts were far from them.

We have many families and step families of the Earth "loving" their parents and siblings to the point of eye for an eye justice toward a step parent or step sibling. Parents have used corporeal punishment to the point of death. Yet, the prophet Malachi told us that Elijah would turn the heart of the fathers to the children, and the heart of the children to their fathers, lest I come and smite the Earth with a curse. (Malachi 4:6) Apparently, eye for an eye justice is not enough to prevent this curse.

Public Example. The natural man has a tendency to make a public example of those they disagree or dislike. Gossip is making a public example of someone. It does not help them however. A great example of blessing others by not making them a public example is Joseph and Mary, the Earthly parents of the Savior. Joseph could have made a public example of Mary when she was found to be pregnant and only betrothed to Joseph. Joseph of Bethlehem could have been blamed for Mary's pregnancy. Both could have been stoned.

It is interesting to note. The Lord knows our hearts. He knows when we are avenging our own blood and anger or coveting something. He knows when someone lies to us to get us to avenge their blood and anger for them. The Lord knows that we are trying to bear the burdens of many generations who are bearing the iniquities of their fathers to the third and forth generation. (Exodus 20:5) We are not doing this so gracefully and tenderly. Yet, The Lord never swears at us, uses eye for an eye justice on us, nor does He want his leaders in his church to make a public example of us. He shared His priesthood with the worthy men of the Earth. Even Christ blesses the families of the Earth through the Abraham Covenant.

In thee all families of the Earth shall be blessed. Each of us has the opportunity to bless families of the Earth. We may not bless all families and step families, but we are to bless the families and step families in which we come in contact. If all of us do our part, all the families and step families of the Earth will be reached and blessed.

The Gospel of Jesus Christ is how families of the Earth are blessed today and how we become the seed of Abraham. The Atonement of Jesus Christ which redeems man from his sins is the greatest blessing for mankind through Abraham. All scripture and all prophets testified or prepared us for His Birth, Crucifixion, and Second Coming. The appreciation of the sacrifice of Jesus Christ is not just for our forefathers. We are asked to appreciate the Sacrifice of Heavenly Father and Jesus Christ through our infirmities, through overcoming many kinds of opposition, and by letting the Savior be the Savior of ourselves and our children.

In other words, the greatest blessing for the world comes by the Atonement of Jesus Christ through the Abrahamic Covenant. Sports, things, and parents will not save our children. If this were not so, the Abrahamic Covenant and the Atonement of Jesus Christ would not be in force for ourselves and our family. Things, people, power, and possessions cannot redeem us.

We bind the Abrahamic Covenant in our lives with a lack of faith in the God of Abraham After we have declared that we have faith in Jesus Christ and taken His name upon ourselves, a low level of commitment to His commandments and covenants binds the Abrahamic Covenant.

There are covenants within the Gospel of Jesus Christ. These covenants are solemn promises with compensatory blessings beginning with: Faith in Jesus Christ, repentance, baptism for the remission of Sins, and the Gift of the Holy Ghost. These basic principles and ordinances are how the Savior blesses us after we comply with our baptismal covenants. (Doctrine and Covenants 130:20-21) We take upon our selves the name of Christ at baptism and promise to bless others. These basic covenants of Christ is how Christ bruised Satan's heels.

When the gospel of Jesus Christ was restored, we learned there is a covenant of marriage that is beyond a civil marriage. (Doctrine and Covenants 132:18-19) This is not a new principle that was conjured up by Joseph Smith. Father Abraham had two wives and concubines. This was the law then. There is a distinction between the marriage of Hagar and Sarai. The Apostle Paul tells us Abraham had two sons, the one by a maid, the other by a free woman. The son of the maid was after the flesh, but the son of the free woman was by promise. The Holy Spirit of Promise seals a Temple Marriage. Ishmael was not born as the result of adultery. Paul tells these are the two covenants, one from Mount Sinai in Arabia, Hagar, which gendereth bondage. The other, Sarai, answers to Jerusalem. (Galatians 4:22 - 31)

190

It is possible that the Apostle Paul is telling us that a civil marriage can lead to bondage, and many of us know this happens, but a temple marriage does not. This bondage begins with the child of a civil marriage persecuting the child born of the Spirit. Even the Apostle Paul said: "That is how it is today." (Galatians 4:29) I suspect the reason that Hagar received a civil marriage over a marriage of the spirit was that Ishmael would receive the birthright, but the Lord knew that Isaac was coming. Abraham did not for a while. Jehovah is a seer.

These laws and covenants of Heaven are also known as the Plan of Salvation. In order to have the Plan of Salvation as a functioning plan on Earth for men to use, there has to be a way to have the power to act in God's name within this Plan of Salvation. We call this authority and power to act in God's name the Priesthood. This is the same priesthood that was given to our Father Abraham.

Blessed Beyond Measure. By both The Holy Bible and The Book of Mormon, we know that Father Abraham paid tithes to Melchizedek, King of Salem (Jerusalem). (Hebrews 7:2; Alma 13:15) Tithing is a miraculous way to bless the people of the Earth, including ourselves. Tithes and Offerings has brought many surprised blessings to individuals. However, we have brought a curse to our lives by the way we pay tithes and offerings. This could be causing our depression. We treat God, our Heavenly Father, like we treat our parents and step parents. We even rob God like we rob parents and step parents.

I am not a judge in Israel. I am not qualified, nor do I have the authority to tell you how much tithing you should pay and how much offerings you should make. No one can tell another person that his or her offering is unacceptable except the judges of Israel. Remember. These tithes and offerings will bless the children of God. I do know from scripture and from many latter-day prophets that tithing is ten percent of our increase or income. The Lord has said that we are robbing God in both tithes and offerings.

If you will reflect on Malachi's teachings and our life styles, you will discover how we rob God in tithes and offerings. I have discovered that tithing is also my time and talents as well as money. I owe God ten percent of my time and talents, too. When this debt was payed, I relieved stress and depression within me. When it is not payed, my schedule became hectic and terribly disorganized–like when my finances get disorganized after skipping tithing.

> *7 ¶ Even from the days of your fathers ye are gone away from mine ordinances, and have not kept them. Return unto me, and I will return unto you, saith the LORD of hosts. But ye said, Wherein shall we return?*
> *8 ¶ Will a man rob God? Yet ye have robbed me. But ye say, Wherein have we robbed thee? In tithes and offerings.*
> *9 Ye are cursed with a curse: for ye have robbed me, even this whole nation.*
> *10 Bring ye all the tithes into the storehouse, that there may be meat in mine house, and prove me now herewith, saith the LORD of hosts, if I will not open you the windows of heaven, and pour you out a blessing, that there shall not be room enough to receive it.*
> *11 And I will rebuke the devourer for your sakes, and he shall not destroy the fruits of your ground; neither shall your vine cast her fruit before the time in the field, saith the LORD of hosts.*

12 And all nations shall call you blessed: for ye shall be a delightsome land,
saith the LORD of hosts.

Malachi 3:7 - 12, The Holy Bible

Tithes and offerings are unusual ways to treat depression. Remember. In verse eleven, the Lord will rebuke the devourer for our sakes. The fruit of our ground will not fall prematurely to the ground which causes depression. The fruit of our souls will not be devoured by guilt, shame, anger, and depression. These are great blessings when one is trying to make ends meet physically, intellectually, spiritually, financially, emotionally, morally, etc.

Blessing others is not a unique way of treating depression. This is called service and sacrifice. Service has always been motivating to both the giver and receiver. Service blesses us beyond measure. Service brings dignity to both the giver and receiver. We shall have as much dignity in this life as we give to others. This is a great offering to the Lord which cannot be taken from us. Thieves cannot break through and steal this dignity. Moth and rust cannot corrupt the dignity that you give to others.

Fasting. The Heimlich Maneuver found in Isaiah will bless us beyond measure when we are choking. Many families and step families are choking as they try to build their Earthly and heavenly homes and try to balance themselves physically, emotionally, intellectually, morally, psychologically, and spiritually in thorny fields. Of course, parents and step parents are still expected to continue to build their home and to work. I went through this period of growth, too. Keep working even though you may be choking with sorrow in your family or step family. This Heimlich Maneuver found in Isaiah will help you.

This Heimlich Maneuver is found in Isaiah 58:6-14. This scripture is about fasting. Fasting is not simply skipping meals. Prayer and fasting with obedience to the Savior's teachings and ordinances will hasten or bring about the desired results that are needed and wanted in our lives. The original Twelve Apostles had to learn about this kind of fasting. We do, too.

6 Is not this the fast that I have chosen? to loose the bands of wickedness, to undo
the heavy burdens, and to let the oppressed go free, and that ye break every yoke?
7 Is it not to deal thy bread to the hungry, and that thou bring the poor that are
cast out to thy house? when thou seest the naked, that thou cover him;
and that thou hide not thyself from thine own flesh?
8 ¶ Then shall thy light break forth as the morning, and thine health shall spring forth
speedily: and thy righteousness shall go before thee; the glory of the LORD shall be thy
rereward.
9 Then shalt thou call, and the LORD shall answer; thou shalt cry, and he shall say,
Here I am. If thou take away from the midst of thee the yoke, the putting forth of
the finger, and speaking vanity;
10 And if thou draw out thy soul to the hungry, and satisfy the afflicted soul; then
shall thy light rise in obscurity, and thy darkness be as the noonday:
11 And the LORD shall guide thee continually, and satisfy thy soul in drought,
and make fat thy bones: and thou shalt be like a watered garden, and like a
spring of water, whose waters fail not.

12 And they that shall be of thee shall build the old waste places: thou shalt raise up the foundations of many generations; and thou shalt be called, The repairer of the breach, The restorer of paths to dwell in.

13 ¶ If thou turn away thy foot from the sabbath, from doing thy pleasure on my holy day; and call the sabbath a delight, the holy of the LORD, honourable; and shalt honour him, not doing thine own ways, nor finding thine own pleasure, nor speaking thine own words:

14 Then shalt thou delight thyself in the LORD; and I will cause thee to ride upon the high places of the earth, and feed thee with the heritage of Jacob thy father: for the mouth of the LORD hath spoken it.

Isaiah 58:6 - 14, The Holy Bible

Cursed with a Curse. Let's return to learning some more synonyms and antonyms. I suspect that if we could do a genealogy of our laws it would be like this: God, Jehovah, Adam, The Abrahamic Covenant, The Law of Moses, The Gospel of Jesus Christ, Magna Carta, Bill of Rights, and our Constitution. Our Constitution is not a curse. Order is not a curse. Each country in which we live has some kind of parliamentary procedure for their citizens to develop agency and have order. I suspect our governments will be returned at the end of time by leaders and latter-day prophets to Father Abraham, Father Adam, Jesus Christ, and our Heavenly Father.

Since we are Children of God and the seed of Abraham either by birth or adoption, the laws of our land will always contain the same principles as those found in the Law of Moses. Moses had many problems leading a large amount of people to safety and then maintaining order. Our leaders do to. We have abbreviated the Law of Moses into the Ten Commandments, but there were more than ten laws given to Moses to manage the seed of Abraham. Our Constitution, its Amendments, Bill of Rights, and other documents have many of the things in the law of Moses. This is because all came from the same source–Jehovah. At various times, things have been added and then taken away by man. Slavery, Civil Rights, liquor laws, and women's right to vote are examples.

Jesus Christ who is Jehovah said if you love me, keep my commandments. (John 14:15) If you love your land and yourself, keep the commandments of the Lord and the statutes governing your land. This includes the land that you own in any country. Obeying the laws of the land and the laws of God has many benefits.

The Ten Commandments. "Thou shalt not make unto thee any graven image, or any likeness of any thing that *is* in heaven above, or that *is* in the Earth beneath, or that is in the water under the Earth: Thou shalt not bow down thyself to them, nor serve them: for I the LORD thy God am a jealous God, visiting the iniquity of the fathers upon the children unto the third and fourth generation of them that hate me." (Exodus 20:1-6)

If you recall, Father Abraham had to leave his family and country over false gods and graven images. Presently, we have an epidemic of children who have attention deficit disorders. I suspect there is a connection with the graven images which they are taken to. Graven images will not soothe them. Graven images will lead them to iniquities. Children will even labor for iniquity. When they become parents, their iniquities will be visited upon their children to show them just what they did to their Heavenly and Earthly Parents to the third and forth generations.

193

If we do not want to be depressed and constantly mending the same curse, this is what we have to do. "Thou shalt not take the name of the LORD thy God in vain; for the LORD will not hold him guiltless that taketh his name in vain. Remember the Sabbath day, to keep it holy. Six days shalt thou labor, and do all thy work: But the seventh day *is* the Sabbath of the LORD thy God: *in it* thou shalt not do any work, thou, nor thy son, nor thy daughter, thy manservant, nor thy maidservant, nor thy cattle, nor thy stranger that *is* within thy gates: For *in* six days the LORD made heaven and earth, the sea, and all that in them *is,* and rested the seventh day: wherefore the LORD blessed the Sabbath day, and hallowed it. (Exodus 20:7 - 11)

We constantly hear of some group insisting by our own courts that we have to remove the Ten Commandments from any public grounds. They may or may not realize this. They are not trying to remove all displays of religion, Jewish History, and Christ, they are trying to remove the icon for our Constitution. It makes you wonder if they are trying to remove the Constitution while hiding behind the Constitution at the same time. With what are they going to replace our Constitution? If they succeed at removing the Ten Commandments, the Abrahamic Covenant will be the next spiritual fortification to be attacked.

Juvenile Law. We will always have juvenile law because children and step children do not honor their father and mother. It does not matter to them if they have decreased their life span. (Exodus 20:12) Children and step children have forsaken parents and step parents which means they gave them up without ever intending to come home again or reclaim their natural parents again. They may only be fifteen years of age. The Savior has said: "And every one that hath forsaken houses, or brethren, or sisters, or father, or mother, or wife, or children, or lands, for my name's sake, shall receive an hundredfold, and shall inherit everlasting life. (Matthew 19:29) Children have not given these things and family up for Christ's sake. They gave them up for their own pride, will, and unrighteous desires. They inherit nothing.

We will always have laws about murder, stealing, and perjury. (Exodus 20:13, 15, 16) The first murder happened when Cain killed Abel. Many books have since been written about murder, theft, and lies or perjury. There are murder mysteries to entertain us, and self help books with ways to protect ourselves or to distinguish when someone is lying. There are books written on how to get away with the perfect crime. The prosecutors, the defenders of the court and the people, have many books to decide if a particular murder was premeditated, accidental, self-defense, from insanity, a felony or manslaughter, or white-collar and blue-collar crime. There are books spelling out the degree of callousness for heinous murders and the number of years of prison which perpetrators should obtain. There are books on abortion.

We still do not get the message. Do not kill a child of our Heavenly Father! It does not matter how angry, hurt, threatened psychologically, or cheated we feel. Do not steal something from God or His Children! This behavior has stolen the hearts of the people and the hearts and attention capacities of the thieves and murderers. Murderers and thieves may have bravado, but they will never have the self-esteem and confidence that they would have had if they obeyed the law of the land. Parents cannot give thieves and murderers, etc., self-esteem. I do not believe our Heavenly Father will allow parents to give self-esteem to children under these circumstances. Children would become so prideful and dangerous that parents and society would be bankrupted spiritually, emotionally, intellectually, and financially all the time. In many cases, this is what is happening in the world today.

Our Constitution and Bill of Rights endow us with certain unalienable rights such as life, liberty, and the pursuit of happiness, freedom of religion, press, and expression. Many feel this happiness and expression will come by adultery and fornication and coveting everything our neighbors and friends have. (Exodus 20:14, 17) It does not matter who we betray to pursue this type of happiness and expression. Wickedness is not happiness. This is a state contrary to happiness and contrary to God. The Abrahamic Covenant restores our lands of inheritance. God cannot and will not restore evil for evil to us. (Alma 41:10 - 13) We are left with the press or media deciding our fate. This is not what God, Jesus Christ, or the framers of our Constitution had in mind for us. Parent and step parents did not have this in mind for their children either.

Jehovah prepared the way for us way back at the time of Abraham with the Abrahamic Covenant for us. Christ came to fulfill the laws that He gave to prophets since the time of Adam. Since the laws of civilization are similar, he came to fulfill the laws of our land as well as the laws of our Heavenly Father. These laws were given to men under Jehovah's inspiration. This is why we are to obey the laws of our land as well as the laws of God. (Matthew 5:17 - 18)

The synonym for fulfill is to perform. If we fulfill our responsibilities in parenthood and at our jobs, we perform the desired tasks of our employer. To fulfill oneself means to realize one's ambitions, potential, and intellectual capacities. Christ fulfilled certain laws so we could fulfill our righteous or spiritual potentials.

Anyone trying to paralyze the laws of our land as well as the laws of God does not have liberty in mind. Any mother or step mother struggling with children or a spouse over drugs, fornication or adultery, alcohol, smoking, theft, and lies knows there is no liberty in this kind of expression by an adult or child. Secrets, lies, intimidation, manipulation, stonewalling behavior, isolation, force, and weapons of rebellion are waged against the parents of the world, the ones who want to bless their families and step families. Yet, the mothers and the fathers of the world must walk on egg shells, or they will be beaten physically and emotionally by their children and step children. Parents and step parents probably are beaten down to keep them walking on egg shells. In addition, the parents of the world are worried sick that a child of theirs will commit murder, be a serial rapist, or a serial robber. Individuals can divorce a spouse. They cannot divorce their children. Fathers, mothers and step parents have become beggars at their own gates and cannot fulfil their patriarchal blessings. Where is the liberty and agency for parents and step parents?

The Laws of Depression. Christ feels these two commandments in the following verses are the most important commandments in scripture. All laws of Heaven and all prophets, including Abraham, hang on these two scriptures. If all laws of Heaven and all prophets hang on these laws, then these two great commandments are the first laws of curing depression, too. We do not have to settle for a bruised, depressed life.

> *37 Jesus said unto him, Thou shalt love the Lord thy God with all thy heart,*
> *and with all thy soul, and with all thy mind.*
> *38 This is the first and great commandment.*
> *39 And the second is like unto it, Thou shalt love thy neighbour as thyself.*
> *40 On these two commandments hang all the law and the prophets.*

> *Matthew 22:37 - 40, The Holy Bible*

The key word in this group of scriptures is "hang." Hang is a good choice of words for the first two great commandments. My husband has hung many pictures on a wall for me. He attached wire to the pictures, found the studs in the wall, and carefully measured how far down he would place the nails. If I was lucky, he put the nail where I wanted. The pictures needed this wire and nails because they had no means of support below. I lean on my husband for support, and I listen carefully to what he and other individuals are saying. This is what hanging means.

Naturally, there are many things that prevent us from "hanging on" or fastening to the two great commandments that should be imminent in our life. When there is no support below us, and there will be times like this, there will be support from above–not from an anti-depressant, endless counseling, or a death watch. This is one of those many tests that we are here for.

When the times of depression come, remember the laws of depression. I would think an artist would paint a picture representing the two greatest Commandments. I suspect the painting of The Last Supper is also a painting of the Two Greatest Commandments. (Matthew 22:37-40.) Christ had not suffered and died yet. The Apostles did not understand the meaning of the bread and wine. The Apostles were hanging on to the Laws and Words of Christ. Individuals can use this painting as a mental visualization of themselves hanging onto the Laws and Words of Christ like the prophets were. It helps one control their tongue and thoughts and actions–even in anger.

The Abrahamic Covenant is another way in which we divide the Darkness from the Day in our life. Heavenly Father and Jehovah gave Abraham their priesthood at a very difficult time in Abraham's life. The priesthood of our Heavenly Father is going to help us so we keep the Day in our life instead of keeping Darkness.

First, you may have to leave your home like Abraham did. It is okay to leave your home like Father Abraham did for safety reasons. You do not need an excuse to allow yourself or your children to be safe or receive kindly treatment. Let your abusive spouse and step children cleave to the idols of this world. In this day, men cleave to cars, women, property, alcohol, drugs, and sports rather than their wife, children, and parents. Do not be concerned with taking things other than your children with you. Repair your physical and emotional wounds in you and your children. As you begin to think clearly, relax, find safety, you will be taught new job skills which you can add some comforts of this world. Be careful what you take from your home. GPS, Global Positioning System Transmitters, can be hidden in your car or possessions. Cell phones can be traced.

Each community has resources now to leave an abusive spouse or step family. I know you wanted to bless your family, particularly your spouse and children differently. Frankly, not only will you be blessing yourself and children if you leave. It is a blessing for your spouse if you leave. Your abusive spouse must learn when they have it good and learn by receiving opposition instead of giving so much opposition. They must learn who the real light of this world is and how to restrain and subdue themselves, not others. Abusive spouses must learn that they are being treated in this world in the manner they treated others, especially their parents, spouse, and children. They have as much dignity as they gave their spouse and children. This is that curse of the Abrahamic Covenant.

The Lord will bless them that bless thee and curse them that curse thee in your step family. The seed of Abraham will always be blessed by the gospel of Jesus Christ. There is a line of authority to relieve your burdens and to be blessed beyond measure. Stop profanity. Pay tithing and pray and fast often. It is difficult for even the Lord to bless someone who cannot accept a compliment or any kind of affection. It is likewise difficult to pay tithing when you have no income, or you will be beaten for doing so. Read the scriptures so the Lord can inspire you. Pray for the revelations that will help you. They will come.

We have learned how we bless and curse others and ourselves. We know how to pay tithes and offerings to the Lord. We know how to pray and fast when we are choking. (Depressed) You do not have to make a public example of someone who offends you. You are now ready for some independence in this world. However, you will still be dependent on the Savior. The Abrahamic Covenant which you keep is your personal Declaration of Independence and Constitution.

How are you and each family member inspired to bless others? How are you tempted to curse others? Are you forcing anyone to become a beggar at his gate? A blessing does not make anyone a beggar at their own gates. Do you know the difference between blessing and opportunity? What may be advantageous for you may not be a blessing for the families of the Earth.

How do you and family members avenge hurt feelings? Is there a gulf between you and your parents and step parents, your spouse, or Christ? (Helaman 5:12) Do you have a desire to fix this gulf or increase the gulf that exists between you, family, step families, or Christ?

Is profanity retiring you and your patriarchal blessing prematurely in your home and neighborhood? Is your gossip causing yourself and neighbors to retire their patriarchal blessing, an offering to the Lord?

How are you trying to make an increase in your self and your family or step family? Is this a legal increase? The Abrahamic Covenant is how we receive our increase. (Isaiah 51:2) If we want to have an increase, that increase guaranteed to the seed of Abraham, then we do the works of Abraham. (John 8:39; Doctrine and Covenants 132:32) Many prophets have told us that if we want to prosper in the land, keep the commandments. (1 Kings 2:3; 1 Nephi 2:20.) This includes the statutes of the land that we live in.

Do you want to be blessed beyond measure? Examine the way you pay tithes and offerings to the Lord. Do you pay tithes and offerings to the Lord? If so, decide if you are robbing God in your time, money, and talents. Are you also robbing your family of these same things?

Father Abraham was given the Abrahamic Covenant so we are not helpless as the many kinds of opposition increase in our homes in the last days. Remember. The Abrahamic Covenant includes faith in Jesus Christ, repentance, remission of sins by the Atonement of the Savior, and the Gift of the Holy Ghost as well as charity, mercy, gratitude, forgiveness, and justice. The Holy Ghost needs an orderly way to function till the end of time, too. The covenants within the Abrahamic Covenant are renewed each Sabbath Day by partaking of the sacrament.

The seed of Abraham continues this covenant until the end of time. You are not helpless in your step family with the Lord's covenants and the priesthood functioning in your life. You can be married for all time and eternity which gives additional strength to your marriage. I realize that many of you do not feel worthy, or you may have spouses who have no desire to become a member of the seed of Abraham. Become a member of the seed of Abraham. It is quite an experience. Never give up. Before you can accomplish the task of endurance, discover how you give up. Is it fatigue or have you given up on the Constitution of your land and the Commandments of the Lord? The Abrahamic Covenant is your personal Declaration of Independence and Constitution.

We have been asked to give up the Ten Commandments and the Atonement of Jesus Christ. Do you want to give up the Abrahamic Covenant, too? The Lord will not forget this covenant. Why? Through the Abrahamic Covenant, the Atonement of Jesus Christ blesses all mankind.

Chapter Twenty

The Atonement of Jesus Christ

When I was a child, I was taught about the Atonement of Jesus Christ. I was told that Christ's Atonement happened in a Garden called Gethsemane where Christ sweat great drops of blood for the sins of mankind. Christ was betrayed, taken prisoner, mocked, and whipped at His trial in the night. His judge, Pilate, tried to wash his hands of the incident. At the request of the Jews, an infamous prisoner called Barabbas was released in place of Christ. Christ was stripped of His clothing. A red robe and a crown of thorns were placed on Him. He was forced to carry His cross to the place of execution, but only made it part way. He was crucified on a Hill called Golgotha. He resurrected on the third day, as He said He would.

Christ's Atonement is why we celebrate Easter. The day of worship has been changed to Sunday in honor of this Day of Resurrection. We assemble to partake of the sacrament which consists of bread and water, a symbol of the bread of life and living water which Christ is for us.

I still do not like to think of the suffering of the Savior. However in my trials, I have learned that the Atonement of Jesus Christ is more than His suffering in Gethsemane, on the Cross, and His Resurrection. As a nurse, I have witnessed severe suffering, but not of this magnitude. A man suffering like this for me and you–with composure–has gotten my attention.

The Alpha and the Omega. Christ's Atonement has a beginning and an ending. Revelation tells us about the ending. Let's begin with the beginning of His Atonement. His Atonement began in the life before Earth, known as the pre-existence. We have to depend on scripture to inform us about what happened in the pre-existence. John the Revelator tells us about the war in Heaven in Revelation, Chapter 12. Christ is called the Alpha and Omega in Revelation, Chapters 1, 22, and 23.

A War in Heaven occurred in the pre-existence. Satan wanted to take over His Heavenly Father's throne and saw the Plan of Salvation as the easiest way to do this. I suspect Satan did not believe that anyone could carry out the law of Atoning Sacrifice. There were so many children of our Heavenly Father. No one could bear all of the sins of Heavenly Father's children. They would have to be forced into salvation. Satan saw opportunity. Satan would do the forcing.

Isaiah states Satan said in his heart that he would also rule over the stars or angels of God. Satan did not agree with the appointment of Jesus Christ as administrator of Heavenly Father's estate and Plan of Salvation for His children. (Isaiah 14:12-14) Satan claims he wanted the honor of saving us, but he had no Plan of Salvation other than compelling us away from Christ.

Satan did not want us to have agency, the freedom to choose for ourselves. He wanted the honor of compelling us to salvation. Naturally, individuals who are compelled do the exact opposite of what you want them to do. I suspect Satan knew this would happen. Heavenly Father lost one-third of His children in this battle over administrator and agency.

The other two-thirds of God's children were waiting to progress to the state where they could obtain bodies and obtain knowledge and wisdom which would allow them to become like their Father in Heaven. Since many children have different abilities and levels of commitment, it became obvious that many of God's children would not be saved even though they voted in favor of The Plan of Salvation, voted to be accountable, and supported God's Choice of executor of His estate, Jesus Christ. Heavenly Father needed someone to give Himself as a ransom for his children. Jesus Christ, our oldest brother, volunteered to do this. This is how Christ became known as the great I AM. With all of our murmurings, Christ was the only one worthy to perform this sacrifice. Satan and his followers were banished from Heaven.

Adam's Fall. Christ prepared the Earth for us to have a dwelling place during our mortal probation. Eve was tempted by Satan and ate the forbidden fruit of the tree of the knowledge of good and evil. Adam ate the forbidden fruit of the same tree to remain with Eve. This is a good example that compelling children and compelling parents does not work. As a result, Adam and Eve were cast out of the garden. They were commanded to make sacrifices of the firstlings of their flocks in similitude of the Sacrifice of the only Begotten Son of God.

Blood Sacrifice. The first murder happened sometime after Adam and Eve were cast out of the Garden of Eden. Cain killed his brother Abel. This murder occurred over a sacrifice that was in the similitude of the Sacrifice of the only Begotten Son of God. At a time in the future, Christ's blood would be shed for us. This time would be known as the meridian of time.

Cain was a tiller of the ground, a farmer. Abel kept sheep. When the time of Sacrifice came, Abel brought the firstlings of his flocks. Cain brought fruit of the ground. His offering was not respected or accepted, and Cain became angry–so angry his countenance fell. (Genesis 4:2 - 6) Think about these two offerings. Imagine a beautiful white horse that has been cleaned and brushed or a sheep that has been washed and sheared. Abel brought the firstlings of his flocks, probably sheep. Cain brought fruit taken off the ground or fruit from a bush growing in the ground. The fruit could be small, partially pollinated, damaged, or starting to decay. The fruit could be beautiful fruit. Horses, sheep, and man have something which fruit does not have. Fruit does not have any blood. A sacrifice of fruit would not be accepted or receive any respect for a blood sacrifice.

Our Heavenly Father had a Plan of Salvation for us. In the beginning, our first parents ate of the forbidden fruit, the mysteries of the world. The first murder occurred over a sacrifice which was meant to remember Jesus Christ. The children of our Heavenly Father was consigned to eternal spiritual death for their misdeeds without the Atonement of Jesus Christ. Little children who died before the age of accountability, would have been sent to hell without the Atonement. At our deaths, our bodies would remain in the grave forever. Our spirits would remain in spirit prison without the Plan of Salvation. There would be no life in the kingdom that was to come.

A Ransom. Jesus Christ ransomed His imperfect brothers and sisters. He saved us from an eternal mortal death–the endless separation of body and spirit. Because of Christ's Resurrection, death, a result of the fall of Adam, could no longer trap us after our mortality.

In the pre-existence, Jesus Christ offered Himself as a Sacrifice to satisfy the many laws which were broken by Satan's temptations, our falls, and our own wills. However, if Satan had not opposed the administrator of the Plan of Salvation and our agency to choose this Plan of Salvation, we would have been in a bigger mess. There would have been no opposition. We would have no desire to mature or become whole.

Ransom notes have been left for families and organizations in this day. These notes have specific instructions which have to be carried out. The persons receiving the ransom note may or may not rescue their loved one or prevent a catastrophe. Our Savior has left instructions for us to follow which will enable us to be saved. He asks us to be repentant, to have a broken heart, and a contrite spirit, and to be baptized by one having authority to baptize and to give us the Gift of the Holy Ghost. His notes are found in scripture.

Repentance, a Broken Heart, and a Contrite Spirit. From my experiences, I do not want to be redeemed in my sins. One cannot be saved from an awful state or redeemed by placing themselves or others in another awful state. I want to be redeemed from my sins and their consequences. I do not want to feel the same or worse. I want myself and my family to feel better. I may have to live with the consequences of my sins temporally, but I can be free from my sins eternally. The improvements and progressions which I make spiritually are called sanctification or cleansing by religion. Our Heavenly Father and Jesus Christ achieves this cleansing and sanctification of His children with forgiveness and mercy mixed with some justice, and the principles and ordinances of the Gospel of Jesus Christ.

I do not know how obedience to God's laws accomplishes a broken heart and a contrite spirit or a cleansing of my spirit. I just know that a tenderness happens within us when we are obedient and repentant. Some families get to experience this while living on Earth. When their children are obedient and repentant with their parents and step parents, all achieve a maturity that many individuals do not have. Because of Christ's Atonement, all mankind has a period of time to live on Earth to develop their personality, their agency, and the tender branches which Christ has asked all of us to develop. With Satan's plan, we would not be a branch of our Heavenly Father. It would be a surety that we would not be a tender branch in His Kingdom.

The Atonement of Jesus Christ is an Infinite Sacrifice. (Alma 34:10) Infinite means Christ's Atonement applies to all created beings–even those beings who give you grief and heartache. I suspect when Jesus was calling himself Alpha and Omega, the beginning and the end, He was referring to this last sacrifice for the world, an infinite Sacrifice. (Doctrine and Covenants 54:1) The Atonement of Jesus Christ applies to all beasts and fowls of the Earth as well as all humans. Beasts and fowls of the Earth will also be resurrected to give us variety in heaven.

The Atonement of Jesus Christ is the last blood sacrifice. We cannot live our lives from ransom note to ransom note. Christ wants to restore us as well as save us. The Gospel of Jesus Christ restores us in our trials and many questions in this life. Thus, Christ's Great Sacrifice is the last Sacrifice. Since, this Sacrifice was for all mankind and all creations till the end of time, Christ's Sacrifice is an Eternal Sacrifice. (Alma 34:10)

Human and animal blood sacrifice is meaningless now because the Last, Infinite Blood Sacrifice has occurred. Human sacrifice for other humans is not part of our laws or God's law. This is why human and animal sacrifice does not restore us and bring peace to God's children that commemorative sacrifices did in Old Testament Times. Sacrifice by a Divine Being satisfied the law. Christ fulfilled those requirements with the divine nature of his birth.

There are too many people on the earth to do animal sacrifices. We would deplete the world's food supply rapidly if we continued making animals sacrifice in remembrance of the Only Begotten Son's Sacrifice. Besides, animals are not sinning. We are. We appreciate the Savior's Sacrifices through our infirmities and sacrifices for our families, step families, and acquaintances.

Though there were many wars where many people were killed defending themselves, the Plan of Salvation and the Law of Moses has always forbidden the shedding of innocent blood. We call this murder. Christ knew that many countries would be forming. As countries with

200

Constitutions and Parliamentary Procedures formed, there would be laws to keep and to restore order which included the law of murder. Human sacrifice is murder. Thus, Jesus Christ's Sacrifice is the last and Eternal Sacrifice for all mankind and all beasts and all fowl of the Earth.

Saved By Grace Alone. As a child I heard of the doctrine of being saved by grace quite frequently. It did not matter what I did or said to others. If I believed there is a Christ, I was saved by His grace. Then I was told to shape up and fly right or else. The arguments and animosity about grace between religions go on from there. I have never understood why churches have been arguing about grace for so many years. We do not have to argue about grace anymore. Yes, we are saved by His grace. In spite of all of our best efforts combined, only His efforts could save us. This is what is meant by an "Infinite Sacrifice," a sacrifice which covers all mankind, all our ancestors and descendants, us, and all beasts and fowls of the air.

We all have known or maybe even had a child or two who attended school, but did not make any effort. They did well in a one-on-one relationship in elementary school, but failed in junior high and high school. If your child did well, other students' averages were lowered. Their fellow students had to make more of an effort at a time when they did not want to make efforts in school work. Your children discovered that they got isolated and victimized if they were smart. Their schools let failing students graduate. Many received diplomas they did not earn. This was not a favor for them or us. These individuals expected everyone to save them by grace.

Grace with Works. When a mother is about to give birth to a baby, many things are happening in her body to facilitate the birth of her baby. Mother and father only hear the size that her cervix has dilated. During labor, an expectant mother's cervix is softened and erased, called effacement. Mother did not go through nine months of anxiety, discomfort, hours of labor pains, years of caring for a sick or well child in the middle of the night, and all the sacrifices of having children just for a child to harden and erase his spirit and learning parts of his brain with alcohol, drugs, and immoral behavior. Many mothers have laid on their side for many months to make sure that blood flow reaches their babies. Fathers have taken extra jobs and remodeled nurseries over and over. Both mother and father expect effort not betrayal from their children.

Likewise, Jesus Christ told Moses that He (Christ) came to this Earth to bring to pass the immortality and eternal life of man. (Moses 1:39, Pearl of Great Price) These are two great things which Christ's Atonement accomplishes for us. We all will be immortal. However, eternal life requires obedience to the Gospel of Jesus Christ and the ordinances and principles within the Plan of Salvation. The hardened, wicked parts in us are erased by the Atonement of Jesus Christ, our broken heart and contrite spirit, repentance, and obedience to His covenants.

If we are saved after our physical deaths by His grace alone, why did the Savior teach us to pray in this manner? We call these words The Lord's Prayer.

Our Father which art in heaven, Hallowed be thy name.
Thy kingdom come. Thy will be done in earth, as it is in heaven.
Give us this day our daily bread.
And forgive us our debts, as we forgive our debtors.
And lead us not into temptation, but deliver us from evil:
For thine is the kingdom, and the power, and the glory, for ever. Amen.
Matthew 6:9 - 13, The Holy Bible

If we are saved by grace alone, we would have no debts. However, the Lord's Prayer tells us that we not only have debts. We will be forgiven as we forgive our debtors. We also are to pray for our daily bread. Heavenly Father's and Christ's Plan of Salvation includes our daily bread. I suspect we avoid temptation and evil with the ordinances and principles of the Gospel of Jesus Christ. The doctrine of grace alone implies this world is our kingdom, and we can do what we want when we want without any consequences. This is not true. We are living in our Heavenly Father's Kingdom. If we are saved by grace alone, there would be no need to tell us about the Kingdom of Heaven through the Lord's Parables. There would be no need for the miracles which the Lord and others do for us. There would be no need for the principles and ordinances of the gospel which leads to mighty changes for good before we achieve eternal life.

Jesus did not die to save us in our sins. He died to save us from our sins. He and our Father in Heaven gave us the choice to die in our sins or be saved from our sins. Our choice determines the mansion or kingdom that we will receive in eternity after our deaths. His grace saved us, but our efforts in this school of life are rewarded, especially our spiritual efforts.

Eternal Life. Your Eternal life begins with faith in Jesus Christ. Remember. Faith in Jesus Christ is your spiritual blood pressure which gives you the strength to do all the things you need to do for your salvation and the salvation of your family and step family. (Philippians 4:13) These things will come by the inspiration of the Holy Ghost and include faith in Jesus Christ, repentance, baptism, and then the Gift of the Holy Ghost.

It does not do us any good to believe in the value of a good spiritual blood pressure. We have to have a spiritual blood pressure which sustains us. A belief in Christ not a belief of Christ is what we need. Faith in Jesus Christ, our spiritual blood pressure, will sustain us through the steps of repentance, even the steps we seem to keep repeating. Repentance can be painful. When you are baptized with one having the authority in God's Chain of Command to baptize, there will be new things come into your family, new ways to cast your nets, and new ways to sort your nets. This knowledge will come by the Gift of the Holy Ghost. The greatest knowledge that we will ever know is the Savior cast a net over all of God's Children by atoning for our sins.

Spiritual Death. As a nurse, I have witnessed death in some of my patients. We tried very hard to keep them alive with medications, oxygen, surgery, and finally cardiopulmonary resuscitation. If our patients died, their families were heartbroken. The patient and their family experienced the stages of dying–shock, denial, disbelief, anger, bargaining, depression, and finally acceptance. Death is always more painful if we remain in the shock and anger stages.

The Savior and the Holy Ghost are working very hard with us so we are not left with the sting of death eternally. (1 Corinthians 15: 50-58) If Christ's Atonement was only about His Suffering and Death and our grace and justice, His labors and our labors would be in vain. We would become angry instead of tender. The world would experience the stages of spiritual death: shock, denial, disbelief, anger, bargaining, depression, and finally acceptance–of spiritual death.

We must be changed from corruption to incorruption for eternal life. (2 Nephi 9:7) Grace alone cannot do this for us. Christ's Atonement gave us time to accomplish this process of change with dignity though good works and His principles and ordinances of the Gospel.

Your Stewardship. We have been told many times that we could not possibly understand the Atonement of Jesus Christ. We believe this and do not try to understand the Atonement of Jesus Christ. We understand more of the Atonement than we realize, especially if we are struggling with a wayward spouse, wayward children and step children, and wayward members of our community. The size of your stewardship determines how broadly you understand the Atonement of Jesus Christ. Someone who has a large stewardship will possibly understand the Atonement of Jesus Christ more than someone who is raising two children in a family. Someday, we will find out how many people Jesus ransomed by His Atoning Sacrifice.

Glad Tidings. The Savior is quick to say that He can do nothing but what He saw His Father do. (John 5:19) Christ told us that we do things that we see our fathers do. (John 8:38) The Atonement is the foundation of all truth in this world. It is the Gospel of Jesus Christ which all prophets have taught us. When I was young, gospel meant glad tidings. Most of us look for the glad tidings in the Gospel of Jesus Christ and the Crucifixion and cannot find them. They are in the Atonement which saved all mankind from spiritual death and bondage by others. Are parents, especially fathers, noticing the glad tidings in Christ's Atonement?

Depression and the Atonement. We may wonder how can Christ's suffering on a cross help us with our depression. It makes some more depressed to think about Christ's suffering, especially when they cannot pay their bills, and they have demanding children. Let's compare the situations in which you and I and Christ lived in the pre-existence and in mortality.

Satan did not like the choice of Jesus Christ being the Administrator of the Plan of Salvation. He did not approve of the angels who were assisting Christ with the Plan of Salvation. It would not have mattered who our Heavenly Father picked to be Administrator of the Plan of Salvation. Satan would not agree with him. Satan wanted to control Heavenly Father's throne. In order to gain control of Heavenly Father's Kingdom, Satan had to control Heavenly Father's children, too. Thus, Satan did not want us to have agency. He wanted to compel Heavenly Father's children to Satan's side. He stole Heavenly Father's assets by stealing His children.

Likewise, in many families and step families, no one can agree on who the administrator of the family or step family should be. It certainly is not going to be the father or step father who toils for the family. A step mother is not qualified because she is a step. It does not matter who their biological parent marries or how nice and accommodating the new spouse is. Children and step children want control of their parent's and step parent's assets. In order to control the household of their parent and step parent, neither parent or child, step parent or step child can have the use of their agency. Family members are not allowed to use the Gift of the Holy Ghost if this gift has been conferred upon them. Children are compelled by older siblings to the side of older siblings. Again, the families and step families of the Earth are fighting over the administrator and agency within their families and step families. Children are compelled, not loved. It is no wonder the Lord established a Chain of Command for us to follow.

If your duties of administrator and your agency are controlled and your children and step children are compelled by secret combinations, manipulation, stonewalling behavior, isolation, and intimidation, it is not your imagination. This is the natural man that is an enemy to God. It is that plan that Satan had for us. Heavenly Father, Jesus Christ, and the Holy Ghost has experience with the behavior of the natural man. They teach us how to reconcile with God. We do not have to make sin offerings to ourselves or others over the slightest of infractions to find the peace of mind that we want. If we seek the mysteries of the world, the forbidden fruits which hurt us, instead of the mysteries that God has prepared for us, we will be cast out from our Heavenly Father's presence and become neither root nor branch. The Atonement of Jesus Christ assures that we are always root and branch with our Heavenly Father, Christ, our parents, step parents, spouse, children, and step children.

Love. It is difficult to understand why our Heavenly Father would send His only Begotten Son to die for the rest of His children. This concept is not new to human beings. Our soldiers fight for us, and many die for us. They know this has to be done to keep each generation going in their country. Parents and step parents fight each other for their children and step children. When two friends fought, a third friend was dispatched to smooth things over. When a parent and child are arguing, a sibling visits the parent to get more information and to see what the parent is going to do to their sibling. They report back to their sibling. These temporal battles of life usually occurred over jealousy and anger. The amazing thing about our rescue from Satan is that Christ's Atonement for us was out of the pure love of Christ, called charity.

I have always wondered how Christ could accomplish the painful task of His Atonement for us. Our painful tasks are so small in comparison. Yet, Christ told us that the works I do shall be greater if you believe on me. (John 14:12) Our Heavenly Father withdrew His power from His Son so no one could say this was not Christ's Sacrifice alone. (John 19:11) I suspect that the Savior could endure His Crucifixion because He forgave His perpetrators. (Luke 23:34) With the kind of love which the Savior had for us, there is always forgiveness and mercy.

Resurrection. Remember. Christ is not still hanging on that cruel cross. He has resurrected and completed the Atonement for all of us, adults as well as children. He is waiting as we all are for the time of our resurrection. One day, He will present the seed of Abraham to our Heavenly Father and tell him that the seed of Abraham has made the necessary steps for eternal life and He has interceded in our behalf to satisfy the law. (2 Nephi 9:25-26) Give back to Christ His stewardship and take back your stewardship by experimenting on His words.

Adam and Eve fell over the mysteries of the world. You and your family members will fall, too. List the mysteries of the world which beguile you and your family members. What do you have to give up for these mysteries? Is your family making any sacrifices in remembrance of the Sacrifice of the Only Begotten Son? Are you doing all that you can do, but not achieving success in your family? Remember. Others are having a trial of their faith, not just you. Children and step children are just beginning their trial of faith. You are further along.

Is your family having problems trying to decide who the administrator of the family is? What is interfering with the agency in each member of your family or step family? How do you and others compel you and your children and step children? Are these things the cause of your depression? Are you aware that just before Jesus Christ performed His painful, Atoning Sacrifice, He gave the world a Comforter? This Comforter is known as the Holy Ghost.

Do you see the glad tidings in the Atonement of Jesus Christ? Are you and your family members looking for other things to save you by grace without effort? If so, what will be your Alpha and Omega? Because of Christ's Atonement for us, we have hope as well as agency. Most of us can choose if we want to be custodial, trainable, or educable while in mortality.

8 ¶ For my thoughts are not your thoughts, neither are your ways my ways, saith the LORD.
9 For as the heavens are higher than the earth, so are my ways higher than your ways, and my thoughts than your thoughts.   Isaiah 55:8 - 9, The Holy Bible

Epilogue

Custodial, Trainable, or Educable. When I was in nurses' training, a mentally-challenged child or disabled child was classified in three ways: They were either custodial, trainable, or educable. This usually depended on their Intelligence Quotient and their ability to take care of themselves. As I recall, a custodial child usually had an IQ ranging from under 50-60, a trainable child had an IQ ranging from 61-70, and an educable child had an IQ of 71-80. Two of the sad things of this life are that teenagers and adults are custodial although they have an IQ ranging from 100 - 120. Husbands become trainable or are custodial when they have an IQ ranging from 100 - 140.

Normal Custodial Care. We all begin life in a custodial state. We began life in the custody of our Earthly parents, especially mother, or we would have died. Our fathers worked to provide food, clothing, and shelter for us, or we would have suffered terribly or died. Mother fed us, kept us warm, and stimulated us, or we would have died. We began our training state. We had brief periods where we returned to a custodial state because of sickness or injury. We quickly returned to a training state or an educable state when we recovered from our illness. Wives are in the custody of their husband and children are in the custody of their parents.

Abnormal Custodial Care. Some individuals milk an illness to remain in a custodial state as long as they can. We use to call these individuals hypochondriacs. Now, we call them alcoholics and drug addicts. Broken wing acts may be common to childhood. In adulthood, this is abnormal custodial care. What we eat and drink can make us uneducable and un-trainable.

An adult who lives off others' light is really custodial even though he or she is wealthy and has many Earthly mansions. They are in our custody because they depend on our money. We support them. They control us like children who controlled their parents. They begin with parents' assets. Governments can become custodial out of choice, or citizens can force governments to be custodial because neither will make the transition from care-receiver to care-giver. Those who depend on vigilante justice to appease their anger and fears are returned to a custodial state. In the Lord's chain of command, children do not have custody of their father and mother unless their parents are advanced in age and are incapacitated. Fathers are not in the custody of wives. Custodial interference is abnormal custodial care.

Normal Care in Training. After birth, several years of training occurred until we reached school age to be educated. Our first hurdle was to be trained to sleep through the night. This was easier to learn if we were transferred from bottle or breast feeding to table food. Potty-training is even easier if a child no longer requires a bottle. Children learn to depend on speech instead of grunting, whining, and crying. Of course, fathers like to teach their children how to toss a ball, usually in the living room. Father gets some re-training, too.

Abnormal Care in Training. Parents and step parents may spend the entire youth of children trying to train children to come home for dinner or before dark, attend school regularly, do homework, and abstain from smoking, swearing, fornication, alcohol, and drugs. This custodial behavior leaves little time to train and educate a child academically. We learn wisdom in our youth by being educable. (Alma 37:35, The Book of Mormon) Parents and step parents have to let their children grow up, experience, and overcome opposition, not embrace opposition.

Normal State of Educable. Once we reach school age, we learn many new things in each year of schooling. Each year of our schooling has a review of things learned in past years of schooling. With this kind of repetition, hopefully, we remained educable through out our years of schooling. Hopefully, we remained educable although the things that we were learning gradually become harder and harder to learn. The idea of schooling is for us to take over our own education when we reach adulthood. This is why reading is so important to learn. If you are living with parents because you are not of age, but you are learning from parents and teachers, you are considered both educable and trainable.

Abnormal Care in Educable. It is hard to believe that there is a deviation in being educable. There is. If you are always learning, but not able to come to the knowledge of the truth, you may think that you are educable or trainable. You are custodial. We call this intellectualizing. Individuals avoid a lot by intellectualizing. They earn many degrees which are expensive. Parents and step parents can become paralyzed by these college degrees if parents and step parents are paying for the degrees. Normally after learning knowledge, a person yearns for experience, a place to use their knowledge, and a way to earn a paycheck.

At sometime in the transitions from custodial to trainable to educable, family members switch from being pampered to care-giver, first for ourselves and then for others. This is called independence. We discover that it is better to give than to receive. If we avoid this important transition, we will always remain in a custodial state. Our spirits become handicapped with selfishness. Spirits do not thrive if we insist that others provide for us when we can provide for ourselves. Depression will overtake you.

Everyone of us has a handicap to overcome. Some handicaps are more pronounced and painful than others. It is normal for the sick to become custodial and need some re-training in personal care, speech, eating, and walking. They can remain educable in their attitude although other things have to be provided for them. I have had patients who had many tubes going in and out of their body. They were very sick. The recovery period was easier for both patient and nurse when the patient remained educable about their illness and in attitude. This did not mean they did not shed many tears about their illness and situation. They also had to limit their spending.

Remaining Educable. How do we remain educable when we have so much opposition to overcome? How do we know who to believe and which path to follow? Nicodemus, a ruler of the Jews told Jesus: "...No man can do these miracles that thou doest, except God be with him. Jesus answered and said unto him, Verily, verily, I say unto thee, Except a man be born again, he cannot see the kingdom of God." Nicodemus asked: "How can a man be born when he is old? Can he enter the second time into his mother's womb, and be born?" Jesus replied: "Verily, verily, I say unto thee, Except a man be born of water and of the Spirit, he cannot enter into the kingdom of God...The wind bloweth where it listeth, and thou hearest the sound thereof, but canst not tell whence it cometh, and whither it goeth: so is every one that is born of the Spirit." (John 3:1 - 8) Our miracles and education will come from being born of the spirit.

Born of Water and the Spirit. Born of water refers to our physical births and baptism. We had to be born on this Earth to progress. Our bodies formed in a bag of waters. This bag of waters ruptures at the time of birth. At the age of accountability, we progress with baptism by one having authority to baptize in the Lord's chain of command. Baptism is symbolic of a spiritual rebirth after one repents of their sins. Born of the spirit refers to the Gift of the Holy Ghost. If you do not have the gift of the Holy Ghost, you are poor in spirit. (Matthew 5:3) The Kingdom of God may be yours, but you have to make efforts for it.

Our spirits will now be molded and guided by the Comforter, the Holy Ghost. There are many tiny miracles in our births and baptism which we cannot see until there are visible growth spurts. Like the wind, we do not know where these miracles came from or where they will lead us. With the gifts of the spirit, we do not have to fight for spiritual breath. (1 Corinthians Chapter 12, Moroni Chapter 10, and Doctrine and Covenants Chapter 46) The world calls this struggle for spiritual breath depression, personality disorders, and suicidal tendencies.

Re-Training of the Spirit. After our spirits are reborn and are cleansed by repentance and baptism, our spirits need to be trained. Let's turn to the Beloved Beatitudes given on the Sermon on the Mount by our Savior. The Sermon on the Mount Chapters include Matthew 5-7. These chapters follow the chapters where John the Baptist has been baptizing, including Jesus. The Sermon on the Mount follows the time that Christ was tempted by Satan. John was also cast into prison, and Jesus chose His twelve apostles.

Christ saw a multitude on a mountain. They may have been baptized by John the Baptist prior to his imprisonment. The multitude may have wondered what was in store for them. They may have just wanted to linger near Christ and feel that peace which He has. This is what Christ taught in that day and continues to teach to the multitudes in this day.

> 3 *Blessed are the poor in spirit: for theirs is the kingdom of heaven.*
> 4 *Blessed are they that mourn: for they shall be comforted.*
> 5 *Blessed are the meek: for they shall inherit the earth.*
> 6 *Blessed are they which do hunger and thirst after righteousness:*
>   *for they shall be filled.*
> 7 *Blessed are the merciful: for they shall obtain mercy.*
> 8 *Blessed are the pure in heart: for they shall see God.*
> 9 *Blessed are the peacemakers: for they shall be called the children of God.*
> 10 *Blessed are they which are persecuted for righteousness' sake: for*
>   *theirs is the kingdom of heaven.*
> 11 *Blessed are ye, when men shall revile you, and persecute you, and shall*
>   *say all manner of evil against you falsely, for my sake.*
> 12 *Rejoice, and be exceeding glad: for great is your reward in heaven: for so*
>   *persecuted they the prophets which were before you.*

Matthew 5:3-12, The Holy Bible

The Salt of the Earth. Christ called His children the salt of the Earth. If we view people from high places, we see each other as ants, but Christ sees us as the salt of the Earth. Christ asked: "If the salt lost its savour, how shall people use salt to flavor their food. If salt has no flavor, salt is good for nothing, and is cast out, and trodden under foot of men. (Matthew 5:13) Remember. We are talking about people, God's children and our children. They are the salt of the Earth who has been divided into twelve tribes. Nothing can change which tribe you belong.

Most parents and step parents are worried to the point of depression that their children and step children will not develop any savour. Their children and step children have wayward behavior. Parents and step parents are often stonewalled so children and step children cannot develop any savour. Children blame parents and step parents for their lack of savour. Naturally, parents and step parents are afraid their children and step children will be good for nothing, cast out, and trodden under the foot of many people. This happens to children who are disobedient to parents and step parents and children who do not keep the Lord's commandments. It especially happens to children and step children who succumb to drug and alcohol abuse.

If you are depressed, you have lost your savour. You have lost your identity and your enthusiasm for life. If life is blah, hopeless, and painful for you, it is blah, hopeless, and painful for your children, step children, and spouse. Your depression may be from being trodden under the foot of children, step children, a spouse, siblings, friends, etc. You may trod yourself or your children under your own feet. Young children and step children do not have the experience to think and act like an adult. They are not going to respond like an adult with wisdom instantly.

If you are depressed from trials in your home, people do not know what to say. They have heard many rumors about you and your family. Some want to know all about what is happening in your home. Some would like to stop your pain, but they cannot. They do not know where your pain comes from. Your neighborhood does not know who to believe anyway. If you want savor back in your life, begin with The Beatitudes. Gradually add them back into your life.

The Opposites of the Beatitudes. Individuals may be thinking they are trying to include an individual Beatitude in their life. They wonder why they have an increase in their depression instead of an increase in successes. They are adding the opposites of the Beatitudes to their life. List the synonyms and opposites of the Beatitudes. For example, poor in spirit is not healed instantly by being rich in spirit. The synonyms for poor in spirit would be fatigue, sadness, hopelessness, and despair. Adding more fatigue and sadness to hopelessness increases despair.

There is quite a bit of emotion in the Beatitudes. This is where our emotional buttons are found. These emotional buttons are the opposites of the Beatitudes and are how you lose your savour which causes depression. Naturally, If someone cannot push one of your emotional buttons, they will move onto the next button, or Beatitude. This takes you from sadness to mourning. We become angry and too brisk and hard-hearted. We feel emptiness all the time. We know we are not so pure so we feel guilty. We may experience the fight or flight reflex with good all the time. The Lord called this situation "feet running swiftly to mischief." (Proverbs 6:16 - 19) We no longer hunger for good and righteousness. We demand justice because we feel we are persecuted, have to endure mocking, and hear lies about ourselves. The Savior has blessings for those who are poor in spirit, mourn, are meek, hunger for righteousness, have mercy for others, are pure in heart, and who endure rivilings, mocking, and falsehoods. Discover them.

Everyone has their idea of what the popular savour of the day should be. This could be smoking, pornography, homosexuality, fornication, adultery, drugs, and alcohol. When you begin collecting this kind of savour, the popular savour always changes to another savour. This is not savour. This is pollution of your salt. The savour of the Savior is the flavoring of the day and always. It never changes, and is suitable for each trial in your life.

I have many spices in my cupboard to season our food. What do I use most? Salt. Sit a pretty, full salt shaker on your shelf to remind you to become a person who has savour. The salt shaker may travel all over the house, depending on what you eat and where you eat it. Sometimes, you will have to look for it, but you now have something to focus on.

Light Under a Bushel. In our Solar System, we have the sun, moon, and stars, but the Savior told us that we are the light of the world. A city that is set on a hill cannot be hid. Men do not light a candle, and then put the candle under a bushel basket. They put the candle on a candlestick so all can benefit from the light in the house. The Savior told us to let our light shine before men, that they may see our good works, and glorify our Father which is in heaven. (Matthew 5:14-16)

Everyone is going to receive rain and sunshine in their life. (Matthew 5:45) Do not be depressed and angry because someone has the light you think you should have. If you stonewall, intimidate, manipulate, and isolate them, you may get their rain and your rain, too. Recognize the light in your life and the benefits of the rain in your life. We all have to learn how to deal with opposition and good in order to develop strengths we did not know we had.

Ought with Thy Brother. I suspect the major cause of depression is not a chemical disorder. The cause of depression is someone has ought for their self, brother, sister, husband, wife, child, sibling, or God. They are angry with family, but feel obligated to do something for them which they do not want to do. Ought also means zero. People may feel pressured into reconciling with someone they do not want to reconcile with. They have zero feelings for them.

These hard feelings and zero or empty feelings cause divisions in families which can range from a mole hill to a mountain. The sexual sins of child abuse, rape, adultery, fornication, and homosexuality, etc. being a mountain. It is very difficult to reconcile with a father, wife, child, or sibling who will not stop committing child abuse, adultery, fornication, theft, or who feels that homosexuality and addictions are okay. Your loved one is not concerned about the impact on the family or themselves. Of course, the law will have to first reconcile some of these situations for your loved one with the public laws on record. It is very difficult when someone you love has to go to prison for their crimes or has zero feelings for themselves and their family and step family. Its makes one angry when they cannot be at home to care for you.

I have had patients who confided in me that their loved one broke the law. Naturally, my patients were terribly embarrassed and hurt. They said they could not get over it. They were also terribly depressed. Some were bedridden. They were sick with a broken-heart. Some blamed themselves. Their broken heart began to accumulate an autoimmune disease, heart trouble, or Diabetes II. My patients were angry and hurting terribly, and the offender did this to them. I have heard of people never going outside their home again after this kind of tragedy occurs in a home. My patients said they refused to cook for their spouse, eat with them, and wash their clothes. The husband took care of the house. The wife stayed with her husband so she and her children could have a house, but not a home. The wife was barely civil with her husband. Her affect, the tone of her voice, was not a normal tone between husband and wife.

When these individuals tried to recover, there was always a commentator to warn the community how wrong this situation was and how terrible the person is every five or ten years. They had their excuses. They enjoyed "shaking the trees again and again to see what would fall." Only the leaves and fruit had already fallen. The commentators were looking at a bare tree and could not recognize the tree was bear. The commentators never seemed to remember the difficulties in their families or colleagues. The neighbors respond as the commentators wanted.

There are errors in this way of handling horrible experiences in personal and family relationships. First, victims and commentators are asking or forcing the offender to remain forever in their sins. If you recall, this is what our Heavenly Father was concerned about in the Garden of Eden. Victims and their commentators are going to make sure their victimizers remain forever in their sins. This is what they deserve. Second, murder cannot be forgiven. Murderers will not receive the Celestial Kingdom. The same commentator often feels abortion is okay. Since victims and commentators cannot forgive, they remain forever in their sins also. Third, the commentators have no idea if the offender has repented. They just want their idea of justice or a good story. It does not matter that courts and psychologists have examined the situation and made their decision according to the laws on record. The commentators claim their idea of justice is for our good. The courts, judges, and legislators are always wrong.

Fourth, Elijah the prophet has a mission to plant in the hearts of the children the promises made to the fathers. This will turn the hearts of the children to their fathers. Turning back to family is a way our families will repent and forgive each other for the disobedience and debts with family members. If Elijah cannot accomplish this task, we will be smitten with a curse and the whole Earth will be wasted at Christ's coming. (Doctrine and Covenants 2:1 - 3, Malachi 4:6) Sower, seed, and land are being destroyed for those who want to repent and forgive by commentators and those who will not repent or forgive? The key to this situation is found in Matthew 5:22. "Who ever is angry with his brother *without a cause* shall be in danger of judgement." We are to forgive even if we have a cause.

"Shaking the trees" to look for a cause many years after an incident has happened does not create a cause for you. This isolates and manipulates you as well as others. This behavior can become a habit at home, school, or your workplace. It takes a great deal of effort to lose this habit. If you easily become angry without a cause for years, you most likely will be angry with children who may have left their toys in the middle of the living room floor, a dog in the middle of the floor, or someone driving slower than you on the freeway.

Offenders of the laws of our land may have satisfied the courts of our land. However, to ease this pain in family relationships, the offender must repent. There are steps to repentance: recognize the impact of your sins on others and yourself; be remorseful; confess with your spouse, church leaders, or civil leaders; refrain from the behavior; make restitution if you can. Keep the Lord's commandments. Find out about the commandments and their blessings in scripture and through prayer and experience. Read your scriptures daily. Be merciful. This is the only way you can stop the pain. This is the only way you can be root and branch again in your family.

Make new friends. Do not watch movies and television programs showing the same situations which you are now enduring, are complaining about, and are trying to forgive or obtain from. Your imagination will run away with itself. Soft pornography in books will not take the place of normal marital intimacy. Soft pornography increases your anger and isolation.

Forgiveness. It does not take a rocket scientist to realize in families and step families that much forgiveness needs to occur for any peace and order to happen in our homes and our lives. (Matthew 18:22) Yet, we really do not know how to forgive nor are we quick to forgive. Your level of forgiveness can be classified as custodial (Never!), trainable, (Maybe, under certain circumstances.), or educable, (I will forgive.)

We have heard of tragic car accidents by drunken drivers and tragic murders. The remaining family members forgive the perpetrator. This is not only a beautiful example of forgiveness. These actions are a perfect example of not judging. (Matthew 7:1-2) Murder cannot be forgiven by another man. God even does not forgive murder in this world or the world to come. (Doctrine and Covenants 42:18-19) The remaining family are letting the courts do the judging, and there is more order in the court. This is what we are seeing and feeling. Examples of forgiveness in the scripture are: Joseph of Egypt and the Savior. Joseph forgave his brethren and ministered unto them. (Genesis 50:15 - 21) The Savior forgave those who crucified him because they did not know what they did. (Luke 23:34)

One may wonder why the Lord would ask us to forgive someone seventy times seven. They are just going to offend us again. (Matthew 18:23 - 35) We do not know men's hearts and fears. We also do not know of the lies that sway men's hearts and create their many fears. So we are to forgive all men. (Doctrine and Covenants 64:10) The Lord forgives our debts, as we forgive our debtors. (Matthew 6:9 - 15) We learn to be merciful this way. We also learn not to be two-faced or speak with a forked tongue. Forgiveness is how we are kind and tenderhearted with each other. (Ephesians 4:32) Step families may feel they need to keep their guard up or ride shotgun over others. Forgiveness is how we do not become taskmasters over others simply because they exist.

We may want to forgive and have no desire to punish others. Like Joseph of Egypt, forgiveness is not complete until we begin to offer an offering to our family on behalf of the Lord again. Fix meals for your family again. Work regularly again. Husbands should do what husbands promised and are expected to do, and wives should do what they promised and are expected to do. Assist children with the things which mothers and fathers help children.

Do not punish your family by not fixing them meals, not showing affection, not washing their clothes, or by not giving them a clean house to live in. If you have to endure this kind of situation, either in yourself, or as a child, spouse, or parent, do not retreat to your bed. Get out of bed. I repeat. Get out of bed. If you take too many anti-depressants, you will not be able to get out of bed and serve your family as you should. You will develop unnatural affections.

I suspect this is why the Lord told us to not sleep longer than is needful. In this same scripture, the Lord also tells us to cease to be unclean and cease to find fault one with another to invigorate your bodies and minds. (Doctrine and Covenants 88:124) Finding fault is part of having ought with your brother and the ought is usually without a cause.

Many of us has stated that Jesus has cleansed us from our sins. Yet, there are many with whom we are angry and many whom we will not forgive. Life without forgiveness and mercy is like taking a bath in dirty water without soap. Jesus has told us that those who will not forgive has the greater sin.

Be faithful to your spouse and parents or step parent. I have had patients who had spouses or children or siblings commit major sexual sins. If the couple was able to remain married, the offending spouse waited on an angry spouse or child to keep peace in the family. I have also had patients where the repeated offender waited on their spouse or child hand and foot long after the incident happened. They could not repent enough, and this is how they were repenting. The helpless spouse or child expected others to wait on them as their sinning spouse did. These individuals had no connection to the major sexual sin. I suspect these spouses were

211

waiting hand and foot on a spouse or child before they or their family members committed a major sexual sin. Everyone needs to be loved and likes to be pampered.

Sin Offering. The spouse or child being waited on had no kind words for their spouse or parent who betrayed them and was now waiting on them hand and foot every day. Both spouse and child lose their identity in this kind of pampering. This is not pampering. You are asking a member of your family who has sinned to make a sin offering repeatedly. (Exodus 29:26) Of course, they can never make the kind of sin offering that will alleviate your pain completely. So you or your child feel you must tell the world what kind of person they are and how miserable they have made you. The Savior does not accept blood sacrifice or sin offerings anymore even in betrayal. He is the Sacrifice which takes the pain of our sins and those who betray us away. You must follow the steps of removing your pain which the Savior provided in the Plan of Salvation. You do not have to victimize someone who has victimized you with their sins by becoming helpless. This is not the kind of fidelity that our Savior has told spouses to have for each other. If your husband is waiting on you twenty-four hours a day, he cannot make the sacrifices he should be making for his family.

Do things that you are proud of and which builds your self-confidence again. Give dignity back to your spouse and parents and step parents. Find a job. Obtain an education. Many women obtain educations so they would not have to be constrained and embarrassed by a deceiving, unfaithful husband. Of course, if a child is the offender, both father and mother and possibly a step parent have to endure the situation.

Do not become dependant on hate or a slave to hate. Sort this out with some counseling with a psychologist and with the scriptures. There are many miracles in forgiveness and mercy. This is why the Savior taught us how to sort things out with prayer in the Sermon on the Mount. This is why he is known as the Mighty Counselor as well as the Everlasting Father. We all have debts to pay. We can pay for our debts and forgive debts of others with His help. Moreover, we do not have to keep accumulating debts by having ought feelings for our family.

> *21 ¶ Ye have heard that it was said by them of old time, Thou shalt not kill;*
> *and whosoever shall kill shall be in danger of the judgment:*
> *22 But I say unto you, That whosoever is angry with his brother without a cause*
> *shall be in danger of the judgment: and whosoever shall say to his brother, Raca,*
> *shall be in danger of the council: but whosoever shall say, Thou fool, shall be in*
> *danger of hell fire.*
> *23 Therefore if thou bring thy gift to the altar, and there rememberest that thy brother*
> *hath ought against thee;*
> *24 Leave there thy gift before the altar, and go thy way; first be reconciled to thy brother,*
> *and then come and offer thy gift.*
> *Matthew 5:21 - 24, The Holy Bible*

At which level does each member of the family function most of the time? Are they custodial, trainable, or educable? What handicaps and broken wing acts do you and your children and step children experience in each of these stages? What temptations are they overcome with by not being educable?

If you or any family members are poor in spirit, do you and your family know what it means to be born of the spirit? Are you willing to retrain your spirit beginning with faith in the Lord Jesus Christ, repentance, baptism, and the Gift of the Holy Ghost? What emotional buttons in the Beatitudes are hardest for you to overcome? Are you retraining your spirit with the opposites of the Beatitudes causing more depression? Does each member of your family know how to pray and are they willing to pray?

Are you aware that you and your family and step family are part of the great salt shaker of the Earth? Has the salt within you been polluted and lost its savour? If so, how have you and each member lost their savour? How are you trying to regain your savour individually and as a family group? Are children and step children allowing parents and step parents to educate them? Have you hidden your light under a bushel? Is the light within you and your family worthy to be put on a candlestick? Is their enough light to last an eternity?

Do you have ought with your self, brother, sister, parent, step parent, spouse, child, step child, or God without a cause? Do you have ought with your brother, sister, parent, step parent, spouse, child, or step child for good reason? Are you asking them to pay tribute to you while you sleep twenty-two hours a day because you are depressed? How is this affecting you and your family? Are you asking yourself, your family members, and others to make a sin offering for your depression and your own sins?

After All That We Can Do. The percentage of biological and step parents change in the world as they marry, divorce, remarry, or die. The prophet, Isaiah, told us that there would be more children of the desolate than children of the married wife. (Isaiah 54:1) From various statistical reports, there are now more step families than nuclear families, and both kinds of families are devastated. The Savior and all of the prophets have given up their lives to teach us how to handle this desolation.

Many families and step families are without form and live in a void of sorrow and ought which they cannot escape. They have no Fuel Source to escape. Families and step families are not willing to divide the Night from the Day to discern their Right Hand from their Left Hand. Like Pilate, families and individuals cannot wash their hands of the Right Hand or the Left Hand. Families and step families are part of the Right Hand. If we make the wrong choices, more ice than warmth and light is accumulated. It is no wonder that we suffer from depression and suicidal thoughts, and we only have confidence in sports, drugs, alcohol, and pornography.

There are many wolves dressed in sheep's clothing. They isolate individuals and then keep track of the ways parents and step parents, children, and step children treat their loneliness, depressions, feelings of isolation, and where their confidence lies. Naturally, these things become expensive. Families and step families are tempted with devises that give more attention deficits and dysfunction. These devises are also expensive. There are other ways to treat your loneliness and dysfunctions. The Savior has provided enough scripture that the uniqueness of individuals and families can be maintained as well as their agency.

Most individuals are struggling with several kinds of depression at the same time. They have poor self-esteem from waywardness in themselves. They compare themselves or family to other wayward children, wayward spouses, sick children, or mentally-challenged children. Mothers who are already depressed are stressed with pregnancy and postpartum depression in themselves or a pregnant teenager. Husbands become depressed as the bills pile up. Every family and step family experiences illness, deaths in the family, financial distress, family feuds, divorce, alcoholism, prescription and drug addiction, suicide, etc. We can feel what it really means to have your light under a bushel of depressions. Our bushel basket of troubles multiplies if we keep filling these kinds of bushel baskets.

The Savior has many ways to assist us in emptying these bushel baskets of trials. We empty these bushel baskets with faith in Jesus Christ, repentance, love, mercy, forgiveness, prayer, fasting, and His covenants. We control what goes into our baskets by soft answers, yes or no answers, saying nothing, turning the other cheek, or ignoring hurtful things, and silence. This gives the Holy Ghost a time to inspire us. Some trials will remain such as illness and handicaps. Children are not always going to listen to you until they have their children. These baskets are easier to carry with the Lord's help. It takes practice and time to coordinate these things for a smooth performance. We learn by doing, not screaming and manipulating. (James 1:22-26)

One thing is for sure. If we make the seed of Abraham, the world's resources, become beggars at their own gates because we have invested in other types of resources, our offerings to our families, step families and others will not be accepted before the Lord. Families and step families, the world's resources, cannot be treated like they have been for thousands of years.

Intercessory Prayer. Before the Savior entered the Garden where He would take upon himself the sins of mankind, He uttered The Great Intercessory Prayer. Though the hour was come for His suffering, He thanks His Heavenly Father for those that He gave him, the apostles, and for those who believe on his name, us. As stated in The Lord's Prayer, He kept everyone in thy name. Life eternal is knowing the only true God and Jesus Christ whom thou hast sent. Christ is glorified in what we do. We are glorified in what He did for us. We are sanctified by His truths and made perfect by becoming one like the Father and the Son are one. This is where joy is found. Our Savior was given power over all flesh. Our Savior completed His mission.

Likewise, parents and step parents have made many prayers on behalf of their children and step children. It would be nice if our children and step children would believe in our answers to our prayers and leave parents and step parents with a good name. Our Savior and the world has given parents and step parents power over their children and step children until they become of age. The greatest things we can teach our children and step children is that God, our Eternal Father, sent Jesus Christ, His Beloved Son, into the world to save us from our sins. Jesus volunteered for this mission. We teach this truth by teaching prayer and repentance and avoidance of dissension. Our children and step children are glorified in what we do for them. Children and step children are glorified in what they do for parents and step parents. Both parent and child, step parent and step child are made perfect by becoming one in purpose like the Father and the Son and the Holy Ghost are one. This is where our joy is found.

Don't retire the Lord"s Intercessory Prayer and your patriarchal blessing in your callings as parents and step parents and as children and step children with unworthy dreams and schemes, depression, and dissension. It is okay to discern the Right Hand from the Left Hand and to establish the words of Christ in each generation of your family and step family. Parents, keep your treetop equal to your roots. Children are not your roots and should not be stronger or higher than you, the parents. Keep your parental powers intact as you, your family, and step family make the many transitions from birth to fig tree to olive branch. You will be blessed for not seeking your life in your trials and while trying to establish the words of Christ in your generation and your children and grandchildren. (Helaman 10:4-5) *Mary Jane Grange, R.N.*

INDEX

Author of Our Salvation

15 Behold, I am Jesus Christ the Son of God. I created the heavens and the earth, and all things that in them are. I was with the Father from the beginning. I am in the Father, and the Father in me; and in me hath the Father glorified his name.

16 I came unto my own, and my own received me not. And the scriptures concerning my coming are fulfilled.

17 And as many as have received me, to them have I given to become the sons of God; and even so will I to as many as shall believe on my name, for behold, by me redemption cometh, and in me is the law of Moses fulfilled.

18 I am the light and the life of the world. I am Alpha and Omega, the beginning and the end.

19 And ye shall offer up unto me no more the shedding of blood; yea, your sacrifices and your burnt offerings shall be done away, for I will accept none of your sacrifices and your burnt offerings.

20 And ye shall offer for a sacrifice unto me a broken heart and a contrite spirit. And whoso cometh unto me with a broken heart and a contrite spirit, him will I baptize with fire and with the Holy Ghost, even as the Lamanites, because of their faith in me at the time of their conversion, were baptized with fire and with the Holy Ghost, and they knew it not.

21 Behold, I have come unto the world to bring redemption unto the world, to save the world from sin.

22 Therefore, whoso repenteth and cometh unto me as a little child, him will I receive, for of such is the kingdom of God. Behold, for such I have laid down my life, and have taken it up again; therefore repent, and come unto me ye ends of the earth, and be saved.

–Jesus Christ
3 Nephi 9:15 - 22, The Book of Mormon

AUTHOR

MARY JANE GRANGE

Mary Jane Grange was born in Sheridan, Wyoming in 1946. She graduated from the University of Wyoming in 1970 with a Bachelor of Science Degree in Nursing. She has worked in doctors offices and several hospitals in Wyoming and Utah. She worked ten years at LDS Hospital in Salt Lake City, Utah, in obstetrics, neuro-intensive care, and the PRN Pool. She is a member of The Church of Jesus Christ of Latter-day Saints and worked in several organizations as a teacher and as an officer. She is proudly a cub and boy scout first-aid merit badge counselor in her ward. She is a member of the Utah Fife and Drum. Mary Jane is a beekeeper and has been an officer in the Wasatch Beekeepers Association for many years.

She is married to Joseph E. Grange. She has one daughter, eight step children, and many grandchildren and step grandchildren from which she has learned several PH.D. degrees from the University of Step Parenting (Hard Knocks). Mary Jane has learned several degrees from the University of Attention Deficit Disorders (Harder Knocks) with many individuals. This book on depression is Mary Jane's third book. She is now working on her fourth book.

OTHER BOOKS BY MARY JANE GRANGE

Mary Jane Grange's first book is on the many trials of step parenting. It is a guide when someone has more rights in a step parent's home than step parents have.

The Medicine Wheel for Step Parents

A Disaster Manual When Someone Has More Rights Than Step Parents

by Mary Jane Grange, R.N.

Mary Jane Grange's second book is on attention deficit disorder and attention deficit disorder with hyperactivity.

So... You Are Tired of Being a Lameduck

The Disaster Manual for Attention Deficit Disorder and Attention Deficit Disorder with Hyperactivity

By Mary Jane Grange, R.N.

Mary Jane Grange's third book is on tips for parents and step parents to relieve and control depression when they have been retired prematurely by children, step children, and extended family and society.

Neither Root Nor Branch
The Disaster Manual for Depression

Mary Jane Grange's fourth book is about her experiences in caring for President Spencer W. Kimball and other patients.

The Nurse and the Prophet
By Mary Jane Grange, R.N.

Mary Jane Grange is currently working on her fifth book which is about her experiences in tutoring her children and grandchildren. It is titled:

Gramma's School.
By Mary Jane Grange, R.N.